Pragmatics in Persuasive Discourse of Spanish Television Advertising

SIL International and
The University of Texas at Arlington
Publications in Linguistics

Publication 137

Publications in Linguistics is a series published jointly by SIL International and the Universtiy of Texas at Arlington. The series is a venue for works covering a broad range of topics in linguistics, especially the analytical treatment of minority languages from all parts of the world. While most volumes are authored by members of SIL International, suitable works by others will also form part of the series.

Series Editors

Donald A. Burquest
University of Texas at Arlington

Mary Ruth Wise
SIL International

Volume Editor

Marilyn Mayers

Production Staff

Bonnie Brown, Managing Editor
Karoline Fisher, Compositor
Hazel Shorey, Graphic Artist

Pragmatics in Persuasive Discourse of Spanish Television Advertising

Karol J. Hardin

SIL International
and
The University of Texas at Arlington

© 2001 by SIL International
Library of Congress Catalog No: 2001093718
ISBN: 1-55671-150-6
ISSN: 1040-0850

Printed in the United States of America

All Rights Reserved

08 07 06 05 04 03 02 01   10 9 8 7 6 5 4 3 2 1

No part of this publication may be reproduced, stored in a retrieval system, or transmitted in any form or by any means—electronic, mechanical, photocopy, recording, or otherwise—without the express permission of SIL International, with the exception of brief excerpts in journal articles or reviews.

Copies of this and other publications of SIL International may be obtained from

International Academic Bookstore
SIL International
7500 W. Camp Wisdom Road
Dallas, TX 75236-5699

Voice: 972-708-7404
Fax: 972-708-7433
Email: academic_books@sil.org
Internet: http://www.ethnologue.com

Contents

List of Tables ix

Acknowledgments xi

1 Introduction 1
   1.1 Media language 1
   1.2 Goals of this study 3
      1.2.1 Preliminaries. 3
      1.2.2 Purpose of the study 5
   1.3 Advertising and persuasive discourse 6
      1.3.1 Lakoff (1982) 7
      1.3.2 Geis (1982) 8
      1.3.3 Other studies 9
   1.4 Overview 10

2 Procedure and Method. 15
   2.1 Design of the study 15
      2.1.1 Sources for data 16
      2.1.2 Data collection 18
      2.1.3 Variables 19
   2.2 Method of analysis 22
      2.2.1 Speech acts 22
      2.2.2 Indexicals and politeness 24
      2.2.3 The Cooperative Principle 25
      2.2.4 Implicature 28
      2.2.5 Novelty 29
      2.2.6 Other strategies 31
      2.2.7 Contribution to persuasion 32

	2.3 Sample analysis of an ad	33
	2.3.1 Speech acts	35
	2.3.2 Novelty, flattery, and humor	36
	2.3.3 Politeness, indexicals, and implicature	37
	2.3.4 Grice's Maxims	37
	2.4.5 Summary	38
3	Analysis and Results	39
	3.1 Introduction	39
	3.2 Pragmatic strategies reflected in the data	40
	3.2.1 Context	40
	3.2.2 Speech acts	44
	3.2.3 Indexicals and politeness	46
	3.2.4 Grice's Maxims	47
	3.2.5 Speaker considerations	48
	3.2.6 Pragmalinguistic variables	48
	3.2.7 Other strategies	49
	3.2.8 Summary	50
	3.3 Linguistic realization of strategies in the data	51
	3.3.1 Speech acts	51
	3.3.2 Indexicals	71
	3.3.3 Politeness	74
	3.3.4 Implicature	86
	3.3.5 Grice's Maxims	93
	3.3.6 Novelty	102
	3.3.7 Minor categories	105
	3.3.8 Summary	106
	3.4 Distributive patterns	107
	3.4.1 Context and similarities	107
	3.4.2 Differences in general pragmatic strategies	109
	3.4.3 Differences in individual pragmatic strategies	110
	3.4.4 Summary	127
	3.5 Summary of analysis and results	128
4	Pragmatics and Persuasion	133
	4.1 Introduction	133
	4.2 How pragmatic strategies effect persuasion in the data	134
	4.2.1 Goals of persuasion	134
	4.2.2 Results: speech acts	136
	4.2.3 Results: novelty	148
	4.2.4 Results: indexicals and politeness	153
	4.2.5 Results: implicatures and violations of maxims	156
	4.2.6 Results: speaker considerations	166

>   4.2.7 Results: minor categories 170
>   4.2.8 Summary 172

5 Conclusions and Implications 173
    5.1 Conclusions 173
        5.1.1 Reorganization of categories 173
        5.1.2 Summary of pragmatics and persuasion 181
    5.2 Support of existing literature 184
    5.3 Applications, limitations, and implications 186
        5.3.1 Applications for teaching 186
        5.3.2 Limitations of the study 188
        5.3.3 Implications of study and further research 188
    5.4 Conclusion 189

Appendix A: A Critical Review of Literature 191
    A brief history of advertising 191
    The language of advertising 193
        Copywriting 193
        Pragmatics in advertising discourse 194
        Studies of Spanish advertising 197
    Pragmatic categories addressed in this study 199
        Speech acts 199
        Indexical expressions 205
        Politeness 206
    The Cooperative Principle and Grice's Maxims 209
    Other strategies in advertising 212

Appendix B: Database Sample 215

Appendix C: Number of Comparable Ads by Product
    in Each Country 219

Appendix D: Distribution of Pragmatic Strategies:
    Preference by Country 223

References 227

List of Tables

1.1 Examples of implicature from Geis (1982:43–48) 8
1.2 Features of persuasive discourse from four studies 10
1.3 Pragmatic categories included in analysis 11
2.1 Days represented by time segments
(Spain schedule: June 1997) 18
2.2 Schedule for recording 19
2.3 Variables in study 20
2.4 Pragmatic categories included in analysis 21
2.5 Classification of types of ads 32
3.1 Proportion of product categories in database (n=723) 41
3.2 Product categories by country (n=241) 42
3.3 Frequencies for audience categories (n=723) 43
3.4 Audience by country (n=241) 44
3.5 Distribution of common speech acts (n=723) 45
3.6 Distribution of indexicals and politeness strategies (n=723) . . 46
3.7: Distribution of Grice's Maxims and implicature (n=723) . . . 47
3.8: Distribution of speaker considerations (n=723) 48
3.9 Distribution of pragmalinguistic variables (n=723) 49

3.10 Distribution of speaker considerations (n=723) 50
3.11 Frequencies of pragmatic variables (n=723) 50
3.12 Summary of speech acts 69
3.13 Preferences for types of personal reference 73
3.14 Types of violations of Grice's Maxims 94
3.15 Products by country (n=241) 108
3.16 Audience by country (n=241) 109
3.17 Categories by country (n=241) 110
3.18 Individual strategies by country (n=241) 110
3.19 Strategies that violate Grice's Maxims 118
5.1 Reclassification of major and minor pragmatic strategies . . . 175
5.2 Summary of pragmatics and persuasion 183

Acknowledgments

I would like to primarily thank the supervisor of my dissertation, Dale Koike, for her many hours of input and suggestions and for being extremely prompt in both reading and returning manuscripts. I wish to thank my committee members, Carlos Solé, Chiyo Nishida, Keith Walters, and Albert Bickford for their input, encouragement, and scholarly examples. Special appreciation also goes to Paul Larson and Francis Palisson for taking a month out of their busy schedules to help me with data collection in Spain and Chile.

I am especially thankful for the help of my husband, Mike Hardin, in creating the database spreadsheet and layout for this study, for reading versions of each chapter, and for patiently supporting me in countless ways. I am also grateful to my parents, Karl and Joice Franklin, for their editing input and for their examples throughout the years, both linguistic and otherwise. I am indebted to the many Spanish speakers (Fátima Alfonso-Pinto, Mimi Bagnasco, Guillermo García-Corales, Baudelio Garza, Julio Jiménez, Paul Larson, Lupita Limage-Montesinos, Fred Loa, María Mayberry, Linda McManness, and Delia Montesinos) with whom I conferred on small and large issues. Finally, I wish to thank the many friends who have encouraged me and who have been willing to listen to me discuss ideas regarding pragmatics and persuasion.

1
Introduction

1.1 Media language

Media, and advertising in particular, generate much of the public language that is heard in society. Of special interest to the linguist, media language offers advantages for analysis and study in that it is available in large quantities and is easily observable in context. As Bell (1991) pointed out, one advantage of media language over face-to-face communication is that sociolinguists are not constrained by Labov's "Observer's Paradox" (1972:209), in which the assumption is that the researcher wishes to observe and record speakers talking the way they do when not being observed and recorded. Instead, media language is intended for mass public consumption and is already monitored in the form of editing, regardless of whether or not the linguist records the material. Perhaps one of the greatest advantages of advertising language for the linguist is that advertising has the singular goal of convincing its audience to buy or use a product or service. It is, therefore, easier to identify clear characteristics of advertising language than ordinary conversations, in which primary goals may vary considerably. Media language offers other advantages: multiple originators, a mass simultaneous and fragmented audience, absence of feedback, and general public accessibility (Bell 1991:2). Thus, advertising language is valuable in providing data from more than one source aimed at varied, yet specific, target audiences and in providing clear style shifts.

Assuming that "one's view of language is shaped by the most readily available examples of it," it is likely that advertising both reflects and influences language (Bell 1991:7). While we may disdain its effect, advertising, along with other media, education, and government, form one of the primary influences on language. Given the active role of media language in even the least technologically advanced and most isolated societies, it seems vital to examine not only the ideology and manipulative intent of advertising but also how advertising reflects the language strategies of a given society—specifically, the pragmatic strategies by which persuasion is effected in that culture. Indeed, it has been suggested that mass communication represents the medium for the collective speech acts of modern societies and reflects the differences in the "constitution of consciousness within different cultures" (Bjerg 1979:332).

In this study, I attempt to combine the diverse fields of pragmatics, semantics, discourse analysis, sociolinguistics, rhetoric, and advertising by providing a pragmalinguistic analysis of data from one type of media language—television advertising. I also examine how pragmatic strategies found in Spanish advertising contribute to persuasion. Although much has been written on the age-old art of the rhetoric of persuasion as well as on the psychology and abuses of advertising, to date there have been few large-scale studies of the pragmatics of advertising and none that I know of in Spanish.

Among linguistics studies of media language, Bell (1991) provided an excellent overview of previous research on media language, emphasizing sociolinguistic approaches to the language of the news in English. Van Dijk (1983) also presented discourse and semantic analyses of mass media discourse, with examples from various languages.[1] One of the few cross-cultural pragmatic analyses of television advertising is that of Kumatoridiani (1984), who compared the structure of persuasive discourse in American and Japanese commercials. The few specific studies of Spanish advertising language tend to focus on

- corrupting phonological and lexical influences on the Spanish language by television ads (Fernández 1988; Avila 1994),
- the rhetoric of persuasion with examples from advertising (Briz Gómez et al. 1987; Delbecque and Leuven 1990; Moreno Fernández 1990), or
- a particular discursive element (Sanchez Corral 1991).

---

[1]For sample in-depth linguistic analyses of a particular type of media language, see Lipski (1985) on phonology and style shift in Spanish language radio of the Americas; Jucker (1986) on the pragmatics of news interviews; and Bruthiaux (1996) on syntax in the discourse of classified advertising in American English.

In the present study I provide a pragmatic analysis of Spanish advertising language that seems to be absent in previous research. (Hereafter, I use the terms ad and advertisement to mean television commercials.)

Though not explicitly emphasizing pragmatics, perhaps two of the best known linguistic descriptions of advertising language occur in *English in advertising: A linguistic study of advertising in Great Britain* by Leech (1966) and *Language—The loaded weapon: The use and abuse of language today* by Bolinger (1980). Both present a detailed survey of the linguistic devices found most often in advertisements and have provided insights for this study. The model most closely related to the present study, however, is that of Geis (1982), who offered a pragmatic study of language use in American television advertising and how it is understood by consumers. A few other pragmalinguistic works regarding the ideology of power and its relationship to advertising, which contributed ideas for this study, include that of R. Lakoff (1982, 1990) and Mey (1985).

1.2 Goals of this study

1.2.1 Preliminaries

Before discussing the general questions and approach of this study, it may be helpful to define the terms PERSUASIVE DISCOURSE and PRAGMATICS. Persuasive discourse is defined by Lakoff (1982:28) as the nonreciprocal "attempt or intention of one party to change the behavior, feelings, intentions, or viewpoint of another by communicative means." Similarly, Schmidt and Kess (1986:287), in their comparison of the language of televangelists and television advertising, defined persuasion as the "process of inducing a voluntary change in someone's attitudes, beliefs or behavior through the transmission of a message." Advertising, propaganda, political rhetoric, and religious sermons are obvious examples of persuasive discourse. Other types of discourse involving unequal distribution of power or manipulation include therapeutic and courtroom discourse, job interviews, examination situations, "academese", and adult speech directed at children (Lakoff 1982; Mey 1985). Lakoff (p. 216) considered power to be a frequent product of persuasiveness because people "who can use linguistic skills to win others over to a point of view, and get them to act in accordance with their interests, are likely to achieve power." She further noted that societies generally have clear ideas about what is persuasive and how to speak in such a way. Furthermore, she suggested that even though persuasiveness appears to be universal in its emphasis upon emotional appeal and intellectual argument, rhetorical practices are not the same in every culture.

Numerous definitions have been promoted for the term "pragmatics", ranging from the "waste-basket of syntax" (Bar-Hillel 1971) to the "study of the relations of signs to interpreters" (Morris 1938:6). A more specific definition was proposed by Levinson (1983:9), who suggested, "pragmatics is the study of those relations between language and context that are *grammaticalized,* or encoded in the structure of a language." The broadest interpretations of pragmatics may be "that it is the study of understanding intentional human action" (Green 1989:3) or that it is "the science of language seen in relation to its users" (Mey 1993:5). Linguistic pragmatics, then, consists of the intersection of linguistics, cognitive psychology, cultural anthropology, philosophy, sociology, and rhetoric. Its central notions include the

- *belief* about a speaker and context, the message, and its effect,
- *intent* of a speaker,
- *plan,* or intended verbal realization, and
- *act* or how the message actually comes out and is understood (Green 1989:2–5).

Note that in this study I do not presume to know or describe how individuals in an audience actually react to TV commercials and which ads are most successful in changing buyers' product preferences. For the purpose of my study, I focus instead upon the

- general beliefs and intents of advertisers,
- plans with regard to pragmalinguistic strategies, and
- acts insofar as they may be generally understood.

Furthermore, rather than viewing pragmatics as a subset of semantics or as a complement to it, the theoretical framework for this study is essentially pragmatic. That is, pragmatics is seen as an umbrella for the realization of explicitly linguistic devices. More specifically, the context of utterance (persuasive discourse in Spanish television advertising) is the key to understanding the pragmatic strategies or devices by which advertisers convey more than is actually said. These pragmatic strategies are expressed linguistically via the syntax, lexicon, and phonology. Thus, the context of persuasive discourse is essential to understanding the relationship between pragmatic strategies and the linguistic means by which they effect persuasion. The general definition for pragmatics I use is "the study of the relationship between language, its communication, and its contextualized use" (Koike 1996).

1.2.2 Purpose of the study

Having explained what I mean by persuasive discourse and pragmatics, I turn to the research questions and approach of this study. In the present study, I generally purport to examine which pragmatic strategies occur most frequently in Spanish television advertising, such as violation of the Cooperative Principle (Grice 1975) and appeal to POSITIVE or NEGATIVE FACE, following Brown and Levinson (1987). I also wish to address how such pragmatic devices are encoded linguistically in the data. There are differences, for example, in pragmalinguistic strategies used by Spanish ads directed at U.S. audiences versus those that address a South American or European audience. There is also variation in the selection of informal versus formal commands or deictic reference, depending on the context. Haverkate (1984) and Koike (1992) demonstrated how deictic reference can "defocalize" or distance the speaker and hearer, depending on the degree of politeness desired. Finally, I examine how pragmalinguistic features of television advertising, including deixis, politeness, illocutionary force, and implicature are used to effect persuasion. Of particular interest are pragmatic strategies that distinctly reflect the Spanish language and cultures, in this case, of Spain, Chile, and the United States.

The general questions to be addressed are as follows:

1. Which pragmatic devices occur most frequently in Spanish television advertising?
2. How are these pragmatic devices linguistically encoded in the data?
3. Are any pragmatic differences evident between dialects of Spanish?
4. How are pragmalinguistic features of television advertising used to effect persuasion?

I initially hypothesize that Spanish advertising language is highly conventionalized and that indirectness and violation of Gricean Maxims via implicature play an important role in persuasion.[2] I also expect to find some intralanguage differences in pragmalinguistic strategies employed in advertising as well as interrelationships between these strategies. Finally, I propose a classification of strategies and their relationship to persuasion in Spanish as they occur in the corpus. The general goal of the study is to describe Spanish advertising language and the various methods and forms it employs to facilitate its function of persuasion. While language cannot

---

[2]Obviously, Grice's Maxims must be interpreted very broadly when dealing with a language and culture other than English. In this study I assume, without attempting to demonstrate, that the Gricean maxims apply to Spanish as well as English. (See the discussion on pages 209–212 on the Cooperative Principle and Grice's Maxims.)

literally carry commodities to their prospective buyers, it is able to facilitate the buying and selling processes (Mey 1985:55).

Even though theoretical concepts underlying Spanish advertising may be influenced by English advertising concepts, pragmatic devices are linguistically encoded in different ways in different languages (Jensen 1982; Blum-Kulka, House, and Kasper 1989; Wierzbicka 1991). Thus, it would be simplistic to assume that Spanish advertising language is identical to that of English. Even when English advertising is used as a model for Spanish ads, the linguistic and pragmatic expression of ideas is not identical. Jensen, for example, found that the verbs *come* and *go* have different deictic referents in Spanish and English. Blum-Kulka, House, and Kasper's (1989) well-known research of cross-cultural pragmatics in requests and apologies demonstrated, among other things, that languages differ in the way they judge the appropriateness of conventional indirectness. Wierzbicka (1991) also examined pragmatics in a wide variety of cultures and found differences in areas such as speech acts and the cultural values they reflect, illocutionary force, interjections, particles, tautologies, and conversational routines. Her examples even included intradialectal pragmatic differences, for example, between Australian and American English, such as use of the diminutive in Australian English as a mark of good humor. In light of such research, in this study I enlarge upon previous work by providing a description and analysis of pragmatic ways in which the Spanish language is used to achieve persuasion within a specified context, that of consumer television advertising.

1.3 Advertising and persuasive discourse

An important influence in the language of advertising can be found in the use or nonuse of Grice's Maxims (see appendix A for a listing of maxims). These seem particularly appropriate in studying advertising language because of the appeal to the Cooperative Principle and the pretense of cooperation that ads contain. Briefly, the Cooperative Principle suggests that there is a tacit understanding between speakers and addressees in a conversation—that all participants are cooperating—which allows for comprehension. Furthermore, Grice's Maxims are adhered to in conversation unless the speaker chooses to violate one for effect or to create a nonconventional meaning that the hearer must work out using contextual or background knowledge. Both VIOLATION and FLOUTING of these maxims may mislead the addressee. However, knowledge of the Cooperative Principle generally provides the hearer with a rational means of comprehension when such violations occur. Lakoff (1982), Geis (1982), and Schmidt and Kess (1986)

1.3 Advertising and persuasive discourse

considered violations of Grice's Maxims and indirectness to be the overarching methods of achieving persuasive discourse in advertising.

1.3.1 Lakoff (1982)

Lakoff (1982) argued that, unlike ordinary conversation, clear examples of persuasive discourse involve violations of Grice's Cooperative Principle and the Maxim of Manner. She considered clear examples of persuasive discourse to be nonspontaneous and to thrive on novelty. She, therefore, suggested that neologisms in advertising, such as lexical, morphological, syntactic, semantic, and pragmatic novelty, flout the Maxim of Manner by attracting attention and making the audience remember. Hence, Lakoff claimed that the violation of maxims in persuasive discourse is covert and that the audience is tricked into assuming that an act of information is occurring. She maintained that persuasive discourse, particularly advertising, superficially adheres to the Cooperative Principle in order to conceal appeals to the audience's emotions. They, therefore, contain an appeal to our knowledge of how the Cooperative Principle works. Some of Lakoff's examples of neologisms are presented in (1).

(1) Lexical novelty/neologism *(devilicious)*

Morphological/syntactic novelty *(The soup that eats like a meal.)*

Syntactic innovation involving
  - absence of subjects/verbal auxiliaries, and... *(Tastes good! And nutritious too!)*
  - odd uses of the definite article *(Next time, I'll buy the Tylenol!)*

Semantic anomaly *(Cleans better than another leading oven cleaner)*

Pragmatic novelty (unusual dialogue: *Fill it to the rim. With Brim.*)

The purpose of Lakoff's article was to consider distinguishing features of persuasive discourse and to contrast them with ordinary conversation, although she acknowledged that this dichotomy is not necessarily the primary distinction between the two. The fact that characteristics of both persuasive discourse and ordinary conversation occur in advertising makes Lakoff's preliminary analysis relevant to this study. She argued that the goal of ordinary conversation is rapport and that it is considered to be good if "we come away feeling that a good interaction has been had by all, that we all like each other, and that we wouldn't mind talking to each other again" (1982:27). She noted, too, that familiarity and ritual serve to clarify ordinary conversation as opposed to the nonspontaneous and novel character of advertising, a subset of persuasive discourse. I found, however, that advertising is highly conventionalized despite its attempts at novelty. Lakoff also viewed rules of rapport as being more important than Grice's Maxims in ordinary conversation because speakers prefer to be unclear rather than offensive. Nevertheless, her claim that rapport does not play a role in persuasive discourse does not address the role of endorsers on television ads and other features in my corpus that indicate the importance of rapport in persuasive discourse as well.

1.3.2 Geis (1982)

Geis (1982) provided a thorough pragmatic analysis of media language in American advertising and ways in which advertisers use conversational implicature to persuade or manipulate their audience. His study placed particular emphasis upon the language of television advertising aimed at children and their ability to understand conversational implicature. He detailed a pragmatist theory of truth in advertising by which advertisers might also be held responsible for what they conversationally implicate. He noted that it has been established experimentally that people tend to recall pragmatic inferences with at least as much frequency as they recall direct assertions (p. 239). Some of the strategies for persuasion he examined included conventional, theoretical, and conversational implicatures, use of modal verbs, comparatives, special words and phrases, styles and registers, and disclaimers. I present a few of Geis's examples of theoretical, conventional, and conversational implicature in table 1.1. Note that only conventional and conversational implicatures were examined in the present study.

Table 1.1 Examples of implicature from Geis (1982:43–48)

a.	*Choosy mothers choose Jif.*	(premise)
b.	If a mother is a choosy mother, she will choose Jif.	(from a)
c.	If a mother doesn't choose Jif, she isn't a choosy mother.	(from b by Contraposition)
d.	If a mother isn't a choosy mother, she isn't a good mother.	(premise)

Theoretical Implicature:
e. If a mother doesn't choose Jif, she isn't a good (from c and d
mother. by Transitivity)

This Atra face-hugging action keeps twin blades at the perfect angle.
Conventional Implicature: Atra twin blades are at the perfect angle.

After all, who knows more about the taste of meat than Alpo?
Conversational Implicature: No one knows more about the taste of meat than Alpo.

1.3.3 Other studies

Expanding Lakoff and Geis's lists of pragmatic devices in persuasive discourse, Schmidt and Kess (1986) examined methods of persuasive communication in the language used by television evangelists and compared their discourse to persuasive language in television advertising. Their results generally supported the categories outlined by Lakoff and Geis, even though their data consisted of a different type of persuasive discourse. They found lexical, morphological, syntactic, and semantic novelty, as well as adjectivalization processes and product names as mini-ads to be characteristic of both televangelism and advertising.

In a strictly linguistic analysis, Bruthiaux's dissertation on linguistic simplicity (1996) examined 800 classified advertisements drawn from two Los Angeles newspapers. He noted that even simple registers require linguistically sophisticated strategies anchored by the context of use. Therefore, superficial simplicity does not always indicate a simple message, as was evident in classified ads. Although his primary purpose was to demonstrate the distinctiveness of the Classified Ads Register and he focused upon syntactic economy with little reference to the register's social context or goal of persuasion, some of the linguistic devices he found may be related to observations from the Lakoff, Geis, and Schmidt and Kess studies. I present corresponding salient features of these studies on persuasive discourse in table 1.2.

Table 1.2 Features of persuasive discourse from four studies

Lakoff (1982)	Geis (1982)	Schmidt and Kess (1986)	Bruthiaux (1996)
	Introducing/ Announcing		
	Product names as mini-ads	Product names as mini-ads	
Lexical novelty/ neologism		Lexical novelty	Creative compounding
Morphological/ syntactic novelty	Count nouns as mass nouns adjectivalization	Morphological/ syntactic novelty adjectivalization	Adjective and nominal chains
Syntactic innovation		Syntactic innovation	Fragments, listing
Semantic anomaly	Elliptical comparatives	Semantic anomaly	
Pragmatic novelty	Imperatives as suggestions rhetorical questions implicatures	Implicatures	Maximum use of shared context

1.4 Overview

In the present study I apply these and other models to television advertising from three Spanish-speaking countries and present a basis for reclassification of features related to persuasive discourse that encompasses characteristics of all four studies. I also applied pragmatic theories regarding nonconventional implicature and violation of the Cooperative Principle (Grice 1975), deixis (Fillmore 1971), politeness (Levinson 1983; Brown and Levinson 1987), speech acts (Searle 1969, 1975), and other pragmatic devices to the data in order to determine the pragmalinguistic means by which persuasion is effected and to propose a classification of such features.[3] I included previous applications of pragmatic theories to Spanish, with particular reference to Haverkate (1984, 1990) and Koike (1989a, 1989b, 1992) regarding speech acts, deixis, and politeness. I analyzed each ad in the corpus for pragmalinguistic features including implicature, deixis, politeness, different types of speech acts, illocutionary force, use of humor, flattery, and endorsements, violations of Grice's Maxims, certain phonological features, lexical selection, and sociolinguistic considerations (such as gender/speaker considerations and the target audience). Appendix A gives a review of the literature I examined. The most important pragmatic strategies examined throughout the study appear in table 1.3.

Table 1.3 Pragmatic categories included in analysis

General category
Speech acts/illocutionary force
Cooperative principle/violations of Grice's Maxims
Implicatures
Indexicals/politeness
Information structure
Phonological features
Lexical selection
Speaker considerations

Although advertising generally tries to make its products and services appear novel, the language and pragmatic strategies of Spanish ads were highly conventionalized. These strategies were related to three primary goals of persuasion: memory, force, and participation. Furthermore, all of the pragmatic categories used for analysis were found in the majority of ads and were reflective of advertising discourse. The pragmatic strategies found in the data also revealed distributive patterns according to the type of ad, country of origin, and contribution to persuasion.

The present study into the pragmatics of persuasion in Spanish is organized as follows. In this first chapter I have provided an introduction and overview of the study, including a general outline of its theoretical basis. In chapter 2, I present a brief history of advertising and detail a literature review of studies of pragmatics and relevant issues, including both background

---

[3]In the present study, I benefit from an earlier paper on the discourse of advertising for a sociolinguistics class (LIN 380S) at the University of Texas at Austin. The pilot study was based on a sociolinguistic analysis of 100 ads from Univisión in the fall of 1996. The ads were only compared for occurrences of linguistic and pragmatic features found by Lakoff (1982) and Geis (1982).

discussions of general pragmatic theoretical concepts and specific applications to language data, particularly to Spanish. I present the procedure and method of analysis in chapter 2 and the analyses and results in chapter 3. In chapter 4, I discuss the relationship between persuasion and pragmatic strategies in the data. Finally, in chapter 5, I present conclusions, including a classification of pragmalinguistic strategies and devices found, their interrelationship, and their relation to persuasion. I also suggest some implications which include applications to the teaching of Spanish for business and for other purposes. In appendix A, I give a critical review of the literature which includes a brief history of advertising, the language of advertising, and pragmatic categories addressed in this study. These categories are speech acts, indexical expressions, politeness, the Cooperative Principle, and Grice's Maxims. Appendices B through D are comprised respectively of: a database sample used in this study, a list of comparable ads by product, and a list of pragmatic strategies according to preference by country.

I hope that this study will contribute to the cross-linguistic understanding of the pragmatics of persuasion by providing an application of supposed universal pragmatic concepts to the Spanish language and by providing another large database from which to compare other languages in future research. In addition, this study adds to a cross-dialectal understanding of Spanish pragmatics, an area in which there is little information in the literature. It also provides a detailed account of a specific genre or register of Spanish discourse, that of television advertising, and offers further insight into ways of persuading in Spanish. Furthermore, I offer a systematic method of analysis that is replicable for other languages and genres of discourse.

The study also contributes to the teaching of pragmatics in Spanish language classrooms, with applications to the teaching of Spanish for business, particularly in how to persuade, sell, and appeal to a given Spanish-speaking audience. It also has potential implications for the teaching of Spanish for

- special purposes (such as law),
- Spanish linguistics (pragmatics and persuasion),
- introductory Spanish (basic pragmatic concepts such as distance and solidarity, directness and indirectness), and
- conversation classes (discussion of ads and teaching of pragmatics).

The ability to appropriately weave linguistic form around meaning in a given context is an essential part of functioning successfully in a language and culture.

1.4 Overview

Advertisements may provide a clear context for examples of language in use and, as such, real-life examples for language teaching. Given the vital role of the media in society and on language, Spanish television advertising reflects the pragmatic and sociolinguistic communication of persuasion by and to Spanish speakers. As Lakoff (1990:2) stated: "Knowledge of special language is power, normally reserved for the professionals; but there is no law that prevents the power from being spread around the larger community through greater understanding.... The trick for all of us is to grasp the generalizations, the larger picture" between the form of a communication and the power it provides its user.

2
Procedure and Method

2.1 Design of the study

In this chapter I provide a description of the procedure by which data were collected from each country and analyzed for the present study. I give an explanation of each variable with examples from Spanish ads as well as a sample in-depth analysis of one advertisement.

In previous extensive linguistic studies of advertising, sample sizes varied from

- 617 television ads collected from December 1960 to May 1961 (Leech 1966),
- 800 commercials gathered between 1978 and 1981 (Geis 1982), and
- 800 classified ads from two newspapers (Bruthiaux 1996).

I base the present study on an allotted time frame of a constructed week and, therefore, the total number of ads was not predetermined. Instead, I gathered 281 ads from the United States, 241 from Chile, and over 242 from Spain. For comparative purposes, I analyzed the same number of advertisements from each country. Thus, the corpus included 241 television advertisements for products and services from each of three countries: Chile, Spain, and the United States. I examined only commercial consumer advertising, or "advertising directed towards a mass audience with the aim of promoting sales of a commerical product or service," (Leech 1966:25). Thus, I did not include public service advertisements (announcements) against smoking, drugs, and other perceived public ills in the corpus.

Selection of the above countries was not arbitrary but based on a desire for samples encompassing a broad spectrum of Hispanic language and culture. Their location on three different continents, dialectal differences among audiences in each country, and differences in historic and economic ties were taken into account. I expected that data from the United States would be most similar to Mexican and possibly Caribbean dialects of Spanish (particularly those of Cuba and Puerto Rico) because these three geographical segments represent the largest Spanish-speaking populations found in the United States. I also expected the commercials to reflect the influence of English and North American societal values. I selected Chile as a country representative of South America because of its geographic distance from the United States and ease of collection.[4] I expected that Chilean advertisements would have fewer ties to English advertising strategies than those of the United States and would contain South American or perhaps European influence. Spain was selected as being optimally different from the United States commercials and because of its likely influence from surrounding European countries.

2.1.1 Sources for data

We[5] recorded the advertisements in the summer of 1997 from one privately owned television station with a wide audience in each country. I chose terrestrial (nonsatellite) and noncable television stations that held the largest viewing audience for private stations within each country. They were as follows: Chile (Teletrece), Spain (Antena 3), and the United States (Univisión). Since Spanish television stations in the United States are not owned or subsidized by the government, only private stations in Chile and Spain were considered valid for comparative purposes. The largest television networks in Chile and Spain are both owned and managed by the government and, therefore, it was possible that they might contain fewer advertisements or commercials that were different in nature from those on private stations due to differences in funding. Thus, Teletrece, Antena 3, and Univisión were the most similar networks in terms of audience penetration, audience preference, and private ownership.

The Corporación de Televisión Universidad Católica de Chile, or Teletrece (Channel 13), is the second largest station in Chile, following Televisión Nacional de Chile (TVN), a public broadcasting network. Teletrece offers many science and educational programs, and is home to

---

[4] I in no way wish to imply that Chilean advertising language is identical or necessarily representative of other parts of South America.

[5] Data was collected in Chile by Dr. Francis Palisson in July 1997, in Spain by Dr. Paul Larson in June 1997, and in the United States by the author in June and July 1997.

2.1 Design of the study

"Mario Kreuzberger" (Don Francisco) of *Sábado Gigante* (IBOPE 1997). Although Televisión Nacional de Chile has a larger viewing audience and more varied programming, Teletrece was chosen for consistency, since the other two stations in this study were privately owned. Also, based on a schedule of programming by IBOPE, the equivalent of the Nielsen ratings in Latin America, Teletrece appeared to offer enough of a variety of programming to be comparable for this study. Furthermore, Teletrece held nine of the top twenty programs in Chile in August 1996, while TVN held eight positions (P&D Net 1997).

Antena 3 TV is a private terrestrial television station based in Madrid, Spain, with a 48.5 percent household penetration, broadcasting 150 hours per week. In 1992, 45 percent of Antena 3 was bought out by Rupert Murdoch, Banesto Bank, and the Zeta Publishing Group (Moore 1992). Antena 3 was chosen for this study because it is private, and because from May 1996 to May 1997, it was the second most watched Spanish television station after TVE-1, a national, government-run station. For May 1997, Antena 3 represented 22.4 percent of the TV viewing audience in Spain, slightly behind TELE 5, another private station, which held 22.8 percent of viewers and behind TVE-1, which held 23.6 percent. Advertising restrictions for Antena 3 include alcohol, tobacco, and medicine, and the sources of import include Europe, the U.S.A., Venezuela, and Hong Kong. Programming is composed of children's programs, news and public affairs, series, sports, and telefeatures (SRDS 1997:1377).

Univisión is a private television network headed by Henry Cisneros and formerly owned by Hallmark. In 1992, A. Jerrold Perenchio bought Univisión from Hallmark with Mexican and Venezuelan billionaire partners who wanted a share of the U.S. television market but faced foreign ownership restrictions (Newcomb and Lataniotis 1997). The network has branch offices in Atlanta, Chicago, Dallas, Detroit, Los Angeles, Miami, Irvine (California), San Antonio, and San Francisco. The closest station to Austin, Texas is KUVN Channel 23 in Dallas. Univisión ranks number ten in terms of the top twenty-four television companies, based on the percentage of total U.S. households reached, and it reaches the largest audience of the Spanish-speaking stations in the United States (SRDS 1997:1161).

Univisión also has a higher audience loyalty, lower audience segmentation, and flatter seasonal audience fluctuation curves than that of other major U.S. networks. The U.S. Hispanic market tends to be younger than the market for non-Hispanics; 58 percent of Hispanic viewers are under 30 years of age. The average age of Hispanic viewers is 26 years, as opposed to 33 years of age for non-Hispanics. Daypart breaks for Univisión (categories reflecting the cost of advertising at a given time of day) parallel those of

English television, and prime time is defined as 7–11 P.M. Seventy-five percent of commercial spots are 30 seconds, followed by 20 percent at 60 seconds and 5 percent at 10–15 seconds. According to ROSLOW Research Group (1994), advertising to Hispanics in Spanish is 40 percent more effective at increasing ad recall, 5.2 times more persuasive, and 56 percent more effective in terms of message comprehension than advertising in English (SRDS 1997:A31–34).

2.1.2 Data collection

The instruments for data collection were programmable videocassette recorders and twenty-eight three-hour videotapes in each of the three countries. Since only three-hour videotapes were available in Spain and the data collectors were unable to be present to record tapes one after another on any given day, it was necessary to design a schedule that reflected a twelve-hour day in four three-hour increments and that simulated a week of programming (from 10 A.M. to 10 P.M.). A twelve-hour day was chosen to represent the major portion of viewing time, including morning, afternoon, and evening. The videotapes included programming as well as advertisements in order to obtain an accurate context when noting the type of program and audience, the time of day, and degree of repetition of ads.

Bell (1991:23) outlined sample sizes to reflect a week, month, or year of news. He noted that samples consisting of a week of consecutive days were inadequate, but that one frequent sampling pattern was to take every nth day of a given period, in this case, n = 4. Thus, each time period was repeated every four days and each day of the week occurred just once within a given time segment, reflected in table 2.1.

Table 2.1 Days represented by time segments (Spain schedule: June 1997)

10 A.M.–1 P.M.	1–4 P.M.	4–7 P.M.	7–10 P.M.
Monday	Tuesday	Wednesday	Thursday
Friday	Saturday	Sunday	Monday
Tuesday	Wednesday	Thursday	Friday
Saturday	Sunday	Monday	Tuesday
Wednesday	Thursday	Friday	Saturday
Sunday	Monday	Tuesday	Wednesday
Thursday	Friday	Saturday	Sunday

2.1 Design of the study

The simulated week in the present study was complicated by the unavailability of videotapes longer than three hours for the data from Spain and, therefore, was based on a repetition of the four time periods (10 A.M.–1 P.M., 1 P.M.–4 P.M., 4 P.M.–7 P.M., and 7 P.M.–10 P.M.) within a four-week period. Because data collection in the present study required three different collectors following the same schedule on three different continents, the schedule in table 2.2 was the largest amount of data collection possible for all three collectors.

Table 2.2 Schedule for recording

Week 1:	10–1	1–4	4–7	7–10	10–1	1–4	4–7
Week 2:	7–10	10-1	1–4	4–7	7–10	10–1	1–4
Week 3:	4–7	7–10	10–1	1–4	4–7	7–10	10–1
Week 4:	1–4	4–7	7–10	10–1	1–4	4–7	7–10

We converted dated videotapes from data in Spain from the PAL system to the U.S. system (NTSC) for viewing. Each researcher noted the period of day, counter number, and context (program) for each advertisement as well as a transcription of all ads. We then entered the data into a database using Filemaker Pro to allow ease of analysis. We also included the frequency of each ad and available information regarding commercial costs as contextual information in all analyses.

2.1.3 Variables

Recall that the general questions to address were:

1. Which pragmatic devices occur most frequently in Spanish television advertising?
2. How are these pragmatic devices linguistically encoded in the data?
3. Are any pragmatic differences evident between dialects of Spanish?
4. How are pragmalinguistic features of television advertising used to effect persuasion?

Thus, the variables in this study were primarily contextual, (pragma)linguistic, and pragmatic in nature, as depicted in table 2.3.

Table 2.3 Variables in study

Context	(Pragma-)Linguistic variables	Pragmatic variables
Country	Phonology	Speech acts
Product	Lexicon	Indexicals
Audience	Syntax	Politeness
		Implicature
		Violation of Grice's Maxims
		Speaker considerations

I examined each ad for the presence of pragmalinguistic features including:

- implicature,
- deixis,
- politeness,
- different types of speech acts,
- illocutionary force,
- use of humor, flattery, and endorsements,
- violations of Grice's Maxims,
- certain phonological features,
- lexical selection, and
- sociolinguistic considerations (such as gender/speaker considerations and the target audience).

While visual images and gestures are important in advertising, in the present study I primarily emphasize the language of television advertising. Therefore, I note the visual aspect of commercials only as contextual information. Furthermore, I base selection of variables on a pragmalinguistic theoretical model. Since persuasion is not merely code-based, another approach might focus, for example, on cultural, historical, economic, or other related issues.

First, in analyzing the data, I determined the relative frequency of each of the pragmatic features in the total number of ads that included them for each country and overall. Frequencies did not include tallies from ads that were repeated and only reflected the presence/absence of a given item. The purpose for counting the above features was to determine which ones might be considered as reflective of the language of Spanish advertising. I then further analyzed the most common pragmatic devices with respect to the linguistic ways in which each feature was encoded and how (if)

2.1 Design of the study

each contributed to persuasion within the context of advertising. I depict an outline of the specific categories targeted in table 2.4.

Table 2.4 Pragmatic categories included in analysis

Category	Information noted
Target audience	All available information as it relates to strategies
Speech acts/ Illocutionary force	Frequency, linguistic realization, contribution to persuasiveness, dialectal variation
Cooperative Principle	Frequency of violations, types of maxims violated, effect on force of message
Implicature	Comparison of ad types, comparison of types of implicature, effect on force of message
Politeness	Occurrences of deixis and tense, relation to politeness and persuasion, appeals to positive/ negative face; power, distance, and rank of speaker to audience
Novelty	Frequency and type, contribution to persuasion
Flattery	Frequency and type, contribution to persuasion
Humor	Frequency and type, contribution to persuasion
Endorsements	Frequency and type, contribution to persuasion
Information structure	Presence of unusual or unexpected word order for emphasis or effect, contribution to persuasion
Phonological features	Presence of a foreign accent, role of intonation, contribution to force of message
Lexical selection	Effect on force of message
Speaker considerations	Gender, age, physical characteristics, profession, etc.; production of distance or solidarity with target audience; contribution to force of message

As previously mentioned, we entered all of the above information into a database in Filemaker Pro. Once entered, this software allowed searches of virtually any item in the database or combination thereof and allowed comparison of ads by country in order to determine the answer to research question number four. I provide a database sample in appendix B.2.[6]

---

[6]Dr. Mike Hardin constructed the database spreadsheet and layout.

2.2 Method of analysis

While important, I studied linguistic variables (syntactic, phonological, and lexical features) only if they contributed to the impact or persuasiveness of a given message in some way. A foreign accent or a particular colloquialism, for example, might help attract the consumer to a product. A rapid rate of speech might either draw the viewer's attention to the ad or be too quick for the viewer to process (as in some rapid disclaimers). Furthermore, a deep, resonating pitch for an announcer might signal authority, sensuality, humor, and so forth, depending on the context. Jingles and poetic devices such as alliteration and rhyming were also noted at times. Similarly, I noted that the syntax of poems and proverbs were used on occasion, as well as information structure and unusual collocations of words that might draw the audience's attention or help them to remember the item being advertised.[7]

2.2.1 Speech acts

I found that the literature on speech acts (as reviewed in appendix A) is relevant to persuasion in advertising because speech acts convey the conventional meaning or intent of a commercial and because the linguistic realization of particular speech acts and the context of utterance help shape the degree to which a commercial is successful in persuading viewers to buy.

Among the pragmatic variables, I classify speech acts according to the five major categories outlined in Searle (1976, 1979). These categories are

- representatives (state, hypothesize, insist),
- declarations (name, christen, curse),
- commissives (promise, offer, refuse),
- directives (suggest, order, plead), and
- expressives (thank, apologize, congratulate).

Recall that the function of representatives is to convey information, whereas directives attempt to get people to do acts, and commissives create stable expectations about speakers' behavior. Reiss (1985:34–35) further suggested that declarations "create facts of language and classification" and that expressives "convey the feelings and attitudes of speakers toward hearers." I base my determination of categories on the preconditions and felicity

---

[7] I checked my analysis with native speakers of Spanish from Spain, Chile, the United States, Ecuador, Cuba, and Panama and conferred with a number of mother-tongue speakers who hold graduate degrees in Spanish, as well as several nonnative speakers who hold doctor's degrees in Spanish linguistics.

2.2 Method of analysis

conditions outlined by Searle, as well as the context of utterance (in the case of indirect speech acts).

I counted the presence or absence of common speech acts per advertisement and determined the frequency of such speech acts. (Frequency consisted of only one count per ad.) I then categorized these speech acts according to illocutionary force. Finally, I analyzed the most frequently occurring speech acts (those occurring in more than half of all ads) to determine any relationship or contribution to persuasiveness and the degree thereof. For example, infelicitous preconditions might be expected in ads containing orders, since advertisers do not have the authority necessary to form such speech acts. When I perceived that the type of speech act was intentionally ambiguous, as in slogans containing fragments interpretable as either an order or an assertion, I entered both types of speech acts in the data for counting purposes. If it was unclear what type of speech act was intended, I entered no speech act in the database so that frequencies would be valid and not based on guesswork. Furthermore, I noted indirect speech acts as such. A few examples of speech acts along with their illocutionary force in the data appear in (2).

(2) Representatives
El único remedio que necesita es Pepto Bismol que cubre suavemente su estómago. (assertion)
The only remedy that you (FRML) need is Pepto Bismol, which gently coats your stomach.

Declaratives
Presentamos la nueva línea Alfa de Electrolux. (introduction)
We present the new Alfa line from Electrolux.

Commissives
Nuestro compromiso es darles gusto. (promise)
Our promise is to give you all pleasure.

Directives
Disfruten la ocasión. (order)
Enjoy the occasion.

Expressives
Muchas gracias. (thanks)
Many thanks.

2.2.2 Indexicals and politeness

The literature on indexicality and politeness also pertains to persuasive discourse (see appendix A). Indexicals allow hearers to be drawn into the discourse scenario and frame the social, spacial, and temporal context. Similarly, strategies of politeness establish the type of relationship between the speaker and hearer and, in doing so, determine the degree to which a discourse imposes on the hearer. I noted and analyzed devices such as deixis, tense, and person to determine their effect (if any) on politeness and persuasion. One might assume, for instance, that ads tend to attempt conditions for solidarity and closeness rather than distance from the target audience by using deictic elements of both spacial and temporal proximity. Other features I noted included verbal tense, aspect, and mood. In all cases, I recorded personal referents, including number and formal/informal. In some cases, no verbs or personal reference occurred; I also entered such details in the database. Moreover, I noted appeals to positive or negative face and information regarding relative power and distance between the speaker and audience.

FACE is the public self image that one wishes to claim. Hence, appeals to the viewer's positive face express solidarity and the desire to have one's values approved. Negative face, on the other hand, respects the viewer's freedom to act unimpeded and allows distance and preservation of status. Many ads contained both strategies; characters in the ad itself addressed one another using positive strategies and the announcer employed a negative strategy. Such cases were easily recorded in the analysis. The sample dialogue in (3) illustrates both positive and negative face in the same ad. The husband and wife communicate solidarity and the wife's desire for her husband to agree with her selection of a pain reliever. Their use of positive face contrasts with the negative face of the announcer in which he conveys authority, distance, and freedom of choice for the viewer.

(3) [Elderly couple preparing for a wedding.]
Wife: *Apúrate, Ramón.*
Hurry [INFRML], Ramón.

Husband (Ramón): *Tengo un dolor de espalda.*
I have a pain in my back

Wife: *Así no vas a disfrutar la boda. Mejor tomar Advil.*
You're [INFRML] not going to enjoy the wedding that way. Better take Advil.

2.2 Method of analysis

Husband: *¿Lo mismo que usas para el dolor de cabeza?*
The same [medicine] that you [INFRML] use for headaches?

Wife: *Sí, también alivia rápidamente el dolor de espalda.*
Yes. It also quickly relieves back pain.

Ann (M): *Los doctores recomiendan Advil para el dolor de espalda. Advil actúa directamente en el punto de origen del dolor, deteniéndolo donde comienza.*
Doctors recommend Advil for back pain. Advil acts directly on the pain's point of origin, stopping it where it starts.

Face was not addressed in some cases because the ad either communicated strategies that were "bald on record" or that were off record and without obvious personal reference. Since advertising is interactional by definition, the latter cases were counted separately. The viewers who choose not to visit the restroom or press the mute button on their television set are automatically engaged in hearing and paying attention to what the ad is trying to communicate, however passive or limited the scope of the individual's attention may be. Consequently, the advertiser is only communicating to a subset of the universe of viewers, namely, those viewers who actually pay some attention to the commercial. Finally, I examined the overall appeal to either solidarity or power for each ad.

2.2.3 The Cooperative Principle

Grice's Cooperative Principle (CP) and maxims are especially relevant to persuasion in advertising because, via implicature, they allow for more to be communicated than is actually said (see appendix A). I tallied and classified violations of the Cooperative Principle (specifically of Grice's Maxims) according to the type of violation involved. A key hypothesis in this study was that the violation and flouting of Grice's Maxims is a basic pragmatic strategy in advertising to achieve persuasion. Consequently, I examined all violations (in the generic sense) to determine if they contributed to persuasion and how (if) conversational implicature was offered. For counting purposes, I placed both violations and floutings in the same category. Following Grice's examples (1975) and those of Geis (1982), I classified violations as shown in (4). Notice that some examples may overlap and violate more than one maxim.

(4) Maxim of Quantity
　　Ellipsis

　　　Contour. Haciéndote el camino más fácil.
　　　Contour. Making the road/way easier.

　　Repetition

　　　Voice(F):　¿De limón?
　　　　　　　　Lemon?
　　　Voice(M):　*Sí. Y de Frigo. Refrescante y crujiente como ninguna*
　　　　　　　　Yes. And from Frigo. Refreshing and crunchy like no other.
　　　Voice(F):　¿De limón?
　　　　　　　　Lemon?
　　　Voice(M):　*Sí. Y de Frigo.*
　　　　　　　　Yes. And from Frigo.

Maxim of Quality
　　False assertions

　　　Hanes te conoce.
　　　Hanes knows you.

　　Metaphor

　　　Skittles. Saborea el arco iris.
　　　Skittles. Savor the rainbow.

　　Hyperbole

　　　Durante muchos años todos han querido conocer el secreto.
　　　For many years everyone has wanted to know the secret.

　　Understatement

　　　Basta una gota del nuevo jugo fresco Watt's.
　　　Even one drop of Watt's new fresh juice is enough.

　　Irony

　　　Man:　[flexing his muscles in front of a picture of the character Hercules from the recent Disney movie]
　　　　　　La gente dice que nos parecemos.
　　　　　　People say that we look alike.

2.2 Method of analysis

Maxim of Relation

Avoidance

Announcer: *Fonovisa presenta Jefe de los Jefes. Diecinueve nuevos corridos de los Tigres del Norte. Disponible en su tienda favorita.*
Fonovisa presents "Leader of Leaders." Nineteen new ballads of the Tigers of the North. Available at your favorite store.

Singer: *¡Pórtense bien!*
Behave yourselves!

Nonrelevance

Una pluma. Un balón. Así estamos haciendo la reBudlución.
A pen. A ball. That's how we're making the reBudlution.

Implied relations/ comparisons

Con valor, corazón. Cumplir con orgullo. Sólo Miller Genuine Draft.
With courage, my love. Do it with pride. Only Miller Genuine Draft.

Maxim of Manner

Rhetorical questions

¿Grandes problemas con cucarachas?
Big problems with cockroaches?

Ambiguous statements

Middle-aged woman (customer): [eating cookies and looking unhappily at women in tight mini-dresses who gave the cookies to her]
Yo las encuentro muy frescas.
I find them very fresh.

Vagueness

Estás hecho para mí.
You're made for me.
[Who is 'me'? The speaker or the viewer?]

Obscure language	*Budweiser te da las armas **para que hagas el mundo a tu manera**.* Budweiser gives you the weapons **so that you can form the world in your way.**
Euphemism	*Ahora es con más frecuencia y estamos muy, muy felices.* Now it is more frequent and we are very, very happy. [referring to sex]
Redundancy	*otro frasco adicional* another additional vial
Excessive verbosity	*Quiero mucho, mucho, mucho más ketchup.* *Quiero mucho mucho más ketchup Watt's.* I want much, much, much more ketchup. I want much, much more Watt's ketchup.

2.2.4 Implicature

I examined each ad for the presence or absence of implicature and according to its type (conventional or conversational). Conventional implicature is a result of connotations of particular linguistic items and is based on general patterns of meaning assigned to those items. In contrast, conversational implicature relies on meaning that must be derived from the context of utterance, and the hearer must work out the meaning conveyed by the speaker. I reviewed each instance of implicature with regard to its possible impact on the force of the message. It was, therefore, necessary to investigate elements such as presupposition and connotation in claims containing implicature. According to Geis (1982), indirectness via conversational implicature is expected to be the most forceful type of implicature. An example of each type appears in (5).

(5) Conventional implicature
     El único remedio que necesita es Pepto Bismol que cubre suavemente su estómago.
     The only remedy that you (FRML) need is Pepto Bismol, which gently coats your stomach.

     (presupposes that you need the product)

2.2 Method of analysis

Conversational implicature
[advertisement for an astrologer]

Endorser *La primera vez gané quince mil dólares y la segunda veinticuatro mil.*
The first time, I won fifteen thousand dollars and the second, twenty-four thousand.

(implies that viewer can win this, too)

2.2.5 Novelty

Other items addressed in this study include novelty, flattery, humor, and endorsements. Again, I counted these according to their presence or absence in each ad and evaluated them in terms of their type and contribution to persuasion. It was expected that what originally is intended by advertisers as novelty eventually becomes conventionalized. Conventionalization of novelty has occurred, for example, with slogans for products such as Coke ("Catch the wave," "It's the real thing"). Flattery, humor, and endorsements, on the other hand, might prove to be strategies for effecting solidarity or for making the speaker seem more real to the audience. In assessing speaker considerations, I consulted various native speakers to determine their impressions and reactions to advertisements in order to gain additional insights.[8]

Following Lakoff (1982), I subdivided novelty into five categories detailed in appendix A (lexical, morphological, syntactic, semantic, and pragmatic), plus three additional classes (explicit, situational, and novel associations). In addition to Lakoff's examples of Lexical Novelty, which primarily consist of neologisms, this study also includes borrowing from English, French, German, or other languages and complex jargon. Morphological Novelty, as Lakoff described it, refers to category shifts such as "Gentles the smoke and makes it mild" (p. 36). In this study, however, I also examined adjectival chaining or loading and possessive pronouns that were used in unusual ways. Syntactic Novelty (Lakoff's syntactic innovation) is reflected in the absence of subjects or articles and Semantic Novelty (Lakoff's semantic anomaly) consists of elliptical comparisons. Pragmatic Novelty is composed of aberrance in the form of discourse, such as unusual dialogue. In this study it

---

[8]Special appreciation goes to the following Spanish speakers for their comments and insights: Fátima Alfonso-Pinto, Mimi Bagnasco, Dr. Guillermo García-Corales, Dr. Baudelio Garza, Dr. Julio Jiménez, Dr. Paul Larson, Lupita Limage-Montesinos, Dr. Fred Loa, María Mayberry, Dr. Linda McManness, and Delia Montesinos. Any errors are, of course, entirely my own.

is limited to instances where one character completes another's sentence in an awkward or unusual way.

Explicit Novelty consists of lexical items that overtly indicate that a product is in some way new. *Nuevo* 'new', *presentamos* 'we present/introduce', *ahora* 'now', and *por primera vez* 'for the first time' are common examples of Explicit Novelty. Situational Novelty is indicated by an unusual setting, a surprise ending to a mini-drama, or shock tactics. New Associations designate particular comparisons or novel associations not inherent to the product itself, such as emotional or sexual characteristics. A few illustrations of novelty in Spanish ads appear in (6).

(6) Examples of Novelty

Explicit
*Para las feas venas varicosas **nuevo** sistema Venacilin.*
For ugly varicose veins, **new** Venacilin system.

Lexical
Esto es el Disney Music Collection.
This is the Disney Music Collection.

Cuestión de PERTsonalidad.
A question of PERTsonality.

Morphological
El único chocolate extra fino relleno.
The only extra-fine filled chocolate.

*Si tú quieres **tu mug, tu Nescafé,** tómalo del mug, auténtico mug.*
If you want **your mug, your Nescafé,** drink it from the mug, authentic mug.

Syntactic
Siempre Coca Cola.
Always Coca Cola.

Advil. Medicina Avanzada Para Aliviar Dolores.
Advil. Advanced Medicine to Relieve Pain.

Semantic
Te da más. [slogan for Western Union]
It gives you more.

2.2 Method of analysis

Pragmatic
Manager: *Y este es mi McDonald's.*
And this is my McDonald's.

Announcer: *Donde ahora cuando compras cualquier sandwich grande o Happy Meal, puedes comprar uno de tres discos compactos por menos de cuatro dólares.*
Where now when you buy any large sandwich or Happy Meal, you can buy one of three compact discs for less than four dollars.

Situational
Vocalist: *El día amanece. Hoy van a celebrarle con Folgers el cumpleaños a Mamá.*
The day is beginning. Today they are going to celebrate Mom's birthday with Folgers.

New associations
El sabor de Kellogg's Frosted Flakes para un tigre de ti.
The flavor of Kellogg's Frosted Flakes for a tiger in you.

2.2.6 Other strategies

I noted and included sociolinguistic information regarding speaker considerations as a context for analysis. That is, information regarding speakers' gender, age, profession, and physical characteristics was taken into account, particularly as they related to persuasion. Speaker considerations may reinforce the advertiser's message by conveying authority, solidarity, or authenticity to the target audience. In a pilot study of one hundred Spanish ads on Univisión, for example, male speakers were used to express any material of a "scientific" or informational nature or to convey authority about a product. The pilot study contained just two examples of female speakers who were career women presenting pseudo-scientific information, both in advertisements for Tums. In an advertisement for EPT (Early Pregnancy Test), the male speaker conveyed authoritative information such as a description of the product, instructions on how to use it, and statistics, shown in (7). This example was particularly interesting in light of the fact that the product is for women and one might expect a female to convey such information. Thus, speaker considerations were expected to be found throughout ads to convey authority and to strengthen the force of an advertiser's claim.

(7) Announcer (M): *EPT. Es tan fácil de usar y confiable como siempre. Sólo EPT tiene una punta absorbente así de ancha y una ventanilla sellada a prueba de derrames.... Más del 99% correcto.*
EPT. It is so easy to use and as trustworthy as ever. Only EPT has an absorbent point this wide and a sealed waterproof window from spills.... More than 99% correct.

Finally, ads were also compared to see if there are any patterns according to content (clothing, food, footwear, and so forth), based on categories reported in the Standard Rate and Data Service (1997) and other categories. All ads fell into one of the categories in table 2.5.

Table 2.5 Classification of types of ads

Foods	Footwear	Sporting goods
Meals and snacks	Major household appliances	Powered vehicles
Alcoholic drinks		Travel
Tobacco	TV and video	Recreation
Health and beauty aids	Audio equipment	Education
Soap/household cleaners	Furniture	Other services
Mens/boyswear	Kitchenware/home furnishings	Financial
Womens/girlswear		Miscellaneous
Toys	Computer	(multiple categories)
Both mens/womenswear	Medical/social services	

2.2.7 Contribution to persuasion

As previously mentioned, I made notation of any example in any given commercial which contributed to persuasion. Rank (1988:10) adapted Cicero's classical oration and Aristotle's "ethos" into a basic persuasive formula for advertisements. His five components were (a) attention-getting, (b) confidence-building, (c) desire-stimulating, (d) urgency-stressing, and (e) response-seeking. These components roughly correspond to the persuasive goals regularly noted in the present study. When recording contributions of strategies to persuasion, I placed particular emphasis on

- attention-getting devices, mnemonic devices, and other features that made an ad memorable (attention-getting),

- the strength or force of the appeal or claim (confidence-building, desire-stimulating, and urgency-stressing), and
- efforts to evoke participation of the viewer with the speaker or message (response-seeking).

Giora (1993:107) stated that poetry and commercials use ambiguity as a device to force the recipient to invest energy in processing their messages.

2.3 Sample analysis of an ad

A sample analysis of an advertisement from Univisión is presented in (8).

(8) Analysis of commercial for *HBO en Español*

HBO en Español (Univisión, 10/31/96, Papá Soltero)
Type: Television product
Setting: various (outside, gym)
Characters: famous boxers, Hispanic and non-Hispanic

Text:
Announcer (male): *Ahora lo mejor en boxeo le llega totalmente en su idioma por HBO en español.*
Now the best of boxing comes to you totally in your language on HBO in Spanish.
Boxer 1 (Non-Hispanic, American accent): *Boxeo.*   [bakséɪoʊ]
                                       Boxing.

Boxer 2 ("): *Eh, ¿qué pasa amigos?*   [éɪ kʰeɪ pʰása amígoʊz]
    Eh, what's happening, friends?

Boxer 3 ("): *¿Qué hora es?*   [kʰeɪ óɹə ɛs]
    What time is it?

Boxer 4 ("): *Adiós amigos.*   [adióʊs amígoʊz]
    Bye, friends.

Boxer 5 (Hispanic): [laughing] *Eso sí. Hay que mejorar el acento.*
    That's it. The accent needs improving.

Announcer: *Boxeo en español en HBO en español. Los mejores boxeadores pelean...*
Boxing in Spanish on HBO in Spanish. The best boxers fight...

Boxer 6 (non-Hispanic): *Aquí.* [akʰí]
Here.

Announcer: *Llame a su compañía local de cable y ordene HBO en español ahora.*
Call your local cable company and order HBO in Spanish now.

Features: Product: TV and video
Target audience (Spanish-speaking, sports enthusiasts)

Speech acts:
representatives (*Ahora lo mejor en boxeo le llega totalmente en su idioma por HBO en español.*)

directives (*Llame a su compañía local de cable*)

Novelty (explicit): **Ahora** *lo mejor en boxeo le llega...*

Flattery (*en su idioma,* contrast between Spanish speaking of two groups of boxers)

Humor (use of American boxers speaking Spanish)

Endorsements (boxers)

Indexicals/politeness:
deixis *(ahora, le llega, eso, aquí)*
personal reference *(su , llame, ordene* vs. *amigos)*
power *(llame, ordene*)
distance *(su*)

Implicature:
conventional *(en su idioma*)
conversational *(Hay que mejorar el acento*)

Violations of Maxims (relevance, quantity)

Phonology (mispronunciation)

Lexicon (simple)

Speaker considerations (contrast)

2.3 Sample analysis of an ad

This commercial contains examples of novelty, flattery, humor, and endorsements. Examples of special phonological and lexical features and speaker considerations, as well as politeness, violations of conversational maxims, and implicature also are present. Speech acts include representatives and directives. The target audience is obviously Spanish-speaking and likely includes sports aficionados.

2.3.1 Speech acts

The announcer and Spanish-speaking boxer's messages primarily contain representative speech acts, with the illocutionary force of asserting that all information stated is factual. Note that representatives meet three conditions:

1. They commit the speaker to something being described.
2. The speaker believes the stated proposition.
3. The speaker tries to get his words to match the world (Searle 1979).

Examples of representatives primarily occur in the announcer's speech, illustrated in (9a–b). Boxer 5's speech in (9c) is also a representative. Rather than expressing a directive, an attempt to get the other boxers to improve their accent, the Spanish-speaking boxer is instead stating a proposition that he believes to be true. It is unlikely that he expects any future action by the other boxers as a result of his statement. Furthermore, the assertions contained in the ad relate to the persuasive component of force/strength of claim because the speakers presume that their words match both their world and that of the audience.

(9) a. *Ahora lo mejor en boxeo le llega totalmente en su idioma por HBO en español.*
Now the best of boxing comes to you totally in your language on HBO in Spanish.

b. *Los mejores boxeadores pelean...aquí.*
The best boxers fight...here.

c. *Eso sí. Hay que mejorar el acento.*
That's right. The accent needs improving.

Two directives occur in the last line of the commercial, in which the announcer attempts to order viewers to call their cable company and to order HBO in Spanish. These directives are encoded using formal commands. The commands are infelicitous as orders, however, in that they do not meet the preparatory condition of ability. Neither the announcer nor HBO in Spanish have the power to issue orders to their target audience. Although formed as an order, the force is diminished. It may be that commands in advertising are conventionalized forms for suggestions; however, it is unlikely that the passive viewer bothers to consider such a fact. The advertiser attempts to force the viewer into the position of either obeying or disobeying the orders. Nevertheless, it is likely that the viewer takes the orders as suggestions, knowing that the advertiser does not have the power to issue orders. These directives effect persuasion by means of the force/strength of appeal and perhaps by forcing the audience to participate in the message.

The word *ahora* 'now' in the announcer's first line is an explicit example of novelty used to convey the idea that the product is new and implicitly that it was not available before. It is, in effect, an attention-getting device. Lexical novelty occurs with the English pronunciation of HBO in (9a) even though the statement says that the product is totally in Spanish. Flattery and humor, on the other hand, are more subtle in this ad. The viewer is able to identify with and laugh along with Boxer 5 in recognizing the poor Spanish pronunciation of the other boxers. Consequently, the contrast portrayed places the audience in the in group with the Spanish-speaking boxer. The contrast between Spanish versus non-Spanish speakers is further supported by the statement that the best of boxing is now coming to you in **your** language on HBO.

2.3.2 Novelty, flattery, and humor

Although there is an appeal to solidarity in the previous statement, note that the ad also conveys authority by using a male speaker (with a deep voice) and through selection of formal pronouns and commands, illustrated in (10). The announcer's statements contrast with the informality of the non-Hispanic boxers in (11) whose messages communicate very little meaning and primarily provide humor because of their poor Spanish and the fact that they are boxers who are stereotypically depicted as being stupid. Flattery and humor effect persuasion in this ad by both strength of emotional appeal and evoking viewer participation in making them "work out" or infer the humor in the Gricean sense.

(10) a. *Ahora lo mejor en boxeo **le** llega totalmente en **su** idioma...*
 Now the best in boxing comes **to-you** (3SG, FRML) totally in **your** (3SG, FRML) language.

b. **Llame** a su compañía local de cable y **ordene** HBO en español ahora.
   Call (FRML) **your** (FRML) local cable company and **order** (FRML) HBO in Spanish now.

(11) a. *Eh, ¿qué pasa amigos?*   Eh, what's happening, friends?

   b. *Adiós amigos.*   Bye, friends.

2.3.3 Politeness, indexicals, and implicature

Politeness, as stated earlier, is evident in appeals to both positive and negative face. The boxers appeal to positive face in their informality, whereas the announcer communicates distance from the audience, and therein authority, via selection of formal pronouns and commands. Here, both types of face effect persuasion in the degree of force/strength of appeal. Deictic referents such as *ahora* 'now', *aquí* 'here', and *llega* 'comes' serve to foreground the product, HBO in Spanish, both in time and space, as does selection of second person and use of the present tense. Again, these elements are related to attention-getting devices and the impact of the message, components of persuasion.

The announcer's opening statement, "Now the best in boxing comes to you totally in **your** language," presupposes and, therefore, conventionally implicates that the viewer's audience is indeed Spanish. This implication contributes to persuasion by identifying the product with the audience. The expression *hay que* 'it is necessary' or 'one has to' in Spanish does not overtly state who must do the action. Nevertheless, the context and the audience's background knowledge make it clear that it is not Boxer 5 whose accent needs improving. Instead, the phrase conversationally implicates that Boxers 1–4 need to improve their Spanish accents. The implication contributes to persuasion by drawing a distinction between two cultural groups, those that speak Spanish and those that do not. Furthermore, the implication contributes to humor in the ad by utilizing the presupposition that boxers are not very clever and do not have much to say of any significance. The implicature must be worked out and, therefore, relates to the viewer participation component of persuasion. It also effects a forceful message because it is indirect and unlikely to be denied or cancelled by the audience.

2.3.4 Grice's Maxims

Grice's Maxim of Relevance is violated in that the messages of Boxers 2–4 ('What's happening, friends?', 'What time is it?', 'Bye, friends') do not clearly relate to the topic at hand, which is boxing on HBO in Spanish. Furthermore, the selection of simple words and phrases for Boxers 1–4 and 6 is deliberate and reinforces the contrast between them and Boxer 5. Like the example of implicature, the violation forces the audience to participate by staying involved in the ad until it can be understood. The Maxim of Quantity is violated by means of repetition, a strategy prevalent in advertising. Thus, the advertisement is more informative than that which is required. *HBO en español* is repeated three times, and *boxeo* and its derivative, *boxeadores,* occur four times. Repetition is used to contribute to product recognition and to attract the audience's attention.

2.4.5 Summary

In this chapter, I explained the method of data collection and analysis. We saw some of the features in table 2.4 and pragmatic strategies contributing to persuasion in just one advertisement on Univisión. While a particular device such as implicature may not obviously contribute to persuasion in just one ad, a variety of ads more clearly reveals the pattern of ways in which a given feature contributes to persuasion. Analysis of a large corpus (723 ads) from more than one region of the Spanish-speaking world can provide a broad basis for an eventual classification of pragmatic strategies used to effect persuasion in Spanish advertising. I offer a detailed analysis of the complete corpus in chapters 3 and 4.

3
Analysis and Results

3.1 Introduction

As presented in chapter 1, the general questions addressed in this study are:

1. Which pragmatic devices occur most frequently in Spanish television advertising?
2. How are these pragmatic devices linguistically encoded in the data?
3. Are any pragmatic differences evident between dialects of Spanish?
4. How are pragmalinguistic features of television advertising used to effect persuasion?

In this chapter, I address the first three questions, loosely applying Pike's (1982) concepts of contrast, variation, and distribution in analyzing the data. That is, the analysis contrasts the variables chosen for the study, examines variation within each category, and addresses the distribution of each variable among the countries included. The purpose of this approach is to provide a thorough description and analysis of pragmatic strategies as they occur in Spanish television advertising. The analysis in this chapter is particularly important in its application to persuasion, which I will address further in chapter 4.

As discussed in chapter 2, the principal variables selected for examination are context, pragmalinguistic variables, and pragmatic variables. Contextual variables include three countries: the United States (Univisión), Spain (Antena 3), and Chile (Teletrece). Other contextual variables are product, which includes twenty-six classes, and audience, which comprises four major divisions and twelve subgroups.

See table 2.4 for the categories included in the database for analysis. The principal categories of analysis in the database are the variables in (12), as well as novelty, flattery, humor, and endorsements.

(12) Context   (Pragma-)linguistic   Pragmatic

    Country   Phonology   Speech acts
    Product   Lexicon   Indexicals
    Audience   Syntax   Politeness
                               Implicature
                               Violation of Grice's Maxims
                               Speaker considerations

Once the analysis was completed, the categories of novelty, flattery, humor, lexical selection, and endorsements were found to be subsumed by other categories. Furthermore, because special phonological features and special information structure are not present in a majority of ads, I did not consider them to be major factors in this study. Recall that the criterion for factors most reflective of advertising discourse was that they had to be present in more than fifty percent of the data. I present a further discussion of the final classification of major pragmatic strategies in chapter 4.

3.2 Pragmatic strategies reflected in the data

3.2.1 Context

In order to better understand the setting in which data were obtained, I will first examine the contextual variables of product and audience for Spanish advertising. Of these contextual variables, the preference for products/services is depicted in table 3.1. Products are generally categorized following the divisions reported in the *Standard Rate and Data Service* (1997). Although no single category is found in a majority of ads, the combined categories of foods and meals/snacks account for 32.1 percent of the data. Hence, the ads in this study mainly represent foods (of any type). The twelve product categories listed first in table 3.1 (foods through major household appliances) comprise 87.5 percent of the total and each of the other categories represents less than two percent of the total (n = 723). The top three categories of foods, meals/snacks, and health/beauty are most useful for this

3.2 Pragmatic strategies reflected in the data

study, because they account for the majority of ads and, therefore, reflect the most examples of persuasive discourse in the data.

Table 3.1 Proportion of product categories in database (n = 723)

Category	Number of ads	Percent of total
Foods	142	19.6
Health and beauty aids	134	18.5
Meals and snacks	89	12.3
Powered vehicles	57	7.9
Audio	49	6.8
Financial	33	4.6
Recreation	28	3.9
Soap and household cleaners	27	3.7
Education	22	3.0
TV and video	21	2.9
Alcoholic drinks	16	2.2
Major household appliances	15	2.1
Kitchenware and home	13	1.8
Travel	13	1.8
Both men's and women's	12	1.7
Miscellaneous	12	1.6
Toys	8	1.1
Computer	7	1.0
Women's and girls'	7	1.0
Other services (legal, utility)	5	0.7
Footwear	4	0.6
Men's and boys'	3	0.4
Furniture	3	0.4
Medical and social	3	0.4
Tobacco	0	0.0
Sporting goods	0	0.0

The order of frequency for the top five products by country is as shown in (13). Again, regardless of the country of origin, foods, meals/snacks, and health/beauty are preferred and account for over a third of the advertising discourse in this study. The preference in ad categories probably also reveals advertisers' views of what is most important to their respective audiences.

(13) United States: (1) health and beauty, (2) foods, powered vehicles, (3) audio, (4) meals and snacks, (5) recreation

Spain: (1) health and beauty, (2) foods, (3) meals and snacks, (4) powered vehicles, (5) soaps and household cleaners

Chile: (1) foods, (2) health and beauty, (3) meals and snacks, (4) financial, (5) audio, education

A comparison of product categories by country is illustrated in table 3.2. In general, there are no great differences in the distribution of categories by country. Although Teletrece (Chile) contains more ads for foods than the other two stations, all show foods as the preferred category. There are some minor differences between countries, such as the absence of Chilean ads for alcoholic drinks (because of station restrictions), the virtual absence of Spanish ads for educational tools (perhaps because of the country's high literacy rate), and the greater number of travel advertisements in Spain (because the ads occurred during the peak vacation time of year). Nevertheless, these contextual variables illustrate the overall similarity in product preference according to country.

Table 3.2 Product categories by country (n = 241)

Product	U.S.	%	Spain	%	Chile	%
Foods	31	12.9	45	18.7	66	27.4
Meals and snacks	21	8.7	36	14.9	32	13.3
Alcoholic drinks	13	5.4	3	1.2	0	0.0
Health and beauty	39	16.2	46	19.1	49	20.3
Soap and household cleaners	3	1.2	15	6.2	9	3.7
Men's and boys'	2	0.8	1	0.4	0	0.0
Women's and girls'	0	0.0	6	2.5	1	0.4
Both men's and women's	4	1.7	3	1.2	5	2.1
Footwear	3		0	0.0	1	0.4
Major household appliances	4	1.7	6	2.5	5	2.1
TV and video	9	3.7	10	4.1	2	0.8
Audio	24	10.0	14	5.8	11	4.6
Furniture	3	1.2	0	0.0	0	0.0
Kitchenware/home	4	1.7	2	0.8	7	2.9
Computer	0	0.0	2	0.8	5	2.1
Sporting goods	0	0.0	0	0.0	0	0.0

Product	U.S.	%	Spain	%	Chile	%
Powered vehicles	31	12.9	22	9.1	4	1.7
Travel	2	0.8	11	4.6	0	0.0
Recreation	16	6.6	7	2.9	5	2.1
Education	10	4.1	1	0.4	11	4.6
Financial	11	4.6	7	2.9	15	6.2
Medical and social	2	0.8	0	0.0	1	0.4
Toys	0	0.0	4	1.7	4	1.7
Other services (legal, utility)	3	1.2	0	0.0	2	0.8
Miscellaneous	5	2.1	1	0.4	6	2.5

The contextual variable of the audience shown in table 3.3 reveals that the majority of Spanish ads (examples of persuasive discourse) are directed at adults (90.3 percent). This focus on adults reflects the reality that it is adults who control the finances in each society. The audience category was subdivided into age groups as indicated. Some ads (general) were not directed at any particular age group, and some are directed to more than one category of audience, so that the frequencies do not add up to one hundred percent.

Table 3.3 Frequencies for audience categories (n = 723)

Audience category		Number of ads	Percent of total
Children		83	11.5
	children (girls)	4	0.6
	children (boys)	4	0.6
Teens		65	9.0
	teens (female)	2	0.3
	teens (male)	2	0.3
Adults		653	90.3
	adults (young)	78	10.8
	adults (women)	147	20.3
	adults (men)	55	7.6
	adults (parents)	45	6.2
	adults (mothers)	39	5.4
	adults (fathers)	0	0.0
	adults (older)	5	0.7
	adults (all others)	291	40.2
General		15	2.1

When products are compared with audience categories, most ads for older adults (60 percent) and almost half of the ads for women (49.7 percent) are for health and beauty products. Similarly, more than half of all ads for children, teens, parents, mothers, and general audiences are for foods and meals/snacks.

Finally, audience categories are fairly evenly distributed across countries, as shown in table 3.4. Adult women are less targeted in the U.S. than in Spain and Chile; however, far more ads are specifically directed at mothers in the U.S. than in Spain and Chile. That is, regardless of the country, Spanish advertising discourse primarily attempts to persuade women and appears to target a similar distribution of audiences.

Table 3.4 Audience by country (n = 241)

	U.S.	Spain	Chile
Children	28	25	30
Teens	21	18	26
Adults (young)	28	20	30
Adults (general)	100	110	79
Adults (women)	30	59	58
Adults (men)	26	13	16
Adults (parents)	18	11	16
Adults (mothers)	23	8	8
Adults (older)	3	1	1
All	2	2	11

Although I examined the contextual variables of product, audience, and country in detail, the analysis does not yield important information regarding their role in the pragmatics of persuasion. Instead they provide a contextual backdrop for the rest of the study, indicating that the bulk of Spanish advertising in this study is directed at adults (especially women), with a distinct preference for food products of some sort or health/beauty products. Furthermore, the distribution of product and audience preferences are similar and, therefore, comparable when analyzing pragmatics and persuasion in ads from Spain, Chile, and the United States.

3.2.2 Speech acts

Which pragmatic devices occur most frequently in Spanish television advertising? In order to describe the pragmatics of Spanish television advertising adequately, I first examine which pragmatic strategies are

3.2 Pragmatic strategies reflected in the data

major, occurring in more than fifty percent of the data, to determine which strategies are most reflective of the persuasive discourse under consideration. I begin with the category of speech acts in discussing data analysis and results.

Speech acts are present in all but two ads and, therefore, constitute one of the major pragmatic variables in this study. The classes of speech acts that occur most in the data are representatives and directives, as in table 3.5. Less frequent are expressives, commissives, and declarations.

Table 3.5 Distribution of common speech Acts (n = 723)

Category	Percent of total
Representatives	95.7
Assertions	92.5
Directives	58.4
Orders	50.1
Expressives	20.3
Introductions	6.6
Commissives	19.8
Offer	9.1
Declarations	11.2
Introductions	6.6

Representatives, or speech acts that convey information and express the speaker's belief, are found in the majority of ads (95.7 percent). Directives are also found in the majority of ads (58.4 percent). In contrast, commissives (69.8 percent), expressives (20.3 percent), and declarations (11.2 percent) are not represented in a majority of ads. In this study, frequencies are based only on the presence or absence of a given class of speech acts and do not reflect repetitions.

Within classes of speech acts, the overwhelming majority of representatives in ads (96.8 percent) are assertions. The majority of directives (90.7 percent) are orders, and more than half of declarations are introductions. Expressives and commissives do not have one specific type of speech act in the majority of ads. Hence, representatives and directives form the most unified classes of speech acts in the data, and the specific speech acts most used in Spanish ads are assertions and orders. This frequency suggests that Spanish advertising language is primarily intended to present facts or opinions (as if they were facts) to attempt to make viewers purchase or use a product/service.

3.2.3 Indexicals and politeness

Indexicals and politeness are also major pragmatic categories in advertising language. Indexicals (deixis, tense, personal reference) are found in all but twenty ads (97.2 percent). Of these, deixis and personal reference are especially reflected in the data (91.0 percent and 84.2 percent, respectively). Tense is measured as those ads containing any tense other than the present. Therefore, tense (nonpresent) is not a major factor and is found in just 37.4 percent of the ads. Present tense, on the other hand, is found in the majority of ads (95.3 percent). These numbers show that present tense, personal reference, and other deictic items are orientational devices widely used by Spanish advertisers. I examine the purpose of indexicals in Spanish advertising discourse in chapter 4.

Politeness is a major factor in the data and is evident in 714 (98.8 percent) of the ads. Positive strategies for politeness occur in the majority of ads (428 ads, or 60.0 percent), although negative strategies follow in preference (320 ads, or 44.3 percent). Only fifty-five (7.6 percent) of the ads contain both positive and negative strategies. In comparing solidarity versus power, solidarity is found to be more reflective of the data. Markers of solidarity occur in 55.6 percent of all ads, whereas power is reflected in 43.7 percent of the data. What these numbers suggest is that strategies for politeness tend to emphasize the similarity between the desires of characters in ads (or the product image) and the audience. Nevertheless, formal politeness and avoidance of imposition are also very common strategies.

The distribution of politeness strategies and indexicals is shown in table 3.6.

Table 3.6 Distribution of indexicals and politeness strategies (n = 723)

Category	Percent of total
Indexicals	97.2
deictic items	91.0
personal reference	84.2
tense (nonpresent)	37.4
Politeness	98.8
positive	60.0
negative	44.3
positive and negative	55.6
solidarity	43.7

3.2.4 Grice's Maxims

A basic hypothesis in this study is that violation of Grice's Maxims is a key pragmatic strategy in effecting persuasion. Partially to determine whether this hypothesis is correct, I examined ads for the presence of at least one violation. That is, violation of Grice's Maxims had to occur in the majority of ads for it to be considered as an important pragmatic strategy in advertising. All but two ads in the data (99.7 percent) contain at least one violation of Grice's Maxims. Furthermore, each individual maxim is represented in a majority of ads. Of these maxims, I found violation of: relation in 89.2 percent, quantity in 73.2 percent, quality in 70.5 percent, and manner in 64.2 percent. The order of frequency for violations of maxims is relation, quantity, quality, and manner, but there is very little actual difference in the frequency of the last three. Initially, I considered novelty to be a separate category; however, if I include novelty as a violation of manner as Lakoff (1982) suggested, violations of manner become the largest category of violations.[9] In chapter 4, I further discuss how the Cooperative Principle contributes to persuasion in Spanish advertising.

Implicature also occurs in a majority of ads (95.8 percent). Both conversational and conventional implicature are found in a majority of ads, representing 85.1 percent and 60.6 percent, respectively. Thus, violation of Grice's Maxims and both types of implicature are important factors in Spanish advertising discourse and are relevant to the discussion in chapter 4 of strategies that contribute to persuasion. Their distribution is summarized in table 3.7.

Table 3.7 Distribution of Grice's Maxims and implicature (n = 723)

Category	Percent of total
Grice's Maxims	99.7
relation	89.2
quantity	73.2
quality	70.5
manner	64.2
Implicature	95.8
conversational	85.1
conventional	60.6

---

[9]For a further discussion of this recategorization, see chapter 4.

3.2.5 Speaker considerations

Speaker considerations are noted only for actual speakers and not for other characters who, although they contribute to the appeal of a given ad, do not contribute linguistically. I found at least one speaker consideration (gender, age, profession, or physical characteristics) in just over half of all ads in the data (54.4 percent). Of these, no single category is found in the majority of all ads; age, physical characteristics, and profession of the speaker in 22.5, 21.9, and 19.4 percent of all ads, respectively. I measure gender as the presence of an announcer or primary speaker that is either female or mixed in a given ad. Gender, therefore, reflects only 13.7 percent of all ads. Of the ninety-nine ads with female announcers or primary speakers, 21 (21.2 percent) ads also have an equally important male speaker, and 8 percent are ads in which the female "speaker" is a vocalist. Just 1.4 percent of the ads have no speaker at all. Thus, the majority of ads contain announcers or primary speakers who are male (94.9 percent of all ads). This fact illustrates the importance of males rather than females as conveyors of information and authority and the role of gender in Spanish-speaking societies. Gender distribution in ads is especially interesting in light of the fact that Spanish advertising is primarily directed at women viewers. Women are seen as the principal consumers in Spanish-speaking societies, yet men (male announcers) are used to try to convince women to buy.

The representation of speaker considerations in the data is listed in table 3.8.

Table 3.8 Distribution of speaker considerations (n = 723)

Category	Percent of total
Speaker considerations	54.4
age	22.5
physical characteristics	21.9
profession	19.4
gender (female or mixed)	13.7

3.2.6 Pragmalinguistic variables

Of the so-called pragmalinguistic variables (phonological elements, information structure, and lexical selection), I found only lexical factors in the majority of ads. I noted lexical items such as neologisms, foreign words, or particularly unusual word choice in 68.0 percent of all ads. Thus, lexical selection could be considered as a major pragmalinguistic

3.2 Pragmatic strategies reflected in the data

variable. Nevertheless, as I argue in chapter 4, most lexical elements noted in the study consist of some type of novelty and are, therefore, better characterized as such. I found phonological elements and syntax (information structure), respectively, in only 24.2 percent and 18.8 percent of the ads. I consider them as minor variables in this study. Table 3.9 shows the distribution of pragmalinguistic variables in Spanish television ads.

Table 3.9 Distribution of pragmalinguistic variables (n=723)

Category	Percent of total
Lexical selection	68.0
Phonological elements	24.2
Information structure	18.8

3.2.7 Other strategies

The database was initially formulated with the additional categories of novelty, flattery, humor, and endorsement. Some type of novelty occurs in every ad in the data, which means it may be considered as a major strategy in Spanish advertising. Nevertheless, as I argue in chapter 4, most types of novelty occur as violations of Grice's Maxims. The most common types in Spanish ads are syntactic and explicit novelty. Lexical, semantic, and situational novelty, as well as novel association, occur in over one-third of all ads. I found only morphological and pragmatic novelty in less than 33 percent of all ads. The order of preference for novelty is as follows:

- Syntactic (85.2 percent);
- Explicit, e.g., *ahora* 'now', *nuevo* 'new' (55.3 percent);
- Lexical (38.5 percent);
- Semantic (37.9 percent);
- Situational (36.1 percent);
- Novel association (35.7 percent);
- Morphological (11.8 percent); and
- Pragmatic (10.1 percent).

Unlike novelty, flattery is not a major pragmatic strategy in the data and I found it in only 35.3 percent of all ads. Similarly, endorsement is not a major strategy, found in just 39.4 percent of the ads. This number includes both direct and indirect/secondary endorsements by characters in ads. Humor is not present in the majority of ads (26.4 percent) and is a result of implicature in the majority (80.6 percent) of these ads. I present a reclassification of minor pragmatic strategies in the data in chapter 4. Table 3.10 illustrates the distribution of the remaining (minor) strategies in this study.

Table 3.10 Distribution of speaker considerations (n = 723)

Category	Percent of total
Novelty	100.0
syntactic	85.2
explicit	55.3
lexical	38.5
semantic	37.9
situational	36.1
novel association	35.7
morphological	11.8
pragmatic	10.1
Endorsement	39.4
Flattery	35.3
Humor	26.4

3.2.8 Summary

Of the factors analyzed, the major strategies in the data, based on frequency, are speech acts, novelty, indexicals, politeness, implicature, violation of maxims, speaker considerations, and lexicon. Moreover, these are preferred strategies even when pragmatic variables are analyzed according to audience, product, and country, suggesting that these pragmatic strategies are important regardless of the type of ad, the type of viewer, and the dialect of Spanish. Table 3.11 depicts the frequencies for each pragmatic variable in this study.

Table 3.11 Frequencies of pragmatic variables (n = 723)

Variables	Number of ads	Percent of database
Novelty	723	100.0
Speech acts	721	99.7
Violation of maxims	721	99.7
Politeness	714	98.8
Indexicals	703	97.2
Implicature	691	95.8
Lexical items	492	68.0

3.3 Linguistic realization of strategies in the data

Variables	Number of ads	Percent of database
Speaker considerations	393	54.4
Endorsements	285	39.4
Flattery	255	35.3
Humor	191	26.4
Phonological elements	175	24.2
Information structure	136	18.8

Minor variables include flattery, humor, endorsements, syntax, and phonology. Of the major variables, representatives and directives are most reflective of speech acts in advertising, and the most common types of novelty are syntactic and explicit novelty. Deictic elements and personal reference are types of indexicals found in the majority of ads, and positive face and solidarity are the most common strategies of politeness. Finally, both types of implicature in the study and all of the violations of Grice's Maxims occur in the majority of all ads. Thus, there are preferred strategies within each major category that are employed regardless of the country of origin.

In summary, the data indicates that the variables in this study are reflective of advertising in three geographically distant and culturally distinct regions of the Spanish speaking world, a result that allows me in chapter 4 to analyze the link between these variables and persuasion for Spanish advertising language in general.

3.3 Linguistic realization of strategies in the data

The second research question addresses the variation within pragmatic strategies by asking the following: how are these pragmatic devices linguistically encoded in the data? This question is important in order to describe adequately *how* advertising language linguistically achieves its pragmatic, and ultimately persuasive, goals. Furthermore, since the data examples are types of persuasive discourse, the structures contained in them are utilized as a partial means of achieving persuasion.

3.3.1 Speech acts

Each class of speech acts is realized by a variety of individual speech acts and illocutionary forces in ads. As previously mentioned, assertions account for the overwhelming majority of representatives and, indeed, the majority of individual speech acts in Spanish ads. Assertions are primarily encoded in the form of declarative statements expressing opinions as though they were facts and sometimes as assertions of actual or probable facts. Assertions, therefore, are used to make an ad sound like it is presenting factual information rather than opinions. Examples of assertions of fact, whether real or imagined, appear in (14).[10]

(14) Assertions

> *Apple Jacks de Kellogg's. El cereal con chispa.*
> Kellogg's Apple Jacks. The cereal with sparkle. (Apple Jacks, U.S.)

> *Para la mayoría de los malestares estomacales, el remedio es el mismo.*
> For the majority of stomach problems, the remedy is the same. (Pepto Bismol, U.S.)

> *Nuevo Sanex Germen de Trigo alimenta tu piel.*
> New Sanex Wheatgerm nourishes your skin. (Sanex shampoo, SP)

> *El set Arcobaleno incluye todo lo necesario para su cocina.*
> The Arcobaleno set includes everything necessary for your kitchen. (Arcobaleno dishes, SP)

> *Porque nada se parece más al jugo de naranja Sprim, ya son miles los fánaticos de su sabor.*
> Because nothing is more like Sprim orange juice, already thousands are fans of its flavor. (Sprim, CH)

> *La imagen es nada. La sed es todo.*
> Image is nothing. Thirst is everything. (Sprite, CH)

Most slogans also appear as assertions of fact as in (15). Slogans commonly contain pithy, easily remembered assertions that summarize a product's appeal.

(15) Assertions as slogans

> *La más fría.*
> The coldest. (Miller, U.S.)

> *Una inversión para toda la vida.*
> An investment for your entire life. (Century 21, U.S.)

> *Un poco de pasta basta.*
> A little pasta is enough. (Gior, SP)

---

[10]Throughout the remainder of this study, country designations for ads will be as follows: U.S. (United States), SP (Spain), CH (Chile).

3.3 Linguistic realization of strategies in the data

Porque yo lo valgo.
Because I'm worth it. (L'Oreal, SP)

Como una roca.
Like a rock. (Chevrolet, CH)

Mucho más.
Much more. (TV Grama magazine, CH)

Assertions also often contain ellipsis of verbs or subjects, leaving the viewer to infer the meaning. In most cases, ellipsis in assertions merely consists of deletion of the copula *ser* 'to be'. See examples in (16).

(16) Assertions containing ellipsis

Corn Pops de Kellogg's. Dulcemente irresistibles.
Kellogg's Corn Pops. Sweetly irresistible. (Corn Pops, U.S.)

Priority Mail. La decisión más fácil para su negocio.
Priority Mail. The easiest decision for your business. (Priority Mail, U.S.)

Nidos Cinta Gallo. Buenos, buenos.
Nidos Cinta Gallo. Good, good. (Nidos Cinta Gallo pasta, SP)

Nueva fórmula Organics. Una belleza más profunda desde la raíz.
New Organics formula. A deeper beauty from the root. (Organics shampoo, SP)

Fuerte. Vigoroso. Confiable. El pickup Chevy S10 [Sdiez] de 97 [noventa y siete].
Strong. Vigorous. Trustworthy. The 97 Chevy S10 pickup. (Chevrolet, CH)

Reports and announcements of events or facts are other illocutionary forces found in the data for representatives. Most reports are expressed in past tense as events that had already happened at the time the ad was made, as in (17a). A few reports contain present tense and present factual information from an implied study, as in (17b). Like assertions, reports are used in Spanish advertising to suggest that ads are providing important and reliable information to viewers.

(17) Reports

    a. *Financiado por la comunidad europea.*
       Financed by the European community. (Mosto, SP)

       La gente se ha adelantado a la calle a probar el nuevo sabor.
       People have taken the lead in the street to try the new flavor. (Pepsi, SP)

       Me dijo, "Virgo, sacúdete y anda que tu trabajo está allí mismo. ¡Y al día siguiente, ya encontré trabajo!"
       He told me, "Virgo, get up and get going because your work is right there. And the following day, I found work!" (Walter, U.S.)

       La idea de este comercial fue creado por estudiantes.
       The idea for this commercial was created by students. (Starburst, U.S.)

       Julio Barrazo ganó $10 [diez] millones [de dolares] en LOTTO Texas.
       Julio Barrazo won 10 million dollars in Lotto Texas. (Lotto Texas, U.S.)

       Renato y Angel son grandes amigos. Y empezaron acá en la tienda.
       Renato and Angel are great friends. And they started right here in the store. (Wal-Mart, U.S.)

    b. *Los doctores recomiendan Advil para el dolor de espalda.*
       Doctors recommend Advil for back pain. (Advil, U.S.)

       Claro, ocho de cada diez de aquí a Córdoba recomiendan usar tampones.
       Of course, eight out of ten from here to Cordoba recommend using tampons. (Tampax, SP)

Like reports, announcements are generally of an informational nature and are not disputable as opinion, as in (18a), in which the statement is an announcement of a future event that was to begin the day after this particular ad occurred. Other announcements contain declarative statements regarding the existence or arrival of a product, as in (18b). These statements are realized with *haber* 'to be in existence', *ya* (+ *estar*) 'already/now (+ to be)', or *ser* 'to be'. The latter is only used in announcements for *FonoVisa* in the data. The statement *Es FonoVisa* 'It is FonoVisa' occurs at the end of the ad; therefore, it is not considered to be an introduction. All announcements found in

3.3 Linguistic realization of strategies in the data

the data utilize present tense which is another pragmatic means of implying that the information presented is new to viewers and worthy of their notice. Thus, assertions, reports, and announcements are types of representatives used in Spanish advertising to suggest that ads provide factual, reliable, and important information to viewers.

(18) Announcements

    a. *El programa de extensión de la Escuela de Arte de la Pontificia Universidad Católica de Chile abre una nueva temporada de cursos. Pintura, historia, grabado, cerámica, fotografía y escultura, dibujo y computación gráfica.*
The extension program of the Art School of the Pontifical Catholic University of Chile is opening a new season of courses. Painting, history, engraving, ceramics, photography and sculpture, drawing, and computer graphics. (Universidad Católica, CH)

    b. *Ya están aquí.*
They are now here. (Opel Astar, SP)

    Eres ya está a la venta.
Eres is now on sale. (*Eres* magazine, U.S.)

    Anna and the Freebies. Ya en tu tienda de discos.
Anna and the Freebies. Now in your record store. (Pilosa CD, U.S.)

    ¡Y hay tres oportunidades para ganar...de cualquier premio!
And there are three opportunities to win...from any prize! (Harina Selecta, CH)

    Hay cuatro diferentes.
There are four different ones. (McDonald's, SP)

    Es FonoVisa.
It's FonoVisa. (Industria de Amor, U.S.)

Among the class of speech acts known as directives, the most common speech acts are orders. In most cases, these are linguistically realized as direct formal or informal commands, illustrated in (19). Furthermore, the lexical item most often used in direct orders is the verb *llamar* 'to call'. Other frequent commands use the verbs *descubrir* 'to discover', *mirar* 'to look at', and *venir* 'to come'. Even though the illocutionary force contained in the examples in (19) is that of an order, the speech acts are infelicitous as orders because they do not meet the preparatory condition of ability (Searle 1979). Since neither the speakers nor the companies have the power to issue orders to viewers, the force of the intended orders is diminished. Although the advertisers attempt to force the viewer into the position of obeying, viewers likely interpret the orders as strong suggestions since they know that there will not be any unfortunate repercussions from ignoring the orders given in a public advertisement.

(19) Orders

> *Disfruten la ocasión.*
> Enjoy the occasion. (Pepto Bismol, U.S.)
>
> *Para tratar las feas venas varicosas, ordene el sistema Venacilin por tan solo $39.95.*
> To treat ugly varicose veins, order Venacilin system for only $39.95. (Venacilin, U.S.)
>
> *Compre como siempre. Disfrute como nunca.*
> Buy, as always. Enjoy like never before. (Travel Club, SP)
>
> *Descubra el nuevo Fairy Ultra.*
> Discover new Fairy Ultra. (Fairy Ultra dish soap, SP)
>
> *Llama ya y aprovecha las ventajas de la gimnasia pasiva con Gymbody 8.*
> Call already and take advantage of the advantages of passive gymnastics with Gymbody 8. (Gymbody 8, SP)
>
> *Mire. Y ahora se adivinó, mándenos una carta.*
> Look. And now that you've guessed, send us a letter. (Fruit Avena de Quaker, CH)
>
> *Sé práctica. Usa Linic Plus.*
> Be practical. Use Linic Plus. (Linic Plus shampoo, CH)

Other types of directives include suggestions, recommendations, requests, attention-getters, invitations, warnings, instructions, and ultimatums.

Suggestions are generally realized in one of four ways:

- As negative interrogatives;
- As an imperative with the first person plural 'let's';
- With some form of *poder* 'to be able' in a declarative statement; and

3.3 Linguistic realization of strategies in the data

- As other types of declarative statements encouraging future action.

The examples in (20) illustrate these four representations of suggestions. They are all relatively nonthreatening means of persuading viewers to buy in comparison to orders, requests, warnings, or ultimatums.

(20) Suggestions

a. Interrogatives
¿No preferirías una Miller Lite en tu mano?
Would you prefer a Miller Lite in your hand? (Miller Beer, U.S.)

¿Por qué no confiar en la marca que cada uno de dos hogares en el país prefiere?
Why not trust the brand that every one in two households in the country prefers? (Sears, U.S.)

¿No has abierto tu portafolio todavía?
Haven't you opened your briefcase yet? (Polaroid, U.S.)

b. Imperatives
Y ahora veamos el resultado.
And now let's see the result. (Gior pasta, SP)

Vamos a ayudar a mamá a preparar el desayuno.
Let's help Mom prepare breakfast. (Quaker Oatmeal, U.S.)

Pongámonos de acuerdo.
Let's agree. (Nestum, CH)

c. Declaratives (with *poder*)
Ya lo puedes conseguir en compacto o cassette.
Now you can get it on compact or cassette. (Industria del Amor, U.S.)

Announcer: *Y puedes coleccionar a todos sólo...*
And you can collect all of them only...

Man: *en mi McDonald's*
in my McDonald's (McDonald's, U.S.)

Ya podéis divertiros con el video de Matilda.
Now you can already enjoy yourselves with the video of Matilda. (Matilda, SP)

d. Other declaratives that encourage future action
Announcer: *Si no quiere que ésas sean sus últimas palabras....*
If you don't wan't those to be your last words....
(Bayer aspirin, CH)

Ahora queda que empresas privadas e instituciones públicas las contraten.
Now it remains for private companies and public institutions to hire them. (La Once lottery, SP)

Es hora de darle fuerza con los nuevos champús Johnson's pH 5.5.
It's time to strengthen it with the new Johnson's pH 5.5 shampoos. (Johnson's shampoo, SP)

El momento de llamar es **ahora.**
The moment to call is **now.** (Walter, U.S.)

Recommendations are primarily expressed with *necesita* 'you need (to)', *hay que* 'it is necessary', and *tiene que* 'you have to'. Some examples of these expressions are shown in (21a). A few recommendations explicitly employ the verb, "to recommend", as in (32b). Although their illocutionary force is not as direct as that of orders, recommendations are more direct and face-threatening for the audience than suggestions or hints.

(21) Recommendations

a. *Necesitan los nuevos Zucosos de Nestle.*
You (PL) need the new Sugaries by Nestle. (Nestle, CH)

Hay que disfrutar.
It's necessary to enjoy. (Yoplait, SP)

Si has perdido buenos trabajos o te estás preparando para el futuro tienes que aprender inglés.
If you have lost good jobs or you are preparing for the future, you need to learn English. (Hablando Inglés, U.S.)

b. *Aguila recomienda el consumo responsable.*
Aguila recommends responsible consumption. (Aguila Amstel beer, SP)

Y yo se lo recomiendo.
And I recommend it to you. (Aceite Rosa Mosqueta, U.S.)

3.3 Linguistic realization of strategies in the data

One example from each of the other types of directives found in the data appears in (22). Most of these remaining directives are addressed to a character in the ad in order to indirectly encourage viewers to respond, based on the character's example. For example, requests and ultimatums are never directly expressed to the audience, since such utterances would likely threaten the viewer's face. Instead, they are directed at another character in the ad and, by example, to the audience. Similarly, one of the two warnings, for a Jurassic Park dinosaur figure for children, is directly aimed at viewers. The other warning is between characters as an advertisement for Motorola pagers that suggests ways in which the viewer can avoid problems by using a pager.

In contrast, attention-getters, invitations, and instructions are generally addressed to viewers rather than to another character. These speech acts impose less on viewers than do most other types of representatives. Attention-getters are always explicitly expressed with the commands *¡Atención!* 'Attention!' or *¡Mira!* 'Look!' These commands imply that the information to follow is important and noteworthy. Invitations are likewise explicitly realized with the verb *invitar* 'to invite' and are also a fairly nonthreatening means of attracting the viewer's attention. The few instructions in the data are addressed directly to the audience and describe how to use the product in question, suggesting a matter-of-fact and informational appeal. Finally, I did not count hints in the data on speech acts, although they frequently appear as a violation of one of Grice's Maxims. (See §§ 2.3.3 and 2.3.4 on politeness and implicature.)

(22) Other types of directives

 Request: *Yo quiero más ketchup Watt's.*
     I want more Watt's ketchup.' (Watt's, CH)

 Ultimatum: *Pórtate bien o te acuso con tu mamá.*
     Behave yourself or I'll tell your mother. (Secret Ultra Dry, U.S.)

 Warning: *Corre. Padres llegando.*
     Hurry. Parents arriving. (Motorola, CH)

 Attention-getter: *¡Atención! ¡Oferta especial!*
     Attention! Special offer! (Viva Inglés, U.S.)

Invitation: *Amigos y amigas, les invito a mi concierto a través de la revista TV y Novelas.*
Friends (masc., fem.), I invite you (PL) to my concert by way of the magazine, TV, and Soap Operas. (TV y Novelas, CH)

Instructions: *La aplicas templada. La retiras sin esperar y el resultado dura semanas.*
You apply it (while) warm. You remove it without waiting and the result lasts for weeks. (Cera Tibia Veet, SP)

The various types of directives are all different means of persuading the audience to the future action of buying a product or using a particular service. Directives addressed to another character in ads are really indirectly addressed to viewers. By using examples of characters changing their product allegiance, ad writers are unlikely to offend viewers and are able to deliver a message that does not overtly impose on the audience. Furthermore, such anecdotal examples are intended to be generalized to the viewing public and are a means of delivering a sales pitch in a more informational and nonthreatening way. Consequently, different types of directives are selected, depending on the desired degree of imposition and effect on the audience.

As outlined in §3.2, commissives, expressives, and declarations are not as frequent in the data as representatives and directives. Commissives are expressed as offers, promises, guarantees, and disclaimers and are directly aimed at viewers, rather than at other characters within the ad. By nature, commissives force advertisers to be accountable for the veracity of their message. This fact may account for their relative infrequency in Spanish ads when compared to representatives and directives.

Offers are those speech acts that tell what the advertiser will do for the viewing audience. These speech acts are often expressed overtly with the verbs *ofrecer* 'to offer' and *regalar* 'to give a gift' or with the mention of a gift, as in (23a). Generally, such offers are not literally true, since the viewer has to purchase something in order to obtain the so-called gift. Explicit offers involving *ofrecer* are more like announcements than actual offers, as the examples in (23b) illustrate. The primary purposes of these ambiguous commissives are to attract attention and to make it seem as though a product has something new or significant to offer. Offers also commonly involve action on the part of the viewer and are, therefore, linked with suggestions, orders, or some type of required action (whether explicit or implicit) on the part of the audience. Thus, most advertising

3.3 Linguistic realization of strategies in the data

offers are qualified in some way, suggesting that if the viewer does X, the company or product will do Y, as in (23c).

(23) Offers

    a. *Ahora con un curso de ciudadanía gratis.*
       Now with a free citizenship course. (Inglés Sin Barreras, U.S.)

       Con aire acondicionado gratis.
       With free air conditioning. (Opel Astar, SP)

       Además regalamos entradas para el concierto de Enrique Iglesias.
       Furthermore, we're giving away tickets for Enrique Iglesias' concert. (TV y Novelas, CH)

       Aire acondicionado de regalo. U oferta equivalente.
       Air conditioning as a gift. Or equivalent offer. (Rover Serie 400, SP)

    b. *Ahora Danone te ofrece el sabor natural de las naranjas frescas.*
       Now Danone offers you the natural flavor of fresh oranges. (Minute Maid, SP)

       Oferta de lanzamiento.
       Initial offer. (Taller de Escritura, CH)

       A quiénes toman la vida con interés, les ofrecemos una buena inversión.
       To those who approach life with interest, we offer a good investment. (Bonos ICO, SP)

       Camy te ofrece este programa.
       Camy offers you this program. (Maxibon de Camy, SP)

    c. *Cambia a AT&T y recibe dos entradas a un juego de MLX.*
       Change to AT&T and receive two tickets to a game of MLX. (AT&T, U.S.)

       Y si te cambias a Sprint ya, recibirás cien minutos gratis.
       And if you change to Sprint now, you will receive one hundred minutes free. (Sprint, U.S.)

       Lleve seis rollos y pague cinco. Lleve cuatro rollos y pague tres.
       Take six rolls and pay for five. Take four and pay for three. (Confort, CH)

Like offers, promises are linguistically realized as declarative statements assuring the future action of the company. Promises occasionally contain specific details of what the product will provide, as in (24a), but more often they express general ideas and leave the viewer to infer what the statements are intended to mean, as in (24b).

(24) Promises

    a. *Y McDonald's donará dinero a Ronald McDonald House Charities.*
       And McDonald's will donate money to Ronald McDonald House Charities. (McDonald's, U.S.)

       También te los entregamos y te los acomodamos en tu domicilio.
       Also, we will bring them to you and arrange them for you in your home. (Rent-A-Center, U.S.)

       Nuevos precios bajos todos los días.
       New low prices every day. (H-E-B, U.S.)

    b. *Todo lo último para ti.*
       All the latest for you (INFRML). (El Corte Inglés, SP)

       Yo y mis psíquicos atenderán a tus problemas.
       I and my psychics will assist with your problems. (Walter, U.S.)

       Cada experiencia en el nuevo Camry te llevará a la grandeza de sus cambios.
       Every experience in the new Camry will carry you to the grandeur of its changes. (Toyota, U.S.)

       Ponte Hanes y ya verás
       Put on Hanes and you'll already see. (Hanes, U.S.)

       Es una sorpresa tan grande que te dejará con la boca abierta.
       It's a surprise so big that it will leave you with your mouth open. (McDonald's, SP)

       Bocatas Bimbo. Verás qué cambio.
       Bocatas Bimbo. You'll see what a change. (Bocatas Bimbo, SP)

Guarantees are generally explicit in their use of some form of the verb *garantizar* 'to guarantee', as in (25a). The few exceptions are similar to promises, but they contain contingent assurances of what the company will do if the viewer does not like the product. That is, they state, "If you aren't satisfied, we (will) do X." The disclaimers in the data occur in Chilean ads for toys

3.3 Linguistic realization of strategies in the data 63

and Spanish ads for medicines. These disclaimers are most likely required by the stations, since the same announcer produces all disclaimers for medicines in commercials from Antena 3. The few apologies in the data contain either *permiso* 'excuse me' or *perdón* 'pardon me' and contribute to humor in the ads.

(25) Guarantees

    a. *Y con la garantía de una de las casas relojeras suizas de mayor autoridad al nivel mundial.*
And with the guarantee of one of the most authoritative Swiss watch companies in the world. (Christian Duvenet, SP)

    Con la garantía de Editorial Planeta.
With the gurarantee of Editorial Planeta. (Editorial Planeta, SP)

    Vitaminas y sabor garantizados.
Vitamins and flavor guaranteed. (Frudesa, SP)

    b. *Si no queda satisfecho, le devolvemos su dinero.*
If you aren't satisfied, we'll return your money to you (FRML). (Set Arcobaleno, SP)

    Y si encuentra algo en Weiners que no esté en rebaja, es gratis.
And if you find something in Weiners that isn't discounted, it's free. (Weiners, U.S.)

(26) Disclaimers

    Las muñecas no se mueven solas. Se venden por separado.
The dolls do not move by themselves. They are sold separately. (Barbie Fashion Avenue, CH)

    Announcer 2:
Este anuncio es de un medicamento. Lea detenidamente las instrucciones de uso. En caso de duda consulte a su farmacéutico.
This ad is for a medicine. Carefully read the instructions for use. In case of doubt, consult with your pharmacist. (Regaine, SP)

(27) Apologies

    Toilet: *[to audience after burping] ¡Perdón!*
        Pardon me! (Clorox, CH)

Thus, commissives in Spanish ads are usually qualified in some way. Offers generally serve to attract attention to a gift or to require action from the audience. Promises and guarantees tend to be general, leaving viewers to infer what is meant, and the few disclaimers in the data are negative and are likely required by the television stations as a control on truthfulness in advertising. Since commissives force advertisers to be accountable to the audience, they are relatively infrequent in Spanish ads when compared to representatives and directives.

Within the class of speech acts known as expressives, the combined illocutionary forces of flattery, praise, and compliments are most frequent, followed by introductions. Other illocutionary types include insults, thanks, greetings, leave-taking expressions, and congratulations. Since it is difficult to distinguish between flattery, praise, and compliments, I assign these as a single category. This category is expressed via declarative statements of several types to the audience. The first type asserts the viewer's inherent worth, shown in (28a). The second type describes the emotional tie or focus of the product/service on viewers (28b). The third type similarly promises a product or service uniquely for the use of an individual viewer, shown in (28c). The first three types of flattery are also often found in product slogans. The last type is addressed to another character within the ad by means of a complimentary assertion or exclamation, as in (28d). These examples of flattery either directly or indirectly attempt to make viewers feel good about themselves, and by association, about the advertised product/service.

(28) Flattery/praise/compliments

    a. *Tú sí que sabes.*
       You are the one who knows. (Burger King, U.S.)

       Usted merece más.
       You deserve more. (Reyes y Asociados, U.S.)

    b. *Te queremos en Alcampo.*
       We love you at Alcampo. (Alcampo, SP)

       En CTC lo más importante es usted.
       At CTC, the most important thing is you (FRML). (CTC Centro, CH)

       Especialistas en ti.
       Specialists in you. (El Corte Inglés, SP)

       Para su familia, de todo corazón.
       For your family, with all [our] heart. (Wal-Mart, U.S.)

3.3 Linguistic realization of strategies in the data

    c. *Y un programa de beneficios sólo para ti.*
       And a program of benefits just for you. (Banco Santiago, CH)

       Todo para ti.
       All for you. (Sears, U.S.)

    d. *Mamá no daría otra cosa.*
       Mom wouldn't give anything else. (Nestum, CH)

       Mi amor, cocinas delicioso.
       My love, you cook deliciously [INFRML]. (Secret Ultra Dry, U.S.)

       ¡Genial! ¡Mami, nunca fallas!
       Fabulous! Mommy, you never fail! (Dodot Excel, SP)

Almost all introductions employ the explicit speech act verb, *presentar* 'to present/introduce'; however, such statements often sound more like an announcement since the so-called introduction is for a product rather than a person. In a few cases, introductions are accomplished with the verb *ser* 'to be' and refer to people rather than products. These personal introductions serve as preludes to endorsements for a product/service.

(29) Introductions

    a. *Bounty presenta las nuevas toallas reusables 'Rinse and Reuse'.*
       Bounty presents the new reusable towels, Rinse and Reuse. (Bounty, U.S.)

       Nintendo 64 [sesenta y cuatro] presenta lo último en videojuegos.
       Nintendo 64 presents the latest in videogames. (Nintendo, SP)

       Presentamos el último milagro de la hidratación.
       We present the latest miracle of hydration. (Hidro-Genesse, SP)

    b. Young woman: [pointing to man] *El es Carlitos.*
                                          He is Carlitos.

       Young Man: *Y ella es Shakirita.*
                    And she is Shakirita. (Eres, U.S.)

       Yo soy Patricio Cornejo.
       I'm Patricio Cornejo. (Aceite Belmont, CH)

The remaining expressives are less common in the data. Most insults are directed from character to character, since insults are inherently face-threatening acts. The one exception is shown in (30). Generally, insults also contribute to humor in ads. Similarly, congratulations are directed between characters, with the exception of the example in (30) that refers to a raffle winner from the audience. Both thanks and greetings are addressed to the viewing audience and all greetings contain the lexical items, *hola* 'hello' or *bienvenido* 'welcome'. These speech acts serve as an imitation of or pretense at personal conversation with viewers.

(30) Other expressives

> Insult:
> *¿No tienen nada mejor que hacer que ver comerciales?*
> Don't you have anything better to do than to watch commercials?' (Nectar Andina, CH)
>
> Congratulations:
> *Alicia, felicidades [to a viewer after winning raffle].*
> Alicia, congratulations! (Carozzi, CH)
>
> Thanks:
> *Gracias por escuchar y ayudar a hacer mi McDonald's su McDonald's.*
> Thanks for listening and helping to make my McDonald's your McDonald's. (McDonald's, U.S.)
>
> Greeting:
> *¡Hola, Austin!*
> Hello, Austin! (Texas Discount Furniture Outlet, U.S.)
>
> Leave-taking:
> *Y nos vemos próximo viernes.*
> See you next Friday. (Carozzi, CH)

In summary, expressives are linguistically realized as:

- direct and indirect flattery, thanks, and congratulations to make the audience feel good and important,
- greetings and leave-takings to imitate ordinary conversation,
- as ambiguous introductions to attract attention, and
- insults to contribute to humor in ads.

They are audience-focused speech acts that allow ads to sound warm and personal.

3.3 Linguistic realization of strategies in the data   67

The speech act category of declarations by definition is always via overt speech act verbs that describe the illocutionary intent. Declarations found in the data include introductions, offers, welcomes, invitations, recommendations, thanks, congratulations, attention-getters, permission seeking, and one each of a confiscation, promise, and warning. Declarations are relatively uncommon in the data, which perhaps reflects the overall avoidance of explicit speech acts in Spanish commercials.

Some speech acts seem deliberately ambiguous in their illocutionary force and can be easily interpreted in two distinct classes of speech acts, representatives and directives. For counting purposes, I included these in both categories. Consider the following examples, which may be interpreted as assertions in (31a) or as orders in (31b) because of the pause between phrases when spoken. Such interpretations are possible to varying degrees in Spanish because the informal imperative and third person indicative verbs have identical forms. The slogan for Coca Cola in (32) is similarly ambiguous in that it may be an assertion or an order. The viewer is left to fill in the missing verb. Since advertising language is deliberately constructed, the examples below are probably intentionally ambiguous.

(31) a. *Nuevo Palmolive for Pots and Pans* [pause] *despega la comida pegada.*
New Palmolive for Pots and Pans [pause] removes stuck food. (Palmolive, U.S.)

Agua ligera Font Vella [pause] *cuida tu cuerpo.*
Light Font Vella Water [pause] takes care of your body. (Font Vella, SP)

St. Ives Swiss Fórmula [pause] *borra el tiempo de tus manos.*
St. Ives Swiss Formula [pause] erases time from your hands. (St. Ives, CH)

Nintendo 64 [sesenta y cuatro] [pause] *entra en juego.*
Nintendo 64 [pause] gets in the game. (Nintendo, SP)

Súper automática de Sindelen [pause] *mejora la vida.*
Sindelen's super automatic [pause] improves life. (Sindelen, SP)

b. *Nuevo Palmolive for Pots and Pans. Despega la comida pegada.*
New Palmolive for Pots and Pans. Remove stuck food. (Palmolive, U.S.)

Agua ligera Font Vella. Cuida tu cuerpo.
Light Font Vella Water. Take care of your body. (Font Vella, SP)

St. Ives Swiss Fórmula. Borra el tiempo de tus manos.
St. Ives Swiss Formula. Erase time from your hands. (St. Ives, CH)

Nintendo 64 [sesenta y cuatro]. Entra en juego.
Nintendo 64. Get in the game. (Nintendo, SP)

Súper automática de sindelen. Mejora la vida.
Sindelen's super automatic. Improve life. (Sindelen, SP)

(32) a. *Siempre [es] Coca Cola.*
[It is] always Coca Cola. (Coca Cola, CH)

b. *Siempre [bebe] Coca Cola.*
Always [drink] Coca Cola.

Indirect speech acts, when observed, are also noted in the data. In some cases, representatives are also indirect commissives. Many assertions, for example, are also indirect promises, as in (33).

(33) *Te sentirás limpia. Te sentirás bien.*
You'll feel clean. You'll feel good. (SalvaSlip, SP)

En cada pedacito, un gran beso.
In each piece, a great big kiss. (Betty Crocker, CH)

Con Miko Etiqueta Negra tú también ganarás
With Miko Etiqueta Negra, you too will win. (Miko, SP)

Other examples of indirectness are found in questions that imply suggestions (34a) or in assertions containing another party's recommendation (34b).

(34) a. *¿Has visto lo que está pasando?*
Have you seen what's happening? (Ford Galaxy, SP)

¿Por qué esperar?
Why wait? (Snickers, U.S.)

¿Ha revisado ya sus amortiguadores?
Have you checked your shock absorbers? (Midas, SP)

3.3 Linguistic realization of strategies in the data

b. *Para el dolor causado por la cirugía, los doctores recomiendan Tylenol más que otras marcas.*
For the pain caused by surgery, doctors recommend Tylenol more than other brands. (Tylenol, U.S.)

Royal Club Evian recomienda Pantene ProV.
Royal Evian Club recommends Pantene ProV. (Pantene ProV, SP)

Since ads are designed to persuade, ambiguous and indirect speech acts are commonly used in Spanish television advertising to convey more than one message. Ads are deliberately created to be ambiguous or indirect in order to imply more than what is literally said without being literally untruthful. For this reason, Geis (1982) argued that advertisers should be held responsible for what their ads may be easily interpreted to mean.

Table 3.12 contains a summary of the classes of speech acts and how they were linguistically realized in our Spanish commercials.

Table 3.12 Summary of speech acts

Speech Act	Linguistic Realizations		
Representatives			
Assertions	Declarative statements of fact or opinion (as if it were fact)	Declarations containing ellipsis	Slogans (ambiguous)
Reports	Past tense (events)	Present tense (implied studies)	
Announcements	Declarative statements (future events)	Declarative statements (existence/arrival of product)	
Directives			
Orders	Commands (*llamar, descubrir, mirar, venir*)		
Suggestions	Interrogatives	Imperatives	Declaratives (with *poder* or those that encourage future action)

Recommendations	Explicit *(recomendar)*	Implicit *(necesita, hay que, tiene que)*	
Requests	Character to character address		
Invitations	Address to audience	Explicit *(invitar)*	
Attention-getters	Address to audience	Commands *(¡Atención!, ¡Mira!)*	
Instructions	Address to audience		
Ultimatums	Character to character address		
Warnings	Character to character address		
Commissives			
Offers	Explicit *(ofrecer, regalar, gratis)*	If audience does X, the company will do Y	
Promises	Declarative statements assuring company's future action (general or specific)		
Guarantees	Explicit *(garantizar)*	If audience isn't satisfied, then company will do X	
Disclaimers	Declarative statements (negative)		
Apologies	Polite imperatives *(permiso, perdón)*		
Expressives			
Flattery	Assertions of viewer's inherent worth	Emotional and individual focus on viewers	Character to character (assertion or exclamation)
Introductions	Explicit *(presentar)* for products	Explicit *(ser)* for people	

3.3 Linguistic realization of strategies in the data 71

Insults	Character to char-acter (humorous)	To audience (humorous)
Congratulations	Explicit *(felicidades)*	
Thanks	Explicit *(gracias)*	
Greetings	Explicit *(¡Hola!, ¡Bienvenido!)*	
Leave-taking	Explicit *(Nos vemos)*	
Declarations	Explicit *(presentar, ofrecer, invitar, recomendar, dar las gracias, felicitar)*	

3.3.2 Indexicals

Indexicals in this study consist of deictic elements of person, place, and time. They serve to orient the audience to the advertiser's point of view. Spatial deixis is realized in the data primarily by verbs of motion, spatial adverbs, and demonstratives, although no single word appears in the majority of ads. Proximity between the product and viewer is primarily encoded by *aquí* 'here (of the speaker)' and *este/esta/estos/estas* 'this (of the speaker)'. The neuter forms *esto* 'this' and *eso* 'that' are both commonly used, with preference for the former. By employing these words, the Spanish advertiser attempts to unite the 'here' of the speaker with that of the viewer in order to draw viewers into the context of the ad and perspective of the advertiser. The adjective and adverb of uniqueness, *único* 'unique/only' and *sólo* 'only', also occur frequently to distinguish a product from all others of its kind. The most common verbs of motion are forms of *ir* 'to go', *venir* 'to come', *llevar* 'to take', *ganar* 'to win', *dejar* 'to leave (transitive)', *llegar* 'to arrive', and *dar* 'to give'. Again, these verbs are used to reduce the degree of metaphorical distance between an ad's speakers and the audience.

No single item indicating temporal deixis occurs in the majority of ads. Temporal deixis is expressed primarily by the adverbs and adjectives of time, *ahora* 'now', *nuevo* 'new', *ya* 'now/already', and *siempre* 'always', and these items either indicate a product's newness or its continuity. Furthermore, markers of the present and future are preferred over the past. In comparing the triad *hoy-mañana-ayer* 'today-tomorrow-yesterday', *hoy* is employed far more often than *mañana,* and *ayer* never occurs in the data. Moreover, the word *pasado* 'past' is used only in a negative context. Only present and future time carry positive connotations in Spanish ads, as in (35). As Sánchez Corral (1991) suggested, advertisers attempt to unite the present and the (future) act of buying. Advertisers are primarily interested in creating a sense of urgency for viewers to become consumers.

(35) *No se quede en el pasado.*
      Don't remain in the past. (Dualette, CH)

   Abárcate, yeah. El pasado pasó.... Generación Next, Next.
   Get with it, yeah. The past is past.... Generation Next, Next. (Pepsi, U.S.)

Similarly, an analysis of tense markers in the data revealed that present tense is preferred over other tenses and occurs in the majority of ads. Of the ads containing another tense, future is preferred, followed in order of frequency by present perfect, preterite, imperfect, and conditional. The imperfect and preterite generally occur in ads

- to relate a significant first time event (36a),
- to illustrate a contrast or change between the past and present (36b), or
- as a flashback or testimonial relating the speaker's involvement with a given product (36c).

Thus, past tenses are only used in limited contexts to indicate newsworthy events. It is the present and future that are of interest to Spanish advertisers.

(36) Past tenses

   a. Announcer:
      Ponds Institute creó Nueva Limpiadora Dual. Un solo producto para el rostro y ojos.
      Ponds Institute created New Dual Cleaner. A single product for the face and eyes. (Ponds, CH)

   b. *Si se perdió el campeonato de béisbol de Puerto Rico, es porque no tiene Galavisión.*
      If you missed Puerto Rico's baseball championship, it's because you don't have Galavision. (Galavisión, U.S.)

3.3 Linguistic realization of strategies in the data

c. Woman 1:
Mi esposo me quiso quitar mi hija, mi casa, mi negocio. Llamé a la psíquica y me recetó una magia blanca. Al mes en mi casa, estoy con mi hija y sigo en mi negocio.
My husband wanted to take away my daughter, my house, my business. I called the psychic and he/she prescribed for me a white magic. After a month in my house, I'm with my daughter, and I'm continuing in my business. (Walter, U.S.)

Of all the types of social deixis, second person reference is the only pronominal reference which occurs in the majority of ads. The data also reveal a preference for informal versus formal reference in second person. Thus, speakers in Spanish ads are more likely to address viewers as if they are on familiar terms. First person plural reference is both inclusive and exclusive in the data, with a strong preference for exclusion of the television viewer. Finally, third person reference is almost as frequent as ads containing no personal reference at all. Advertisers wish to communicate interest in the viewer above all other people. A breakdown of preferences for the number of ads containing personal reference appears in table 3.13. The numbers generally suggest that advertisers attempt friendly, personal messages as opposed to formal and impersonal ones.

Table 3.13 Preferences for types of personal reference

1st person—183
    1st person singular—124
    1st person plural—76

2nd person—381
    2nd person singular, informal—277
    2nd person singular, formal—92
    2nd person plural, formal—21
    2nd person plural, informal—5

3rd person—116
    3rd person singular—66
    3rd person plural—53

No personal reference—108

3.3.3 Politeness

Recall that positive face allows imposition yet expresses a desire for the speaker's wants to be desirable or appreciated by the hearer. Ads reflecting positive politeness typically express a friendly tone and concepts such as "this product is specifically for you" or "you are going to like this." Such ads generally project solidarity and suggest intimacy with the audience. On the other hand, ads containing negative strategies tend to remain distant from the viewer and to avoid any imposition. Such strategies express notions such as "here is an option that is available, should you so desire" and "this is what the product does."

Positive face is the preferred strategy of politeness and is encoded with both formal and informal personal reference, although the preference is for a familiar tone. Ads containing positive face strategies generally do not attempt to distance the speaker from the audience. When ads containing positive face do attempt distance, it is often to mitigate the effects of a sensitive subject or to soften the illocutionary force of a directive. Flattery, humor, and endorsements are all much more frequent in ads conveying positive politeness.

The examples in (37) illustrate positive face strategies without distance in the data.[11] Such ads are formulated using informal personal reference and either attempt to flatter or to align the product in some way with the viewer's point of view, shown in (37a) and (37b), respectively. The ads in (37b) contain alignment; that is, they attempt to identify emotionally with the audience and show solidarity and similarities between viewers and the speakers in ads. For example, the ad for Linic Plus depicts a woman who says that she is practical and assumes that viewers are like her. Similarly, the ad for Avon Color appeals to viewers who believe that they are unique and fashionable.

(37) Positive face, no distance

    a. Flattery
    (Burger King, Univisión)
    Announcer:
    Burger King presenta ' Tú sí que sabes'. Si algunos te salen muy caros [image of a man receiving a bill for pizza] *y otros te dejan con hambre* [image of a man looking at a tiny taco], *sabes que sólo Burger King siempre tiene una gran comida. El Whopper Value Meal. Justo lo que buscas. Sabor que te encanta y siempre*

---

[11]Information in square brackets indicates actions, images, and sounds in the ads. Written rather than spoken information is indicated by the angle brackets "< >."

hecho a tu manera. Con papitas y refresco, sólo dos noventa y nueve todos los días. Encuentra lo que quieras como lo quieras todos los días. Burger King. Tú sí que sabes.
Burger King presents "You who really know." If some seem very expensive and others leave you hungry, you know that only Burger King always has a great meal. The Whopper Value Meal. Just what you're looking for. Flavor that delights you and always made your way. With french fries and a beverage, only 2.99 every day. Find what you want the way you want it every day. Burger King. You are the one who knows.

(Electrolux, Antena 3)
[Image of man walking toward refrigerator]
Announcer:
Presentamos la nueva línea Alfa de Electrolux. ¿Te gusta? Pues, adelante. Fíjate en sus detalles. Te gusta, ¿eh? Pues, hay algo que te gustará más y es que hemos conseguido reducir aún más su consumo. Frigoríficos Electrolux Gustan más. Gastan menos.
<*Electrolux. Lo hacemos por ti.*>
We present the new Alpha line from Electrolux. You like it? Well, come on in. Notice its details. You like it, eh? Well, there is something that you'll like more and it's that we have managed to lower its electrical consumption even more. Refrigerators Electrolux. <Electrolux.> Enjoy more. spend less. <Electrolux. We do it for you.>

Man:
¿Hmm?
Hmm?

(JC Penney, U.S.)
Woman:
Sólo hay una tienda para todas tus ocasiones especiales. Es JC Penney. [Image of bride and groom]. *Allí quedas bien con tus regalos y también quedas bien con tu bolsillo.* [Images of people opening presents]. *JC Penney nos ha ayudado a hacer nuestras celebraciones más especiales con grandes ofertas y buenos regalos.*
There is only one store for all your special occasions. It's JC Penney. There your gifts suit you and your pocketbook also suits you. JC Penney has helped us make our clebrations more special with great offers and good presents.

Announcer: [Image of a father opening a present].
Ahorre en las marcas favoritas de papá hasta el 14 de junio.
Save on Dad's favorite brands until the 14th of June.

Vocalist:
JC Penney. Te queda bien.
JC Penney. It suits you.

b. Alignment
(Linic Plus, CH)
Woman:
Si eres una mujer práctica como yo, me vas a entender. Y si quieres sentir hermosa y sin caspa, con mayor razón. Aprovecha tu tiempo. Para ti, existe Linic Plus que elimina la caspa porque estuvo aquí en el puro cabello.
If you're a practical woman like me, you're going to understand me. And if you want to feel beautiful and without dandruff, even better reason. Take advantage of your time. For you, there exists Linic Plus, that eliminates dandruff because it was here right on the hair itself.

Announcer: *Linic Plus con autopirox.*
Champú anticaspa y bálsamo todo en uno que actúa directamente sobre el puro cabelludo, eliminando la caspa donde se forma.
Linic Plus with autopirox. Antidandruff shampoo and balsam all in one that acts directly on the hair, eliminating dandruff where it is formed.

Woman:
Y mira como funciona. Mi cabello brillante, fácil de peinar y sin caspa. Sé práctica. Usa Linic Plus.
And look how it works. My hair [is] shiny, easy to comb, and without dandruff. Be practical. Use Linic Plus.

Announcer:
Linic Plus. Tu solución Linic que ahorra tu tiempo.
Linic Plus. Your Linic solution that saves you time.

Woman:
¡Funciona!
It works!

3.3 Linguistic realization of strategies in the data

(Avon Color, CH)
[Image of cosmetics]
Announcer:
Con la nueva línea Avon Color, ahora es tan fácil ser bella. Porque nuevo Avon Color se ha puesto a la vanguardia de la moda con nuevos tonos, diseños y formúlas para realzar tu belleza, tu personalidad y tu estilo. Avon Color les demuestra a tus labios, tus ojos, tu rostro que es tan fácil ser bella. Color. Avon comprende a la mujer.
With the new Avon Color line, now it is so easy to be beautiful. Because new Avon Color has set itself on the edge of fashion with new tones, designs, and formulas to heighten your beauty, your personality, and your style. Avon Color shows your lips, your eyes, your face that it is so easy to be beautiful. Color. Avon understands women.

Ads containing positive face strategies sometimes exhibit distance as well, as in (38). In such cases, formal personal reference or no personal reference is employed in order to soften the effects of commands, as in (38a), or to mitigate any imposition due to the personal nature of the product, as in (38b–c).

(38) Positive face, with distance

 a. (Club Mundial del Vídeo, U.S.)
Man:
¡Atención, mucha atención! Ahora por primera vez en la televisión, El Club Mundial del Vídeo le ofrece las mejores películas del rey de tango. Adivinó–Carlos Gardel. Usted se va a llevar seis de sus mejores películas, originales y garantizadas. Usted se va a llevar un cancionero con más de doscientos tangos escritos para usted. Usted se va a llevar... originales de sus mejores películas por tan sólo sesenta y cinco dólares y noventa y cinco centavos ($65.95).... Y si marca ahora, usted se lleva completamente gratis cincuenta y seis melodias, cincuenta y seis tangos contenidos en dos discos compactos...con mejor calidad. Escuchó bien: 2 discos...del gran Carlos Gardel. ¡Mucha atención! Marque...y ordene.
Attention, much attention! Now for the first time on television, The World Video Club is offering you (FRML) the best movies of the king of tango. You guessed it–Carlos Gardel. You are going to take away six of his best movies, originals and guaranteed. **You** are going to take away a song book with more than two hundred tangos written for you. **You** are going

to take away...originals of his best movies for only $65.95....
And if you dial now, you'll take away, completely free,
fifty-six melodies, fifty-six tangos contained in two compact
discs...with better quality. You heard right: two compact
discs...from the great Carlos Gardel. Much attention!
Dial...and order.

b. (Venacilin, U.S.)
Woman:
*Para las feas venas varicosas, nuevo sistema Venacilin. Su figura lo
merece. Venacilin le puede ayudar. Para las várices, el nuevo
sistema Venacilin. Es completo y fácil de usar. Todo lo que necesita
es crema Venacilin, incluyendo compresas y tabletas. Para tratar
las feas venas varicosas, ordene el sistema Venacilin por tan solo
treinta y nueve dólares y noventa y cinco centavos. Llame gratis
ahora mismo a.... Dígale adiós a las venas varicosas con Venacilin.*
For ugly varicose veins, new Venacilin system. Your (FRML)
figure deserves it. Venacilin can help you. For varicose veins,
the new Venacilin system. It is complete and easy to use. All
you need is Venacilin cream, including compresses and tablets. To treat ugly varicose veins, order Venacilin system for
only $39.95. Call free right now at.... Say goodbye to varicose
veins with Venacilin.

c. (Super Potencia 2000, U.S.)
Announcer:
*¿Se siente cansada o cansado? ¿Tiene falta de interés en los
momentos íntimos con su pareja? Si usted responde sí, la solución
a este problema es Super Potencia 2000 [dos mil]. Un
revitalizador recomendado para la mujer y el hombre que ... de
energía, vitalidad o virilidad. Mejore su actividad sexual con Super
Potencia 2000 [dos mil].*
Do you (FRML) feel tired (MASC, FEM)? Do you lack interest in
intimate moments with your spouse? If you respond, "yes,"
the solution to this problem is Super Potency 2000. A
revitalizer recommended for the woman and the man that...of
energy, vitality, or virility. Improve your sexual activity with
Super Potency 2000.'

Man 1 (with wife):
*Desde que tomo Super Potencia 2000 [dos mil] me siento como
un tigre.*
Since I've been taking Super Potency 2000, I feel like a tiger.

3.3 Linguistic realization of strategies in the data

Woman 2 (with husband):
Mi excusa era "estoy cansada, no tengo ganas." La de él, "no tengo energía," pero desde que tomamos Super Potencia 2000 [dos mil] todo ha cambiado entre nosotros. <Resultados pueden variar en cada persona.>
My excuse was "I'm tired, I don't feel like it." His [excuse] was, "I don't have the energy," but since we've been taking Super Potency 2000 everything has changed between us. <Results can vary in each person.>

Man 2:
Ahora es con más frecuencia y estamos muy, muy felices.
Now it's more frequent and we're very, very happy.

Man 3:
Me siento.... Yo se lo recomiendo a mis cuates.
I feel.... I recommend it to my pals.

Announcer:
Mejore su actividad sexual con Super Potencia 2000 [dos mil]. Frasco de sesenta cápsulas por treinta y nueve dólares y noventa y cinco centavos ($39.95). De regalo con su orden recibe otro frasco adicional con sesenta cápsulas. Llame ya mismo ....
Improve your (FRML) sexual activity with Super Potency 2000. Bottle of sixty capsules for $39.95. As a gift with your order, receive another additional bottle with sixty capsules. Call right now...

Ads reflecting negative politeness are generally encoded with formal personal reference or none at all. The ads for Becel and Biotherm in (39) contain personal reference, whereas the ads for Margaret Astor Integrité and Cucal do not. Exclusion of personal reference in the latter achieves even more distance than ads containing formal personal reference. Most negative strategies also coincide with other devices that distance the speaker from the audience such as formal personal pronouns.

(39) Negative face, with distance
(Margarina Becel, CH)
Announcer:
[Image of words going across screen, like a cardiogram]. *En este mes, de corazón un mensaje de Becel. Una alimentación alta en grasas saturadas aumenta el colesterol y los riesgos de un infarto. Con Becel su corazón está protegido, porque Margarina Becel es baja en grasas*

saturadas y no contiene ácidos grasos trans. Por eso, Becel es reconocida internacionalmente como especialista en cuidar el corazón. Margarina Becel. Baja en grasas saturadas. Y sin ácidos grasos trans.
In this month, a message from the heart from Becel. Food high in saturated fats raises cholesterol and the risks of a heart attack. With Becel, your (FRML) heart is protected, because Becel Margerine is low in saturated fats and doesn't contain transfatty acids. That's why Becel is recognized internationally as a specialist in caring for the heart. Becel Margerine. Low in saturated fats. And without transfatty acids.

(Biotherm, SP)
Announcer:
Biotherm reinventa la hidratación con Hydra-Detox. La primera hidratante detoxificante natural. Y ahora si quiere una piel Biotherm, por la compra de sus productos en El Corte Inglés, le obsequiamos con un tratamiento completo. <Biotherm. El Corte Inglés.>
Biotherm is reinventing hydration with Hydra-Detox. The first natural detoxifying hydration. And now if you want Biotherm skin, with the purchase of its products at El Corte Inglés, we present you (FRML) with a complete treatment. <Biotherm. El Corte Inglés.>

(Margaret Astor Integrité, SP)
Announcer:
Ahora por la compra de una crema Margaret Astor Integrité, un contorno de ojos gratis. Margaret Astor Integrité. Con oxígeno puro.
Now with the purchase of a Margaret Astor Integrité cream, a free eye shadow. Margaret Astor Integrité. With pure oxygen.

(Cucal, SP)
[Image of a cockroach]
Announcer:
Las cucarachas nunca vienen solas. [Image of eggs being left behind]. *Aunque desaparezcan, quedan sus huevos. Por eso, el nuevo Cucal es aún más eficaz. Porque elimina las cucarachas. Y los huevos. Nuevo Cucal. Elimina las cucarachas y los huevos.*
Cockroaches never come alone. Even if they disappear, their eggs remain. That's why new Cucal is even more effective. Because it eliminates cockroaches. And their eggs. New Cucal. It eliminates cockroaches and their eggs.

3.3 Linguistic realization of strategies in the data

Commercials exhibiting negative politeness without any devices to distance the speaker from viewers are far less common than those with distancing strategies. For example, even though the speakers utilize informal pronouns in (40a–b), they allow viewers to choose for themselves and overtly communicate this freedom from imposition. Other ads containing negative face without distance merely describe what their product/service does and leave the audience to decide whether or not they wish to find out more information, as in (40c–d).

(40) Negative face, no distance

a. (Aleve, U.S.)
Grey-haired woman [seamstress]:
[She sighs].
Cuando me duelen las manos no me puedo dar el lujo de parar. Durante el día puedo tomar cuatro Advil u ocho Tylenol. O puedo tomar sólo dos Aleve. Como dice la etiqueta. Tú decides.
When my hands hurt I can't give myself the luxury of stopping. During the day, I can take four Advil or eight Tylenol. Or I can take only two Aleve. Like the label says. You decide.

Announcer:
Aleve. Un gran alivio todo el día.
Aleve. A great relief all day.

b. (Escuela de Investigaciones Policiales, CH)
[Image of police cars, silhouettes, dusting for fingerprints, chessboard]
Announcer:
Estrategia. Desafío. Ingenio. Tu decisión. Escuela de Investigaciones Policiales. Admisión 97 (noventa y siete). <Inscripciones hasta el 31 de agosto....>
Strategy. Challenge. Ingenuity. Your (INFRML) decision. School of Police Investigations. Admission 97. <Registration until the 31st of August.>

c. (Ford Galaxy, SP)
[Image of van pulling into small parking space. Beautiful woman gets out. She closes the door. Alarms go off on other cars surrounding the Ford.]

Announcer:
Ford Galaxy. Otra visión de la vida. <Desde 3.400.000 ptas.... >
¿Has visto lo que está pasando? <Ford. >
Ford Galaxy. Another vision of life. <From 3,400,000 pesetas.... > Have you (INFRML) seen what is happening? <Ford>

d. (Férroli, SP)
[Image of multiple closed vault-like doors]
Announcer:
<Férroli. > Hemos creado algo que no puedes ver. Que no puedes oír. Que no puedes tocar. Algo que sólo puedes sentir. Aire acondicionado Férroli. Creamos el aire.
<Férroli. > We have created something that you (INFRML) cannot see. That you cannot hear. That you cannot touch. Something that you can only feel. Férroli air conditioning. We create air.

A number of ads express both positive and negative strategies of politeness within the same ad. In such cases, negative face is usually conveyed by the announcer's speech or by written phrases on the screen. The commercial for Kalia detergent in (41a) illustrates the change in politeness strategies within the same ad. The characters employ positive politeness, in contrast with the announcer's formal and informational speech. In the portion of the ad in (41b) for Rent-A-Center, only the final order (indicated by angle brackets) is encoded as a formal command. Consequently, the written part of the ad communicates more authority and distance from viewers than the rest of the ad.

(41) Both positive and negative face

a. Announcer
(Kalia, SP)
[Image of children at a birthday party. Child spills chocolate.]
Mother 1: *Este chocolate no saldrá con detergente y aquí no puedo usar lejía.*
This chocolate won't come out with detergent and here I can't use bleach.

Mother 2: *No te preocupes. El nuevo Kalia te quitará las manchas.*
Don't worry. New Kalia will remove the stains for you (INFRML).

3.3 Linguistic realization of strategies in the data

    Mother 1:   *¿Y los colores?*
                              And the colors?

    Mother 2:   ...*ya no tiene lejía.*
                              ...it [Kalia] no longer has bleach.

    Announcer (M): *Añadido al detergente, Kalia puede con manchas que el detergente sólo no elimina.*
                              Added to detergent, Kalia can [do] with stains what detergent alone doesn't eliminate.

    Mother 1:   *Tenías razón. Con Kalia quedó como nueva.*
                              You were right. With Kalia it came out like new.

    Announcer: *Donde no pueda usar lejía, use el nuevo Kalia. El sin lejía.*
                              Where you can't use bleach, use (FRML) new Kalia. The one without bleach.

b. Written
   (Rent-A-Center, U.S.)
   Vocalists: *Rent-A-Center. Llévatelo...¡ya! Llama gratis. 1-800-se renta.*
                    Rent-A-Center. Take (INFRML) it away with you...now! <Call (FRML) free: 1-800-se renta.>

Only a few ads in the data contain no address to face at all. Such ads either reflect bald on-record strategies or are completely off record. Two examples from the six ads that are bald on-record appear in (42). The lack of bald on-record examples in this study suggests not only that the strategy is uncommon in Hispanic advertising, but also that these advertisers generally prefer not to be too frank and explicit in their attempts to persuade. Off-record strategies are accomplished by avoiding reference to the audience and via metaphor or hints to buy. These strategies are exemplified in (43) and are also infrequent in the data. Off-record strategies are used to create an overall image or appeal, such as sensuality (as in the ad for Camy) or mystery and romance (as in the Coke ad). Hispanic advertisers likely prefer on-record, yet indirect, strategies of politeness to off-record ones because they wish to be sure that the message is clearly conveyed without being too overt.

(42) Bald on record

(Bitter Kas, SP)
[Image of beverage, women around a table]
Woman 1: *¿Y tú no tomas Bitter Kas?*
And you don't drink Bitter Kas?
Woman 2: *Me gusta. Pero esta vez se me olvida pedirlo.*
I like it. But this time I forgot to ask for it.
Woman 3: *Pues, no es tan difícil. Aperitivo Bitter Kas.*
Well, it's not so difficult. Aperitif Bitter Kas.
Woman 1: *Bitter Kas aperitivo.* <*Bitter Kas. El aperitivo.*>
Bitter Kas aperitif. <Bitter Kas. The aperitif.>

(El Pozo, SP)
Announcer: [Image of woman kissing child] *Disfruta de lo bueno.* [Image of a couple kissing.] *Disfruta de lo bueno.* [Images of various people winning things—the Olympics, board games.] *Disfruta de lo bueno. Salchichón Nobleza El Pozo. ¡Disfruta de lo bueno!*
Enjoy what is good. Enjoy what is good. Enjoy what is good. El Pozo Noble Sausage. Enjoy what is good!

(43) Off record

(Camy, SP)
[Image of ice cream]
Announcer: *Extreme de Camy. Extremadamente sensual.* [Image of woman in bathing suit lying on beach]. *Extreme de Camy. Extremadamente delicioso.* [Image of woman eating ice cream, kissing a man]. *Extreme de Camy. El placer helado llevado al extremo.*
Extreme from Camy. Extremely sensual. Extreme from Camy. Extremely delicious. Extreme from Camy. Pleasure (from) ice cream carried to an extreme.

Vocalists: *Extreme. De Camy.*
Extreme. From Camy.

(Coca Cola, U.S.)
<El idioma del amor. Una mirada.>
<The language of love. A look.> [Image of Coke bottle].
<Un saludo>
<A greeting.> [Image of coke bottle being opened.]
<Un toquecito>
<A touch.>
[Image of hands selecting one of many Cokes on ice.]
<Un baile>
<A dance. > [Image of Coke being poured in glass over ice.]
<Un secreto>
<A secret.> [Image of bubbles.]
<Un besito>
<A kiss. >
[Image of woman drinking Coke. Sound of a sigh.]
<Siempre Coca Cola.>
<Always Coca Cola. > [Image of a woman's face.]

(Paco Rabanne, SP)
Woman:
    ¡Paco!
    Paco!
Announcer: ¡Paco! [Image of a bottle of cologne. Six other faces.
Each says, "¡Paco!" Announcer repeats after each person.]

Announcers' speech occurs in the majority of the ads (86 percent) and it is their speech that projects authority and power. Of the commercials with announcers, there is a preference for explicitly informal versus formal reference to the audience; 39 percent employed *tú/vosotros* versus 18 percent with *usted*. Nevertheless, roughly a third (38 percent) of the ads containing announcers' speech do not have any overt personal reference whatsoever with respect to the audience, suggesting that when an announcer's speech is formal, the preference is to avoid explicit formality and thus to avoid personal reference altogether. Finally, a small percentage of ads (4 percent) are ambiguous with respect to formality of personal reference. Ambiguous reference to viewers by the announcers is uncommon but includes *ustedes* 'you (PL)', *nosotros* 'we (inclusive)', *para todos/para toda la familia* 'for everyone/for the whole family', *a los que* 'for those who', *quién sabe* 'the person who knows', *mi* 'my', *Mamá* 'Mom (vocative)', and *muchachos* 'boys and girls (vocative)'.

In summary, positive politeness strategies are preferred in Spanish ads which project solidarity and similarity with viewers by flattering and emotionally aligning the advertiser's viewpoint with that of the audience. Nevertheless, negative strategies are also common and generally coincide with distancing strategies in an attempt to offer options to the audience and freedom from imposition. When both positive and negative strategies occur in the same ad, negative politeness is usually accomplished via an announcer or writing. Furthermore, announcers and written messages convey importance and authority in Spanish ads.

3.3.4 Implicature

Both conventional and conversational implicatures are common throughout the majority of ads. These implicatures are related to advertisers' goals of communicating a message that is indirect. It is perhaps easier to describe how conventional implicature is encoded in the data, since it is based on presupposition and implications stemming from the meaning of particular words, phrases, and syntactic structures. Conventional implicatures in the data arise as a result of either presupposition or the semantics of words or phrases. I first examine common types of presupposition.

Presupposition is important in advertising because it assumes that the audience agrees and that it shares the knowledge being communicated. For example, the phrase *saber que* 'to know that' frequently occurs in the data to imply that the speaker's information is factual by presupposing that the embedded information is a known fact to both the speaker and viewers. Consider the interrogative and declarative examples in (44a). The inherent improvement of a product is also presupposed by means of phrases such as *ahora...* 'now...' and *ya* 'now/already', as in (44b).[12] Such statements presuppose that the action or state described did not exist previously. Prior actions or states are also presupposed via *otro* 'another', *de siempre* 'as always', *el mismo* 'the same', and *sigue* 'continue' + verb. These phrases are exemplified in (44c).

(44) Conventional implicature—presupposition

    a. Presupposed factual information
       ¿Sabe usted por qué las camionetas Chevy son las más confiables y duraderas en circulación hoy?
       Do you know why Chevy trucks are the most trustworthy and lasting trucks in cirulation today? (Chevrolet, U.S.)

---

[12]Pertinent phrases are in bold-face type.

3.3 Linguistic realization of strategies in the data

¿Sabe qué tiene en común ahora el té de Chile con el de Londres?
Do you know what Chile's tea now has in common with that of London? (Té Club, CH)

Boy: *Mmmmmm. Quiero saber porque Chocapic tiene tanto chocolate.*
Mmmmm. I want to know why Chocapic has so much chocolate. (Chocapic, CH)

Sabemos la sed que sientes.
We know the thirst you feel. (Coors, U.S.)

Announcer: *Cuando sabes lo que quieres, sobran las razones. Kaliber by Guinness. Por lo que tú ya sabes.*
When you know what you want, there are more than enough reasons. Kaliber by Guinness. For that which you already know. (Kaliber, SP)

b. Presupposed improvement
¿Te imaginas proteger tu pelo a la vez que lo tiñes? **Ahora lo puedes** *con Excellence y Media de L'Oreal.*
Can you imagine protecting your hair at the same time as you color it? **Now you can** with Excellence y Media from L'Oreal. (L'Oreal, SP)

Ahora *Confort rinde mucho más.*
Now Confort yields much more. (Confort, CH)

Ya están en Chile *nuevas toallas Kotex.*
Now new Kotex napkins **are in Chile.** (Kotex, CH)

Ya hay solución *para los cabellos castigados y sin vida.*
Already there is a solution for damaged and lifeless hair. (Genesse, SP)

c. Presupposed prior action/state
Otro World Best de Samsung.
Another World Best from Samsung. (Samsung, CH)

Su protección **de siempre.**
Your protection **as always.** (Atrix, CH)

Para la mayoría de los malestares estomacales, el remedio es **el mismo.**
For the majority of stomach problems, the remedy is **the same.** (Pepto Bismol, U.S.)

Saimaza. **Sigue** *eligiendo lo mejor.*
Saimaza. **Keep** selecting the best. (Saimaza, SP)

Other presuppositions include the audience's desire for change, a knowledge of the audience's personal characteristics, possession, and future action. Advertisers typically portray change as a positive idea. The viewer's presupposed need or desire for change is indicated in the data by the phrases in (45a). Advertisers also frequently assume knowledge, particularly of their viewers' positive characteristics such as inherent beauty or merit, as in (45b). Supposed possession of a favorite place to shop or of a particular product is assumed through use of possessive pronouns for items not normally owned or not yet in the viewer's possession, as in (45c). Future action is also taken for granted by means of phrases such as *esperamos tu llamada* 'we're waiting for your call' and *gracias por....* 'thanks for....' Again, each of the following examples of presupposition are used to assume that the audience is in agreement with an ad's message and that the advertiser/product actually knows the individual viewer's wants and desires.

(45)   Conventional implicature—more presuppositions

   a. Desire for change
   Juega y **cambia** *tu vida.*
   Play and **change** your life. (Loteria Primitiva, SP)

   Para darle a tu pelo todo el brillo y volumen **que necesita.**
   To give your hair all the shine and volume **that it needs.**
   (Timotei, SP)

   Mejora *la vida.*
   Improve [your] life (Sindelen, CH)

   Participe en el sorteo mensual de hasta treinta millones de pesos. Parallevarse **lo que quiera de Falabella.**
   Participate in the monthly raffle of up to thirty million pesos. To get **what you want from Falabella.** (Fallabella, CH)

   b. Knowledge of audience characteristics
   Las finas burbujas de Font Picant despiertan la vitalidad que hay en ti.
   The fine bubbles of Font Picant awaken the vitality that is in you. (Font Picant, SP)

3.3 Linguistic realization of strategies in the data

Sedal. Saca lo mejor de ti.
Sedal. It brings out the best in you. (Sedal, CH)

Completa **lo que te falta.**
Complete **what you lack.** (Redoxon Complex, SP)

Tu **solución** *Linic que ahorra tu tiempo.*
Your Linic **solution** that saves your time. (Linic, CH)

Obtenga el respeto que usted se merece.
Obtain the respect that you deserve. (Capitol Car Credit, U.S.)

Descubre tu propia belleza y la hace durar mucho más.
It [the mascara] discovers your own beauty and makes it last much longer. (All-Day Mascara, CH)

c. Possession/future possession
Disponible en su tienda favorita.
Available at your favorite store. (Fonovisa, U.S.)

Dos vídeos Disney para tu colección.
Two Disney videos for your collection. (Disney videos, SP)

Búscalos gratis en el interior de los envases de tu pan Ideal.
Look for them free on the inside of packages of your Ideal bread. (Ideal, CH)

Si tú quieres tu mug, tu Nescafé. Tómalo del mug, auténtico mug.
If you want your mug, your Nescafe. Drink it from the mug, authentic mug. (Nescafe, CH)

d. Future action
Nuestras operadoras esperan su llamada.
Our operators are waiting for your call. (Inglés Sin Barreras, U.S.)

Gracias por escuchar y ayudar a hacer mi McDonald's su McDonald's.
Thanks for listening and helping to make my McDonald's your McDonald's. (McDonald's, U.S.)

Finally, certain syntactic structures such as those in (46) occur frequently. A prior expression of doubt or surprise (by the audience) is presupposed in many cases by the single word assertion, *Sí* 'Yes.' Also, rhetorical questions are frequently employed when the viewer's assumed answer is affirmative, as in (46b). Thus, advertisers are able to create a pseudodialogue between an ad's speaker and the viewer.

(46) a. *Sí. En sólo cinco minutos, listo su crédito automotriz Corp Banca.*
Yes. In just five minutes, your Corp Banca auto credit [is] ready. (Corp Banca, CH)

Sí. Ganas tres cientos noventa millones con sólo tres números.
Yes. You win 390 million with only three numbers. (Loto, CH)

b. *¿Grandes problemas con cucarachas?*
Big problems with cockroaches? (Combat Plus, U.S.)

¿No preferirías una Miller Lite en tu mano?
Wouldn't you prefer a Miller Lite in your hand? (Miller, U.S.)

¿No te parece que mereces un recreo?
Doesn't it seem like you deserve a break? (Orlea Bon Bon, CH)

Common conventional implicatures derived from the semantics of other lexical items are illustrated in (47). These implicatures include implied scientific information, health, uniqueness, inexactness, small quantities, ongoing action, inclusion, and unimportance. Lexical items connoting scientific information and health are used to suggest the proven and beneficial nature of products, as in (47a–47b). In contrast, phrases such as those in (47d) imply inexact quantities that will be beneficial to viewers. It is likely that viewers are so used to hearing these phrases that they ignore them and only hear actual numbers and amounts. Phrases of inexactness also allow advertisers to defend the veracity of their claims. Another widely-used conventional implicature is derived from the use of small print, which implies information that is of little importance. In reality, small print tends to contain rather important disclaimers and details about a product.

(47) Conventional implicatures—other types

a. Scientific information
*Y es **comprobado** y eficaz a reactivar el crecimiento del cabello en sólo cuatro meses.*
And it is **proven** and effective in reactivating the growth of hair in only four months. (Rogaine, U.S.)

*EPT usa el mismo método que usan **los doctores**.*
EPT uses the same method that **doctors use.** (EPT, U.S.)

b. Health
*Nuevo cereal Cocoa Frosted Flakes de Kellogg's **con diez vitaminas y hierro**.*
New Cocoa Frosted Flakes cereal from Kellogg's **with ten vitamins and iron**. (Kellogg's, U.S.)

Con vitaminas, fibras y minerales.
With vitamins, fibers, and minerals. (Azúcar Moreno de Caña, SP)

c. Uniqueness
***Sólo** Dualette de Elid me da la suavidad que necesito.*
Only Dualette from Elid gives me the softness that I need. (Dualette de Elid, CH)

*Especialistas **en ti**.*
Specialists **in you** (2 sg, INFRML). (El Corte Inglés, SP)

*Usted se va a llevar un cancionero con más doscientos tangos escritos **para usted**.*
You are going to get a songbook with more than 200 tangos written **for you** (2 sg, FRML) (Club Mundial del Vídeo, U.S.)

d. Inexactness
***Más de** cien millones en premios.*
More than 100 million in prizes. (Carozzi, CH)

*Ahorre **hasta** el cincuenta por ciento con el nuevo ciento veintidós Manquehue de larga distancia.*
Save **up to** fifty percent with the new 122 Manquehue long distance. (Manquehue Larga Distancia, CH)

*Y ahora puede disfrutar de una gran variedad de deliciosos omelettes **desde** sólo 2.99 [dos dólares y noventa y nueve centavos].*
And now you can enjoy a great variety of delicious omelettes **from** only 2.99. (Denny's, U.S.)

e. Small quantity
*Cada vídeo por **sólo** nueve cientos noventa pesetas.*
Each video for **only** 990 pesetas. (Editorial Planeta, SP)

*Puntomatic nueva fórmula con **sólo** two pastillas lava más blanco.*
New formula Puntomatic with **only** two tablets cleans whiter. (Puntomatic, CH)

f. Ongoing action
A lo largo siempre es bueno usar pilas Energizer porque su energía sigue y sigue y sigue y sigue....
In the end, it's always good to use Energizer batteries because their energy keeps going and going and going.... (Energizer, U.S.)

Announcer:	...*Te sentirás bien.*
	...You will feel good.
Woman 1:	*Horas*
	Hours
Woman 3:	*Y horas*
	And hours
Woman 5:	*Y horas.*
	And hours (Evax Ultra Star, SP)

g. Inclusion
*Cada día **somos** más los que disfrutamos de esta Silueta.*
Each day **we are** more, those of us that enjoy this Silhouette. (Silueta bread, SP)

*Hay muchos productos que parecen iguales, pero **sabemos** dónde está...la calidad.*
There are many products that seem equal, but **we know** where the quality is. (Simago, SP)

h. Unimportance
Use of small print.

Conventional implicatures are important in advertising because they allow advertisers to communicate ideas beyond what is literally stated. This message embellishment is accomplished by means of presuppositions and implicatures based on the semantics of words or phrases. Presupposed factual information, improvement, prior actions/states, desires for change, knowledge of the audience, possession, and future action are used to assume (and imply) that the audience shares the advertiser's views. Furthermore, lexical items in ads may conventionally implicate scientific information, health, uniqueness, inexactness, small quantities, ongoing action, inclusion, and unimportance in order to make a product sound as positive as possible to the viewer.

3.3.5 Grice's Maxims

Unlike conventional implicatures, conversational implicatures are achieved in a variety of ways and require the audience to "work out" the meaning in the Gricean sense. Furthermore, individual viewers may differ somewhat in their interpretation. By nature, conversational implicatures are difficult to classify other than as results of violations of Grice's Maxims. Grice (1975) suggested the types of violations listed in (48).

(48) Grice's examples of maxim violations

    Quantity: tautology, avoidance via ellipsis
    Quality: irony, metaphor, understatement, hyperbole
    Relation: nonrelevance
    Manner: ambiguity, obscurity via euphemism, failure to be brief/succinct

In the present study, I expand Grice's categories to include other violations in the data, beyond those discussed earlier in this chapter. The types of violations found are shown in (49). Violations besides those outlined by Grice are indicated with italics.

(49) Expanded examples of violations

    Quantity: *repetition,* ellipsis
    Quality: *false assertion,* irony, metaphor, understatement, hyperbole
    Relation: nonrelevance, *implied comparison/relevance*
    Manner: ambiguity, obscurity, verbosity, *vagueness, rhetorical questions,* redundancy

Although not all violations lead to conversational implicature, most do so in the data. Often such implicatures are in the form of what we commonly term "hints". The Maxim of Relation is most frequently violated, followed in order by quantity, quality, and manner. Nevertheless, if we consider novelty to be a subset of manner violations, as Lakoff (1982) suggested, manner becomes the preferred group. (See also chapter 4.) Table 3.14 depicts frequencies for each type of maxim violation. Again, percentages do not add up to 100 percent since several types of violations occur in most ads. Overall, quantity, quality, relation, and manner violations primarily occur because of repetition, metaphors, implied relevance, and vagueness.

Table 3.14 Types of violations of Grice's Maxims

Example	Frequency	Percent of each maxim violation
Quantity—repetition	353	67
Quantity—ellipsis	120	23
Quantity—lack of information	88	17
Quantity—more information than necessary	10	2
Quality—metaphor	287	56
Quality—hyperbole	242	47
Quality—false assertion	61	12
Quality—irony	15	3
Quality—tautology	9	2
Quality—understatement	6	1
Relation—implied relation	605	94
Relation—nonrelevant	40	6
Manner—vague	236	51
Manner—obscure	96	21
Mannerr—hetorical question	93	20
Manner—ambiguous	66	14
Manner—verbose	50	11
Manner—redundant	10	2
Manner—euphemism	6	1

Repetition of lexical items or phrases is a frequent means of violating quantity. Repetition allows the advertiser to reinforce the memorability of a particular phrase and to imply that the repeated information is important. In most ads, the product name is repeated at least three times. Ellipsis is also very common in Spanish ads and generally takes the form of elliptical comparatives, where part of the comparison is omitted and the viewer is left to infer the meaning, as in (50b). In such cases, advertisers attempt to imply the most favorable of all possible interpretations. Ads are only considered to lack information when no verbal information about the product is given whatsoever, as in (50c). Only a few ads contain more information than necessary. All such ads from Spain are at least two minutes long and are highly repetitive. Violations of quantity in the data can suggest that there is not much of substance to say about the product in question, but the more likely intent is to imply that the repeated information is important or to reinforce the

3.3 Linguistic realization of strategies in the data

product name. Repetition, ellipsis, visual distractors with little information, and giving too much information are strategies to distract viewers from considering how little information they are receiving.

(50) Violations of quantity

a. Repetition

(Cereal Milo, CH)
<¿*Tienes que jugar?*>
<Do you have to play?>
[Image of boy playing tennis.]
<¿*Tienes que ganar?*>
<Do you have to win?>
[Image of Milo and an older boy serving in tennis.]
<*Agarra un plato.*>
<Grab a plate.>
<*Come cereal Milo.*>
<Eat Milo cereal.>
<*Es potente*>
<It's powerful>
<*Cereal potente.*>
<Powerful cereal.>
Announcer: Milo. El cereal potente.
Milo. Powerful cereal.

b. Ellipsis
Descubre tu propia belleza y vas a asegurar mucho más.
Discover your own beauty and you're going to insure much more. (All-Day, CH)

Fortalece su cabello un cincuenta y cinco%
Strengthen your hair [by] 55 percent. (Alberto VO5, CH)

c. Lack of information
(Coca Cola, CH)
[Image of button with Coca Cola written on it. Button is pushed and begins a series of chain reactions in a machine. Eventually the machine pours a coke.]
<*Siempre Coca Cola.*>
<Always Coca Cola.>

Violation of quality is primarily achieved through use of metaphor and hyperbole, and to a lesser degree, through literally false assertions. Other violations of quality in the data such as irony, tautologies, and understatement also appear in (51) but are infrequently utilized. Most quality violations result in implicatures suggesting more descriptions of the product than are literally true. As Geis (1982) suggested, strategies for avoiding truthfulness seem to be used so that the advertiser cannot be held responsible for the implied message. Instead, advertisers may argue that their message is indeed truthful to some degree, however small that might be. Thus, in (51a) we see a number of associations being implicated that are not literally qualities of the product advertised. Other quality violations in (51b–51f) also implicate nonliteral qualities about products. The advantage of metaphoric language for advertising is that it allows multiple associations with a product and suggests that these associations are true in some way.

(51) Violations of quality

    a. Metaphor
Kellogg's. El cereal con chispa.
Kellogg's. The cereal with sparkle. (Kellogg's, U.S.)

Y puedes capturar la emoción con cuatro relojes salvajes de Burger King.
And you can capture the emotion with four savage watches from Burger King. (Burger King, U.S.)

Porque todas las vacas del mundo viven en Kraft.
Because all the cows of the world live in Kraft. (Kraft, U.S.)

La banca inteligente
The intelligent bank. (Corp Banca, CH)

<*Come Fútbol. Sueña Fútbol.*>
<Eat football. Dream football.> (Coca Cola, CH)

Vuelve a la sencillez y la belleza de Irlanda en tu tienda de discos.
Return to the simplicity and the beauty of Ireland at your record store. (The Corr's CD, SP)

    b. Hyperbole
Nada más natural que el trigo para alimentar tu cuerpo.
Nothing more natural than wheat to nourish your body. (Sanex, SP)

3.3 Linguistic realization of strategies in the data

El set Arcobaleno incluye todo lo necesario para su cocina.
The Arcobaleno set includes everything necessary for your kitchen. (Arcobaleno, SP)

El lubricante más avanzado del mundo.
The most advanced lubricant in the world. (Mobil 1, SP)

Siempre universal.
Always universal. (Coca Cola, CH)

A cambio de escuchar, Chile tiene el mejor fútbol del mundo.
Contrary to what you hear, Chile has the best football [soccer] in the world. (Nike, CH)

c. False assertion
El refresco que siempre te ha refrescado.
The refreshment that always has refreshed you. (Coca Cola, U.S.)

Quieres un Ford nuevo.
You want a new Ford. (Ford Contour, U.S.)

La retiras sin esperar....Sólo en dos minutos.
You remove it without waiting....In only two minutes. (Cera Tibia Veet, SP)

La preferida de los que se acuestan al amanecer.
The preferred one of those that go to bed at dawn. (Heineken, SP)

Es tiempo de pintar tu casa.
It's time to paint your house. (Sears, U.S.)

d. Irony
Mom 2: *¿Tú crees que a las mujeres nos gustan los zapatos?*
Do you think that we women like shoes?

Mom 1: *No. ¿Cómo crees? Es puro mito.*
No. How can you think that? It's just a myth. (Payless, U.S.)

Y al final de la historia, hasta su suegra lo alababa.
And at the end of the story, even his mother-in-law praised him. (Inglés Sin Barreras, U.S.)

> Mother: *O te comas todo o te quedas sin postre.* [Image of child eating his food, then eating the flowers, tablecloth, chunks of the wall.]
> Either you eat everything or you don't get any dessert. (Postres Caricia, CH)

e. Tautology
Cuando Wieners tiene una venta de "Todo en Rebaja" todo está rebajado.
When Wieners has a sale of "everything reduced," everything is reduced. (Wieners, U.S.)

Y su tecnología aún absorba porque sólo Nova absorba igual que Nova.
And its technology still absorbs because only Nova absorbs the same as Nova. (Nova, CH)

f. Understatement
Un poco de pasta basta.
A little pasta is enough. (Gior, SP)

...cualquier persona puede convertirse en un empresario exitoso. Sólo basta tener una buena idea.
...any person can become a successful businessman. It's enough to just have a good idea. (Curso Creación de Nuevos Negocios, CH)

Violations of relation are primarily accomplished by association of unrelated concepts. The ad for Bayer in (52a), for example, associates the product and a pounding head. The slogans for Hellmann's mayonnaise, Pepsi, and Miller Beer similarly equate the products with a particular quality. Through song, Soprole's commercial suggests a relation between conquering obstacles and the product, a yogurt. Some violations of relation also occur because of nonrelevant statements, as in (52b). The implicatures arising from such violations of relation suggest that the concepts in ads are equal or associated with one another, either merely because both ideas occur in the same ad or because the product has some vaguely similar qualities to the associated item. Thus, violation of relation in advertising allows for virtually any comparison, however remote or ridiculous.

3.3 *Linguistic realization of strategies in the data* 99

(52) Violations of relation

   a. Implied comparisons/relations
   Si ésta es tu cabeza... [Image of pendulum swinging back and forth, hitting sides of something. Woman is groaning.] *éste es un producto para el dolor de cabeza.*
   If this is your head...this is a product for headaches. (Bayer, SP)

   Dales Hellmann's. Dales lo mejor.
   Give them Hellmann's. Give them the best. (Hellmann's, U.S.)

   Pepsi. Generación Next.
   Pepsi. Generation Next. (Pepsi, U.S.)

   Miller Time. Todo puede pasar.
   Miller Time. Anything can happen. (Miller, U.S.)

   Las pequeñas grandes cosas que nos llevan a triunfar. <*Soprole, el yogurt*>
   The small great things that lead us to triumph. <Soprole, the yogurt.> (Soprole, CH)

   b. Nonrelevance
   Julio: *Cuando llegué a la casa después del trabajo...* <*Barrazo ganó $10 millones en LOTTO Texas.*>
   When I arrived at the house after work... <Julio Barrazo won 10 million dollars at LOTTO Texas.>

   Julio: *...en el refrigerador había una ensalada de papas y me agarré un sandwich para comérmelo. De repente oí que alguien tocó la puerta....No lo pude creer porque nunca en mi vida había ganado algo.*
   ...in the refrigerator there was a potato salad and I grabbed a sandwich to eat it all up. Suddenly, I heard that someone knocked on the door....I couldn't believe it because never in my life had I won anything.

   <*Tal vez fue por algo que comió.*>
   <Maybe it was because of something you ate.>

   Julio: *No, no creo que sea la ensalada de papas lo que tuvo la suerte.*
   No. I don't think it was the potato salad that had the luck. (Lotto Texas, U.S.)

Oye, vive más y aprende. Y compra Luv's.
Listen, live more, and learn. And buy Luv's. (Luv's, U.S.)

Finally, violations of manner are generally encoded with the related strategies of vagueness, obscurity, and ambiguity. In (53a), for example, viewers are supposed to infer that Kraft cheese is full of milk, that they know that Burger King is their preferred choice for hamburgers, that Fattaché will accomplish whatever the viewer wants it to do, and that **all** doctors recommend Tylenol. Such interpretations are only possible, however, because of background knowledge and context. Ambiguity is generally achieved via wordplay, as in (53c). Rhetorical questions are frequently employed to implicate a desired response from the audience. Rather than being true questions, rhetorical questions in the data are merely an indirect means of implying the assertions of fact, shown after each example in (53d). Finally, verbosity, redundancy, and euphemism play minor roles in achieving manner violations. Conversational implicatures derived from violations of manner convey "fuzzy" positive notions about products by cloaking suggestion in vague language. Consequently, viewers may watch a given ad and come away with a good feeling about a product without knowing exactly why the product is supposed to be worth buying.

(53) Violations of manner

    a. Vagueness
    Porque todas las vacas del mundo viven en Kraft.
    Because all the cows in the world live at Kraft. (Kraft, U.S.)

    Tú sí que sabes.
    You are the one who knows. (Burger King, U.S.)

    Y si también combinas Fattaché con un poco de ejercicio de grado, vas a obtener estupendos resultados.
    And if you also combine Fattaché with a little of the right amount of exercise, you're going to obtain stupendous results. (Fattaché, U.S.)

    Para el dolor causado por la cirugía, los doctores recomiendan Tylenol más que otras marcas.
    For the pain caused by surgery, doctors recommend Tylenol more than other brands. (Tylenol, U.S.)

    b. Obscure language
    100% café. 100% sabor.
    100% coffee. 100% flavor. (Monterrey, CH)

Woman 2: *Mi Feeling es bailar toda la noche. (Feeling popsicles, CH)*
My Feeling is to dance all night.

Announcer: *Atrapa tú también el sabor naranja Crush. < UNICA con JUGO de NARANJA. > A todo Crush.*
You also [should] trap Crush's orange flavor.
<The ONLY one with [real] ORANGE JUICE.>
For everything, Crush. (Crush, CH)

Piensa en verde.
Think of green. (Heineken, SP)

c. Ambiguity
Mantenemos tu Automóvil.
We maintain your Automobile. (Sears Auto Center, U.S.)

Acércate con confianza con la MENTAlidad de Scope.
Approach confidently with the MINTality of Scope. (Scope, U.S.)

Cuestión de PERTsonalidad.
Question of PERTsonality. (Pert Plus, CH)

Té Club. El club de todos los chilenos.
Club Tea. The club of all Chileans. (Té Club, CH)

Tu dulce compañía.
Your sweet company. (Arcor Golosinas candy company, CH)

d. Rhetorical questions
¿Qué más se puede pedir?
What more can be asked?
Assertion: *No se puede pedir más.*
Nothing more can be asked. (Follow Me to America, U.S.)

¿Buscando la compañía ideal?
Looking for the ideal company?
Assertion: *Estás buscando a nosotros, la compañía ideal.*
You're looking for us, the ideal company. (Town North Suzuki, U.S.)

¿Piel firme de ahora en adelante?
Firm skin from now on?
Assertion: *Puedes tener piel firme de ahora en adelante.*
You can have firm skin from now on. (Vasenol, CH)

¿Que cuántas cremas usa?
You use how many creams?
Assertion: *Usa demasiadas cremas.*
        You use too many creams. (Nivea, SP)

¿Cómo recargas las pilas?
How do you recharge your batteries?
Assertion: *Necesitas más energía.*
        You need more energy. (Bio Clesa Líquido, SP)

e. Verbosity/redundancy
Es el nuevo Rexona 24 horas esfera gigante.
It's the new Rexona 24-hour giant sphere. (Rexona deodorant, CH)

El nuevo envase individual grande de papitas Evercrisp tipo americano.
The new big individual package of American type Evercrisp potato chips. (Evercrisp, CH)

Regaine minoxidil. Tratamiento local sintomático de la caída del cabello, de origen androgénico.
Regaine minoxidil. Local symptomatic treatment of hairloss, of androgenous origin. (Regaine, SP)

...Usted los encuentra en CTC Centro de CTC.
...You find them at CTC Center from CTC. (CTC, CH)

3.3.6 Novelty

The last major category to examine with regard to how it is encoded in the data is novelty. Lakoff (1982) argued that novelty is a violation of manner and is used to attract attention and make the audience remember; however, the data in the present study suggest that certain types of novelty (as defined by Lakoff) accomplish other purposes. The most frequent types of novelty found in Spanish ads are syntactic and explicit novelty. Typically, syntactic novelty consists of omission of verbs and of lists of single nouns or adjectives. Because it is so common in Spanish advertising, it probably no longer attracts much attention from viewers. Instead, syntactic novelty allows for brevity and implicatures arising from both violations of manner and quantity, as in (54a).

Both explicit and lexical novelty are used to make the audience take notice of a product or the ad itself and, therefore, are clear violations of manner. Explicit novelty mainly consists of the lexical items, *ahora* 'now', *nuevo* 'new',

3.3 Linguistic realization of strategies in the data

por primera vez 'for the first time', and forms of *presentar* 'to present', *cambiar* 'to change', and *descubrir* 'discover'. Lexical novelty is achieved by neologisms, jargon, and use of foreign words, particularly from English and French. Semantic novelty is only recorded in the data when it involves elliptical comparisons like those in (54d), which are violations of both quantity and manner. As stated in §2.3.4, elliptical comparisons generally serve to imply the most favorable of all possible interpretations. Situational novelty is contextual and involves a novel event or an unusual or unexpected setting or ending to an ad, both of which are violations of manner to attract attention. Novel associations at times are reflected through use of metaphor or the creation of a new need or association with the product that is not inherent to the product itself. Finally, pragmatic and morphological novelty are infrequent and unimportant compared to other types of novelty.

(54) Novelty

    a. Syntactic

    EPT. Para la respuesta correcta.
    EPT. For the correct response. (EPT, U.S.)

    Té Supremo. Con toda la calidad del mundo.
    Supreme Tea. With all the quality in the world. (Té Supremo, CH)

    Para tener un viaje feliz, sólo autobuses San Luis.
    For a happy trip, only San Luis buses. (Autobuses San Luis, U.S.)

    Preparación. Concentración. Técnica. Destreza.
    Preparation. Concentration. Technique. Dexterity. (AT&T, U.S.)

    b. Explicit

    Ahora hay un nuevo desodorante aún más eficaz.
    Now there is a new, even more effective deodorant. (Sanex, SP)

    Presentamos Aquafresh.
    We present Aquafresh. (Aquafresh, CH)

    Por primera vez envuélvete con lo último de la televisión.
    For the first time, involve yourself in the latest in television. (Showtime en Español, U.S.)

Cambio drástico.
Drastic change. (Toyota Corolla, CH)

Descubre todo lo que te interesa en la revista más completa.
Discover everything that interests you in the most complete magazine. (Vanidades, U.S.)

c. Lexical
Jargon:
GelSec
GelSec (Kotex, CH)

ProVitaminas
ProVitamins (Pantene, SP)

Filtrohelada
Filtercooled (Coors, U.S.)

Neologism:
Hiperrico, hiperbuenos
Hyperrich, hypergood (Hipercor, SP)

Sprimido
Sprimmed (Sprim, CH)

Zucaritas, chocorricas
Sugaries, chocorich (Kellogg's, CH)

Zoorpresa
Zoorprise (Nestle, CH)

McVaso
McGlass (McDonald's, CH)

PERTsonalidad
PERTsonality (Pert, CH)

Lexical borrowing:
Assy (Assy shampoo, CH)

Petit Yopsuiss
Little Swiss Yorgurt (Yoplait, CH)

Hidro-Genesse (Hidro-Genesse, SP)
MoviLine
MobileLine (MoviLine, SP)

3.3 Linguistic realization of strategies in the data

d. Semantic
Summa es más.
Summa is more. (Summa, CH)

Mientras más la use, más puntos y más y mejores regalos.
While the more you use it, more points and more and better gifts. (Paris, CH)

e. Situational
M&M's that talk (M&M's, U.S.)
Surprise party (Miller, U.S.)
Recipe contest (La Lechera, CH)
Cows that dance (Lechera Asturiana, SP)
Images of people kissing each other's underarms (Sanex, SP)
Woman washes her hair outdoors with a hose (Wash & Go, SP)

f. Novel situations
Sexy women and beer (Miller, U.S.)
Relay race and dish washing liquid (Fairy Ultra, CH)
Royal Club Evian health spa and shampoo (Pantene, SP)
Topless woman and vitamins (Revalid, SP)
Freedom and a powered vehicle (Toyota 4Runner, U.S.)

Thus, novelty serves more than one persuasive purpose. Lexical, explicit, and situational novelty, as well as novel associations, all involve manner violations that cause the audience to pay attention to the ad. Besides violating manner, syntactic and semantic novelty are also violations of quantity because information is left out and viewers must fill in missing information based on their background and the context.

3.3.7 Minor categories

With the exception of lexical selection, the remaining pragmalinguistic categories are not found in the majority of the data and are, therefore, relatively unimportant when describing Spanish advertising language. Lexical selection overlaps with lexical novelty and violations of manner. That is, the category "lexicon" in the database includes lexical borrowing, jargon, neologisms, and wordplay, which I have already discussed. Flattery is of three types: self-flattery, character-to-character flattery, and flattery of the audience. Flattery is generally revealed through expressive speech acts, discussed in §2.3.2. Endorsements are of two kinds: direct testimonials by real people regarding a product's effectiveness and indirect testimonials by characters in the ad. Endorsements are used as examples of consumer behavior for viewers to follow. Humor is difficult to categorize because of the variety of strategies for making the audience laugh or be amused. Nevertheless, humor typically is effected as a result of some type of implicature or because of visual antics or a slapstick type of humor. Advertisers seem to use humor to make the audience feel good or to draw viewers into the message of the ad. Syntactic strategies in the data consist of topicalization or left dislocation in order to emphasize a particular element. Finally, phonological devices in ads include alliteration, rhyming, jingles, and foreign pronunciation of words.[13]

3.3.8 Summary

In summary, results for research question (2) suggest that the most common class of speech acts in the data, representatives, are typically encoded as assertions of real or supposed facts. Assertions are, therefore, used to make an ad sound like it is presenting factual information rather than opinions. Like assertions, reports are used in Spanish advertising to suggest that ads are providing true and important information to viewers.

Directives are generally realized as orders, but are really strong suggestions since they are infelicitous as orders; advertisers do not have the inherent power to make viewers act. Suggestions are also common and less face threatening. They are encoded as interrogatives, imperatives, and declaratives. Commissives and expressives are less uniform than directives in their realization. Most commissives are qualified offers requiring action from viewers or vague promises that are unlikely to be challenged. Expressives generally take the form of flattery, praise, and compliments involving emotional alignment with viewers. Furthermore, some speech acts are deliberately formed to be vague or ambiguous, allowing for more than one interpretation.

Spatial and temporal deixis most often refers to notions of "here and now", as opposed to past reference that generally carries negative connotations. Second person is by far the most common form of reference, suggesting the importance of viewers as individuals. Moreover, positive-face, conveying concepts of solidarity and proximity, is the most frequent form of politeness, although negative-face strategies involving distance and power are also common. Furthermore, written messages and the speech of male announcers convey authority and power. When an announcer's message is formal, the preference is to avoid explicit formality by avoiding any personal reference whatsoever.

Conventional implicature is achieved through presuppositions that assume that the audience is in agreement or shares the knowledge presented

---

[13] I found no identical ads from the three countries.

3.4 Distributive patterns

and through implicatures derived from the semantics of lexical items. Conversational implicature, on the other hand, is more difficult to categorize and more often consists of hints or inferences as a result of violations of Grice's Maxims. Thus, the viewer must "work out" meanings of conversational implicatures. Repetition, metaphor, implied relations, and vagueness are the most common types, respectively, of violations of quantity, quality, relation, and manner. Implicatures arising from violations of these four maxims, among other things, suggest importance and a stronger claim or association than can be literally stated without being literally untruthful. The persuasive intent of implicatures is

- avoidance when ads have little real information to present;
- avoidance of responsibility for their literal messages;
- making minor associations constitute inherent similarity between a product and selected notion; and
- conveying a product's positive characteristics via vague language.

All of this information on the linguistic realization of pragmatics shows the ways that advertisers express pragmatic strategies to achieve their persuasive goals.

3.4 Distributive patterns

3.4.1 Context and similarities

I address distributive patterns in the data in this section in response to research question (3): are any pragmatic differences evident between dialects of Spanish? This question has not been addressed in previous literature. In order to better understand the distribution of data among countries, a brief examination of contextual variables is in order. Product preferences by country are presented in table 3.15. Differences in distribution are most apparent between the U.S. and Chile and in the categories of foods and powered vehicles. Despite differences in distribution of product categories, comparable ads are found within most categories on each television station. These subgroups of comparable ads appear in appendix C, by country and the number of comparable ads.

Table 3.15 Products by country (n = 241)

Product	U.S.	SP	CH
Foods	31	45	66
Meals and snacks	21	36	32
Alcoholic drinks	13	3	0
Health and beauty	39	46	49
Household cleaners	3	15	9
Men's and boys' clothing	2	1	0
Women's and girls' clothing	0	6	1
Both men's and women's clothing	4	3	5
Footwear	3	0	1
Major household appliances	4	6	5
TV and video	9	10	2
Audio	24	14	11
Furniture	3	0	0
Kitchenware and home	4	2	7
Computer	0	2	5
Sporting goods	0	0	0
Powered vehicles	31	22	4
Toys	0	4	4
Miscellaneous (variety)	5	1	6
Travel	2	11	0
Recreation	16	7	5
Education	10	1	11
Financial	11	7	15
Medical/social	2	0	1
Other services (legal, utility)	3	0	2

Audience preference by country is similar in most cases, as shown in table 3.16. Teletrece (CH) has fewer ads for a general adult audience, whereas Univisión (U.S.) shows fewer ads for women, more ads for men, and more ads specifically for mothers than do the other two stations. This did not appear to be due to the subject matter of the programs.

Table 3.16 Audience by Country (n = 241)

Audience	U.S.	SP	CH
Children	28	25	30
Teens	21	18	26
Adults (young)	28	20	30
Adults (women)	30	59	58
Adults (men)	26	13	16
Adults (parents)	18	11	16
Adults (mothers)	23	8	8
Adults (older)	3	1	1
All	2	2	11

3.4.2 Differences in general pragmatic strategies

Distribution of general pragmatic strategies by country reveals a few differences, but pragmatics in Spanish advertising is generally more similar than different. In the data, the three dialects employ general categories of speech acts, novelty, politeness, indexicals, implicature, violation of maxims, and lexicon with similar frequencies. This similarity is also true regardless of product or audience categories. Speaker considerations, however, do not occur with a similar degree of frequency in all countries.[14] Speakers in Univisión (U.S.) ads reflect stereotypes of gender, age, physical characteristics, or professional status at least twenty percent more often than do their counterparts on the other stations. Spanish copywriters in the U.S. apparently believe that stereotyping viewers is an effective way to advertise products and services. The minor categories of flattery, endorsements, syntax, and phonology also reveal differences in the degree of preference by country. Variation in these categories appears most between the U.S. and Spain, with the exception of distribution of phonological examples, which varies most between the U.S. and Chile. These general preferences are charted in table 3.17.

---

[14]The focus of this study is on linguistic rather than cultural or social aspects of commercials. In this section I only offer some possible reasons why strategies are used, based on discussion with Spanish speakers from Chile, Spain, and the U.S. Clearly, cultural and social implications are far more complex than the degree to which they are mentioned in this study. I do not pretend to offer a definitive account of social/cultural reasons for differences in the data; instead, I present tentative suggestions.

Table 3.17 Categories by country (n=241)

	U.S.	%	SP	%	CH	%
Speech acts	241	100.0	239	99.2	241	100.0
Novelty	241	100.0	241	100.0	241	100.0
Politeness	239	99.2	236	97.9	239	99.2
Indexicals	238	98.8	230	95.4	235	97.5
Implicature	227	94.2	232	96.3	232	96.3
Violation of maxims	241	100.0	239	99.2	239	99.2
Speaker considerations	166	68.9	116	48.1	111	46.1
Flattery	105	43.6	67	27.8	83	34.4
Humor	64	26.6	65	27.0	62	25.7
Endorsements	120	49.8	71	29.5	94	39.0
Syntax (info. structure)	70	29.0	29	12.0	37	15.4
Phonological elements	71	29.5	50	20.7	174	72.2
Lexical selection	161	66.8	164	68.0	167	69.3

3.4.3 Differences in individual pragmatic strategies

Unlike general strategies, preferences for individual pragmatic strategies within each major category vary considerably in some cases. Table 3.18 depicts the frequencies of each strategy according to country.

Table 3.18 Individual strategies by country (n=241)

Strategy	U.S.	%	Spain	%	Chile	%
Representatives	230	95.4	231	95.9	231	95.9
Directives	165	68.5	123	51.0	134	55.6
Expressives	81	33.6	35	14.5	31	12.9
Commissives	59	24.5	47	19.5	37	15.4
Declarations	33	13.7	27	11.2	21	8.7
Syntactic	176	73.0	228	94.6	212	88.0
Explicit	130	53.9	142	58.9	128	53.1
Semantic	107	44.4	72	29.9	95	39.4
Lexical	99	41.1	99	41.1	80	33.2
Novel association	77	32.0	92	38.2	84	34.9
Situational	70	29.0	97	40.2	94	39.0
Morphological	30	12.4	18	7.5	37	15.4
Pragmatic	50	20.7	9	3.7	14	5.8

3.4 Distributive patterns

Strategy	U.S.	%	Spain	%	Chile	%
Deixis	227	94.2	207	85.9	224	92.9
Personal reference	222	92.1	191	79.3	196	81.3
Tense	116	48.1	86	35.7	72	29.9
Positive face	172	71.4	137	56.8	119	49.4
Negative face	86	35.7	105	43.6	129	53.5
Distance	127	52.7	103	42.7	142	58.9
Solidarity	160	66.4	131	54.4	111	46.1
Power	81	33.6	108	44.8	127	52.7
Conversational implicature	198	82.2	209	86.7	208	86.3
Conventional implicature	168	69.7	138	57.3	132	54.8
Violation of quantity	168	69.7	168	69.7	193	80.1
Violation of quality	180	74.7	160	66.4	170	70.5
Violation of relation	205	85.1	223	92.5	217	90.0
Violation of manner	164	68.0	151	62.7	149	61.8
Gender	45	18.7	33	13.7	22	9.1
Age	80	33.1	31	12.9	35	14.5
Physical characteristic	57	23.7	26	10.8	42	17.4
Profession	73	30.3	30	12.5	33	13.7

Ads from both Spain and Chile reveal the following order of preference for speech act strategies: representatives, directives, commissives, expressives, and declarations. Commercials from the U.S., on the other hand, prefer expressives over commissives. Perhaps advertisers prefer to attempt emotional and personal relationships with viewers as individuals more than advertisers prefer to commit themselves to action. It seems that "free" gifts and offers occur less frequently in U.S. ads. Although the degree of preference for representatives is almost identical in each dialect, the order varies somewhat with other speech-act strategies. Directives, declarations, commissives, and expressives all occur more often in the U.S. ads. Furthermore, individual speech acts within each class (such as orders, suggestions, requests, and invitations in the class of commissives) are most common in U.S. ads, generally followed by ads from Spain.

The larger repertoire of speech acts from the U.S. may reflect the greater complexity found in ads on Univisión than those of Spain and Chile. Furthermore, the greater complexity of Univisión commercials may be due to a larger budget and the fact that ads from Spain are often only ten seconds in length, far shorter than those on the other two stations. Chilean ads also tend to include fewer participants than the U.S. ads, which may contribute to the comparative lack of variety of speech acts found in Teletrece ads.

The examples in (55) depict an ad for Pantene shampoo in all three countries that is representative of some general differences between ads from the three regions. The Chilean and U.S. ads are quite similar in message, but the American ad is more complex in terms of participants and also includes an announcer. The Chilean ad depicts the same woman, but the ad appears to be dubbed. There is no announcer and the assertions are direct, whereas in the U.S. ad, the announcer's first statement implies rather than overtly states that Pantene is the solution, as in the Chilean ad. Even though there is also just one speaker in the commercial from Spain, it is more indirect than that of Chile. The ad indirectly suggests that use of Pantene will contribute to the viewers' overall health, not just that of their hair. Thus, the ad from Spain has more of an appeal to the sophistication of its viewers.

(55) One ad, three countries

United States
Woman: *¿Sabías que pones tu cabello en riesgo cada vez que lo lavas? El cabello es más frágil cuando está mojado. ¿Sorprendida? El sólo peinarlo puede romperlo.*
Did you know that you put your hair at risk each time you wash it? Hair is more fragile when it is wet. Surprised? Just combing it can break it.

Announcer: *Pantene ProV.*
Pantene ProV.

Woman: *Con provitaminas diarias para un cabello fuerte y saludable que se rompe menos.*
With daily provitamins for strong and healthy hair that breaks less.

Announcer: *Pantene tiene una fórmula única con provitaminas que penetra en la raíz mejorando tu cabello hasta la punta.*
Pantene has a unique formula with provitamins that penetrates to the root, improving your hair even at the ends.

Woman: *Fuerte, saludable y brillante.*
Strong, healthy, and shiny.

3.4 Distributive patterns

Announcer: *Pantene ProV. Para un cabello tan saludable que brilla.*
Pantene ProV. For hair so healthy that it shines.

Woman: *Fuerte y hermoso día tras día.*
Strong and beautiful day after day.

Chile
[dubbed]

Woman: *¿Sabes qué puede dañar tu cabello? Lavarlo. ¿Sorprendida? El cabello está más frágil cuando está mojado. Al peinarte, puedes dañarlo. La solución: Pantene ProV que ayuda a mantenerlo fuerte y celebrarlo. Su fórmula con provitamina de cinco nutre desde la raíz y actúa las áreas más dañadas. Ayudando a fortalecer tu cabello hasta las puntas. Dejándola saludable y brillante. Pantene ProV. Para un cabello tan saludable que brilla.* < *Un cabello tan saludable que brilla.* >
Do you know what can damage your hair? Washing it. Surprised? Hair is more fragile when it is wet. When combing it, you can damage it. The solution: Pantene ProV, which helps keep it strong and enhance it. Its [Pantene's] formula with provitamin of five nourishes from the root and acts on the most damaged areas. Helping to strengthen your hair even at the ends. Leaving it healthy and shiny. Pantene ProV. For hair so healthy that it shines. < Hair so healthy that it shines. >

Spain
[Image of person diving into a pool of water that says "Royal Club Evian" at the bottom.]

Announcer: *Royal Club Evian. Conocido en todo el mundo por fortalecer y devolver la salud al cuerpo y a la mente. Y para sanar el cabello, Royal Club Evian recomienda Pantene ProV. Incluso el pelo debilitado cubre a fuerza. Aplica Pantene con un masaje. Así sus provitaminas penetran y nutren el cabello de la raíz a las puntas. Pantene fortalece tu pelo devolviéndole su salud. Pantene ProV. Pelo tan sano que brilla.* < *Pelo tan sano que brilla.* >
Royal Evian Club. Known all over the world for strengthening and returning health to the body and

mind. And to cure hair, Royal Club Evian recommends Pantene ProV. It even covers weakened hair completely. Massage Pantene in. That way its provitamins penetrate and nourish the hair from the root to the ends. Pantene strengthens your (INFRML) hair, returning its health. Pantene ProV. Hair so healthy that it shines. < Hair so healthy that it shines. >

Similarly, the examples in (56) for Minute Maid orange juice further illustrate the differences in complexity of message between the U.S. and Chile frequently observed in the data. Even though the ads' slogans are the same, the Chilean ad has only one participant, the announcer and one major image with which to associate the product.

(56) A comparison of complexity

United States:
[Image of a bullfighter and a woman]
Woman: *Toma, Marián, de un buen jugo.* [Image of product.]
Aquí dice en inglés que sabe como es una naranja más fresca y madura.
Drink, Marian, from a good juice. Here it says in English that it tastes as though it is a very fresh and ripe orange.

Bullfighter: *Pues, por ti, Dora, lo voy a averiguar.*
Well, for you, Dora, I'm going to find out.

[Man leaves the room, goes to airport. Image of a plane flying from Spain to U.S.]

¡Ey!
Hey!

[Man hails taxi. Image of sign saying, "Welcome to Florida". Image of man in an orange grove. Man bites into an orange.]

Sí, Minute Maid sabe como una naranja madura.
Yes, Minute Maid tastes like a ripe orange.'

[Image of a cow. Cow moos. Man speaks to the cow.]

¡Olé!
Olé!

3.4 Distributive patterns

> Announcer: *Minute Maid Premium. ¡Dale un mordisco!* [Image of the bullfighter with a cape in front of cow.]
> Minute Maid Premium. Take a bite!
>
> Chile:
> Announcer: *Ahora Danone te ofrece el sabor natural de las naranjas frescas. Nuevo Minute Maid Premium de Danone. ¡Dale un mordisco!* [Image of a bite being taken out of a car ton of juice.] < *¡Dale un mordisco!* >
> Now Danone offers you the natural flavor of fresh oranges. New Minute Maid Premium from Danone. Take a bite! < Take a bite! >

Use of deictic expressions is similar in the U.S. and Chile and is slightly less frequent in ads from Spain. Personal reference is most common in U.S. ads, followed by ads from Chile and Spain. This pattern may suggest that U.S. advertisers view friendliness and individuality as being more important than their counterparts do from Spain and Chile. Use of nonpresent tense is also most common on Univisión ads, followed by Antena 3 and Teletrece. Again, the complexity of personal reference and tense may be partially explained by the length of the ads. Although ads that are more complex are not necessarily more persuasive, they probably hold the viewer's attention better and are more interesting. Consequently, a greater repertoire of pragmatic strategies may indirectly contribute to the persuasiveness of an ad.

Indicators of both positive face and solidarity are most frequent in the U.S., followed respectively by Spain and Chile. The Chilean ads, however, reveal the most negative politeness strategies and devices indicating distance and power. Antena 3 (SP) ads contain the smallest number of distancing strategies; this finding suggests that a high degree of formality is unappealing to the Spanish public. Pragmatic strategies often reflect ad writers' stereotypes of society, whether real or imagined. Thus, the distribution of politeness strategies and distancing devices suggests that advertisers in Chile view their audience as members of a more stratified society than their counterparts in the U.S. and Spain. Furthermore, advertisers in Spain and the U.S. see their audiences as members of more egalitarian societies.

Previously, I discussed how distancing devices such as formal pronominal address are used in the data along with negative politeness or with positive politeness for a mitigating effect. The following examples illustrate the overall differences in politeness strategies between the three countries in ads for long distance telephone companies. The tone in (57a) is familiar and informal commands are used. The MCI (U.S.) ad's intent seems to be to please viewers by assuring them that their desires and MCI's desires are the same. The ad for Airtel (SP) also conveys positive face, but verbs and the one command are formally encoded, suggesting distance. The ad for Entel (CH) in (57c) attempts a different strategy, by implying status and power and by avoiding imposition on the audience. This ad achieves the greatest distance from viewers in that it contains no personal reference.

(57) Politeness strategies

    a. MCI, United States

       Grandmother: *Llamar por cobrar. Siempre lo hago. <Es tan sencillo.>*
                        Call collect. I always do it. <It's so easy.>

       Mother: [pushing daughter's swing] *Y me cuesta igual que ella me llame por cobrar.*
                And it costs me the same as if she calls me collect.

       Daughter: *Y nosotros la llamemos. <Siempre unidos.>*
                And if we call her. <Always united.>

       Announcer: [Images of family, hugging, smiling, telephone number.] *Sólo con MCI One, la tarifa por país es la misma. Si te llama por cobrar del extranjero con el número MCI o si llamas directo de casa. <La misma tarifa por país> Alégrate. Ahora te pueden llamar por cobrar a tu casa con toda confianza cuandoquiera. Llámanos hoy para más información. MCI. Sí se puede. <Sí se puede.>*
                Only with MCI One, the country charge is the same. If she calls you (INFRML) collect from a foreign country with the MCI number or if you call direct from home. <The same charge for each country.> Be (INFRML) happy. Now they can call you collect at home with complete confidence, whenever. Call (INFRML) us today for more information. MCI. Yes, it's possible. <Yes, it's possible.>

3.4 Distributive patterns

b. Airtel, Spain
   [Black and white image of large building]
   Announcer: Hay personas a las que les gusta hablar mucho. Otras, en cambio, son de pocas palabras. [Image of couple kissing.] Los hay que prefieren escuchar. Porque todos somos diferentes, Airtel Bono ha creado Bono Airtel. El primer sistema de bonos de la telefonía. Ahora cada uno podrá comprar el tiempo que quiera hablar. Y hablar siempre le costará menos. Bono Airtel. <Bono Airtel.> La telefonía que marca diferencias. <La telefonía que marca diferencias.> Si puede imaginar, se puede hacerse. Airtel. <Airtel> ¿Por qué no? <¿Por qué no?> <Infórmese en el....>
   There are people who like talking a lot. Others, in contrast, are of few words. There are those that prefer to listen. Because we're all different, Airtel Bono has created Bono Airtel. The first telephone voucher system. Now each one will be able to buy the time that he/she wants to talk. And talking always will cost him/her less. Bono Airtel. <Bono Airtel.> The telephone company that dials differences. <The telephone company that dials differences.> If you (FRML) can imagine it, it can be done. <Airtel.> Why not? <Why not? Find out (FRML) information at....>

c. Entel, Chile
   [Images of technology, people on phones, throughout ad.]
   Announcer: El más avanzado servicio de larga distancia. <1,2,3> La telefonía local del futuro. Telefonía personal CPCP. <PCS> La magía global del internet. Miles de kilómetros de fibra óptica terrestre y submarina. ['1,2,3']. Conecciones satélitales simultáneas... equipos de técnicos muy profesionales forman la plataforma de telecomunicaciones <1,2,3> más avanzada del país. Es el sistema universal Entel. Que a sólo tres años del tercer milenio pone la tecnología del futuro a servicio de los hombres de hoy. Entel. <Address of web page.> Un mundo sin límites.

'The most advanced long distance service. <1,2,3> The local telephone company of the future. Personal telephone CPCP. <PCS> The global magic of the internet. Thousands of kilometers of ground and underwater fiber optics. <1,2,3> Simultaneous satellite connections... teams of very professional technicians form the most advanced platform of telecommunications in the country. <1,2,3> It is the universal system Entel. Which, at only three years from the third millennium, puts the technology of the future at the service of people of today. Entel. <Address of web page.> A world without limits.

Although conventional implicature is most frequent in American ads, conversational implicature is slightly more frequent in ads from Spain and Chile. This is not surprising for ads from Spain since they are very short in length and, therefore, necessarily include less information. Nevertheless, violations of quantity occur most often in Chilean commercials, and violations of relation are least frequent in the American data. Other violations are similar in their distribution among countries, suggesting that violations of the Cooperative Principle are applied in similar ways, regardless of the dialect of Spanish. Furthermore, their widespread occurrence demonstrates how conversational implicatures arising from violations of maxims are preferred strategies in Spanish advertising discourse.

The distribution of specific strategies that violate Grice's Maxims appear below in table 3.19.

Table 3.19 Strategies that violate Grice's Maxims

Maxim	U.S.	%	SP	%	CH	%
Quantity (n = 529)						
Repetition	124	35	101	29	128	36
Ellipsis	33	28	31	26	56	47
Lack of info.	12	14	47	53	29	33
More info. than necessary	2	20	8	80	0	0
Quality (n = 510)						
Metaphor	101	35	86	30	100	35
Hyperbole	78	32	73	30	91	38

3.4 Distributive patterns

Maxim	U.S.	%	SP	%	CH	%
False assertion	30	49	23	38	8	13
Irony	9	60	3	20	3	20
Tautology	4	44	0	0	5	56
Understatement	2	33	2	33	2	33
Relation (n=645)						
Relations	189	31	213	35	203	34
Nonrelevance	16	40	10	25	14	35
Manner (n=464)						
Vague	80	34	83	35	73	31
Obscure	34	35	28	29	34	35
Rhetorical questions	38	41	28	30	27	29
Ambiguous	23	35	19	29	24	36
Verbose	12	24	20	40	18	36
Redundant	4	40	0	0	6	60
Euphemism	3	50	3	50	0	0

Both repetition and ellipsis are common strategies, regardless of country; all three countries employ repetition more than any other violation of the Maxim of Quantity. Chile applies ellipsis more than any other country, whereas Spanish ads utilize more information than necessary or a lack of information. The latter strategies seemingly contradict each other; however, the overprovision of information only occurs in lengthy two-minute ads and the lack of information is found in shorter ads, usually ten seconds in length. The abundance of ads containing ellipsis in Chilean ads may reflect a more formulaic construction of ads by Chilean advertisers.

Metaphorical language is highly productive in Spanish television advertising. Hence, the preferred ways of violating quality are metaphor and hyperbole, regardless of dialect. Use of metaphor, hyperbole, and understatement are evenly distributed across the data, as previously shown in table 3.19. Literally false assertions and irony are used more often in the U.S. data, and tautology most commonly occurs in Chilean ads. Note, however, that no examples of tautology are found in the data from Spain and that literally false assertions are least frequent on Teletrece. The latter is perhaps due to more stringent restrictions on advertising messages on the Chilean station.

Nonrelevance as a violation of relation is more common in U.S. ads, followed by Chile, then Spain. Vagueness is the preferred strategy by all three countries for violating the Maxim of Manner; however, vagueness is least common in Chilean ads. Again, restrictions on advertising on Teletrece may require Chilean ads to be more explicit. Use of rhetorical questions is more frequent in U.S. ads than in Chile and Spain, whereas verbosity is least frequent in American ads. Furthermore, I found no instances of euphemism in Teletrece ads (CH) or of redundancy on Antena 3 (SP). The lack of tautology and redundancy from Spain may be partially due to the ads' short length (thus, lack of time for excessive verbiage).

With respect to novelty, the most common types, regardless of country, are syntactic and explicit novelty. Syntactic novelty is most frequent in ads from Spain, probably because of their short length compared to commercials from other countries. The examples in (58) are entire texts of just a few of the many ten-second ads in the data from Antena 3. Explicit novelty and new associations are also most common in ads from Spain. Spanish advertisers imply that their audience is desirous of change and tired of the status quo.

(58) Syntactic novelty—Spain
[Image of a woman in a bra.]
<*Gemma Essential.*> *La evolución de la ropa interior.*
Gemma Essential. <Gemma Essential.> The evolution of underwear. (Gemma Esencial, SP)

[Image of pounding metal in shape of a watch] <Irony> [Image of a watch.]
<*Colección primavera/verano 97*>
<97 Spring/Summer Collection>
Announcer: Swatch. <Website.> (Swatch, SP)

[Image of a laboratory.]
Announcer: *Nuevo Gameboy. Más pequeña. Más ligera. Y compatible con todos los juegos de Gameboy.*
New Gameboy. Smaller. Lighter. And compatible with all the games from Gameboy. (Gameboy, SP)

Likewise, ads containing sexual associations such as those in (59) are most common in ads on Antena 3 (SP). It seems that ads with shock value are expected to stimulate interest from the Spanish public, whereas sexual associations are far less common and less explicit in Chilean and American ads. There are also restrictions on nudity and sexual explicitness in U.S. and Chilean commercials. Situational novelty also occurs more often in ads from Spain, followed closely by those from Chile.

3.4 Distributive patterns

(59) Novel associations—sexual
   (Goldstar Air Conditioning, SP)
   [Image of naked woman, hand running ice cube along her body.]
   Announcer: *Hay muchas formas de disfrutar del frío, pero no todas tienen siete años de garantía. Aire Acondicionado LG. El único con siete años de garantía.* <*LG. La nueva cara de Goldstar.*>
   There are many ways of enjoying the cold, but not all have a seven-year guarantee. LG Air Conditioning. The only one with a seven-year guarantee. <LG. The new face of Goldstar.>

   (Impulse body spray, SP)
   [Image of male model posing nude for art class. A female student enters the class late. As she walks by the model, there is an image of her spraying body spray on herself. The man's eyes look uneasy. He looks at his private parts. The female students start laughing at him. The students begin to clap in applause.]
   Announcer (Female): *Un impulso incontrolante.* <*Un impulso incontrolante.*> *Impulse. Desodorante Body Spray.*
   An uncontrollable impulse. <An uncontrollable impulse.> Impulse. Deodorant Body Spray.

   (Axe by Fabergé, SP)
   [Image of a woman at home, rushing to get ready. She grabs a body spray.]
   Vocalist: *Ready baby. The world's gonna find out today....*
   [Woman runs out of house. Various women on the street, on the bus wink and look interested in her. Woman smells her cardigan. Woman returns home and slams the man's spray on table. He smiles.]
   Announcer: *Axe para hombre.* [Image of the product.] <*Fabergé. París.*>
   Axe for men.

(Revalid vitamins, SP)
<Revalid.> [Image of product].
Announcer: *Revalid. Vitaminas para tu cabello.* [Image of topless woman]. *Vitaminas para tus uñas. <Aminoácidos. Hierro. Cobre. Zinc. Vitaminas B1, B2. Oligoelementos.>*
Revalid. Vitamins for your hair. Vitamins for your nails. <Amino acids. Iron. Copper. Zinc. Vitamins B1, B2. Oligoelements.>

Situational novelty is also frequently used in ads from Spain to shock or surprise the viewer, as in (60). It is particularly unlikely that the violent ad in (60) for Pepsi would be appealing in the U.S. or Chile. This ad and others suggest that shock appeals are a pragmatic strategy for ads from Spain. Pragmatic novelty, on the other hand, rarely occurs in Chilean and Spanish ads and is probably a strategy borrowed from English advertising in the U.S. and applied to Spanish commercials. Semantic novelty is also less common in commercials on Antena 3 (SP) than other stations. Its infrequency may reflect the fact that ads from Spain are less formulaic than their counterparts in the study.

(60) Situational novelty
(Visionlab, SP)
[Image of a man running, being chased.]
<Small print: *Les hemos ofrecido este programa.*> <We have offered this program.>
Man 1: [With sunglasses on, chasing someone.]
   ¡Alto! ¡Policía!
   Halt! Police!
      [Image of another man fleeing on a motorcycle.]
      ¡Confiscada!
      Confiscated!
Announcer: *¿Gafas de sol...graduadas?*
   Sun glasses... that are graduated?
[Image of Man 1 on **toy** motorcycle that he "confiscated"] [Image of sunglasses.] *Ocho modelos por nueve mil novecientas.* <*Montura más cristales 9.900.*> *Sólo en Visionlab.* <*Visionlab. Los grandes centros de la visión.*>
Eight models for nine thousand, nine hundred. <Mounting plus lenses, 9,900.> Only at Visionlab. <Visionlab. The great vision centers.>

3.4 Distributive patterns

(Pepsi, SP)
[Image of young man watching a scene, holding a Pepsi.]
Young man: *Los que han probado la nueva Pepsi quieren ver la versión salvaje del spot.*
Those that have tried the new Pepsi want to see the savage version of the spot.
[Image of U.S. flag]
[Image of garbage truck in residential neighborhood]
Older Woman: *¡Buenos días, chicos!*
Good morning, boys!
[Sound of "America the Beautiful" playing in the background]
Garbage Collectors: *Hola, Señora Guzman. ¿Cómo estás?*
Hello, Mrs. Guzman. How are you?
Older Woman: *Hoy, muy bien. Gracias.*
Very well today. Thank you.
[Men drive on to next house. They see a woman in front of her house.]
Woman: *Buenos días, chicos.*
Good morning, boys.
Garbage Collector 1: *¡Nada de Buenos Días, chicos!*
None of that "good morning, boys!"
Garbage Collector 2 [Pointing gun at her]:
…latas y los desechos desorgánicos. ¡Es protesta para tanto y todo el programa federal de separación y reciclaje de basura.! ¡Aparte!
…cans and unorganic garbage. This is in protest against so much [garbage] and the whole federal program of separating and recycling garbage. Move away!

[Image of them with automatic weapons shooting holes in her house. They blow it up]. [Men get back in truck] [Woman is left crying outside].
Announcer: *Recuerda, puedes seguir votando.* <Website.> *Nuevo sabor de Pepsi. El cambiazo.* <*El cambiazo. Nuevo sabor de Pepsi. Pepsi.*> <*GeneratioNext.*>
Remember, you can keep voting. New flavor of Pepsi. The huge change. <The huge change. New Pepsi flavor. Pepsi. GeneratioNext.>

(Halcón Viajes, SP)
[Image of a black cat.]
Fortune teller: *[Answering the phone.] Consultorio de Juliet Margot. Adivino todo lo que quieras saber.*
Juliet Margot's office. I divine everything that you want to know.
Voice: [at other end of phone line.] *Quiero saber dónde está Curro.*
I want to know where Curro is.
[Fortune Teller slams the phone down, angrily.]
Announcer: *¿En Santo Domingo? ¿Cuba? ¿Cancún? <El Caribe. Cancún. Cartagena, Santo Domingo. Isla Margarita. Cuba. Jamaica. Bahamas. Panamá.> Donde sea pero con Halcón Viajes. <Halcón Viajes.> <Air Europa. Telephone number.>*
In Santo Domingo? Cuba? Cancún? <The Caribbean. Cancún. Cartagena de indias, Colombia. Santo Domingo. Margarita Island. Cuba. Jamaica. Bahamas. Panama.> Wherever it may be, but with Halcón Trips. <Halcón Trips.>
Snorkeller: [Popping his head up from under water, laughing.] *¡Ja!*
Ha!

Among the minor pragmatic strategies in the data, devices for flattery, endorsements, and information structure occur most often in American ads, followed by those of Chile. The examples in (61), for example, illustrate the different approaches to ads for L'Oreal hair color. The ad from Univisión (U.S.) flatters the audience by implication, whereas the same speaker in the ad from Spain emphasizes choice and status. This emphasis commonly occurs in ads from Spain, suggesting that ad writers view their audience as being sophisticated and influenced by snob appeals.

(61) Flattery
(L'Oreal, U.S.)
Woman (Nastassia Kinski):
¿ Te imaginas proteger tu pelo a la vez que lo tiñes? <Nastassia Kinski.> <L'Oreal Paris.> *Ahora lo puedes con Excellence y Media de L'Oreal. Una crema rica que protege tu cabello.* <Protege.> *No gotea* <No gotea.> *Y cubre perfectamente las canas.* <Cubre

3.4 Distributive patterns

perfectamente las canas. > Lo que más me gusta es el color. <Cuida.> Y siento mi pelo más sano y cuidado. Can you imagine protecting your hair at the same time that you color it? Now you can with Excellence and Media from L'Oreal. A rich cream that protects your (INFRML) hair. <Protects.> It doesn't drip. <Doesn't drip.> And it perfectly covers gray hair. <Perfectly covers gray hair.> What I like most is the color. <Cares for [your hair].> And I feel my hair being more healthy and cared for.

Announcer: *Excellence y Media.* <Excellence and Media.> <L'Oreal.> *La crema colorante de acción protectora.* <*Crema colorante de acción protectora.*> Excellence and Media. The protective action coloring cream.

Woman: *De L'Oreal* <L'Oreal.> *Porque yo lo valgo.* From L'Oreal. Because I'm worth it.

(L'Oreal, SP)

Woman (Nastassia Kinski):

Cuando me tiño el cabello, sólo uso la crema de la crema. Excellence Creme de L'Oreal. Excellence es una crema especial porque sus ricas humectantes... tan rica que protege como ninguna otra. Tan cremosa que no gotea. <*No gotea. Cubre las canas.*> *Excellence realmente cubre las canas con un color bello y saludable. ¿No es de lo que se trata? Excellence Color de L'Oreal. Es el color para el cabello. Es la crema de la crema. Piénsalo.*

When I color my hair, I only use the crème de la crème. Excellence Creme from L'Oreal. Excellence is a special cream because its rich humectants...so rich that it protects like no other. So creamy that it doesn't drip. <It doesn't drip. It covers gray hairs.> Excellence really covers the gray hairs with a beautiful and healthy color. Isn't that what it's all about? Excellence Color from L'Oreal. It's the color for hair. It is the creme of the creme. Think (INFRML) about it.

Humor is fairly evenly dispersed among the three countries, as are lexical items. Examples of lexical borrowing differ between countries, although most instances of borrowing are from English and occur in all three countries. Chilean ads also exhibit some instances of borrowing from Italian, and ads from Spain contain items from French and German. Phonological elements such as jingles, alliteration, and foreign pronunciation are most commonly noted in Chilean ads, possibly due to the formulaic style of Chilean ads. Only ads on Univisión contain examples of the echoing announcer style commonly found on Spanish radio in the U.S. and Mexico. Finally, elements of nationalism are only found in Chilean ads, such as those in (62). These examples suggest an intense rivalry between Chile and its neighbors, particularly in sports. Apparently, advertisers in Spain and U.S. do not think that nationalism is a selling point for their respective viewers.

(62) Nationalism—Chile
(Rol Top, CH)
Man: Los mejores alfajores en el mundo son los alfajores argentinos. Y claro, el chocolate auténtico usa leche. Argentino. El chocolate argentino. El bizcocho argentino. Debes de probar todos. Y éste. Este es mejor. Es bárbaro. Es Rol Top. Es nuevo. [Looks at wrapper.] ¡Es chileno! The best pastries in the world are Argentinian pastries. And of course, milk is in authentic chocolate. Argentinian. Argentinian chocolate. The Argentinian cookie. You should try them all. And this one. This one is the best. It's awfully good. It's Rol Top. It's new. It's Chilean!'
Announcer: Rol Top. El mejor alfajor es chileno. Y es de Dos en Uno. Rol Top. The best pastry is Chilean. And it is from Dos en Uno.
Man: Déjame llorar. Déjame.
Leave me alone to cry. Leave me alone.

(Entel, CH)
[Image of a man at the top of a tower yelling. Voice of crowd echoes back.]
Man: CHI-LE. <1,2,3>
CHI-LE
Crowd: Chi, chi, chi, le,le,le. ¡Viva Chile!
Chi, chi, chi, le, le, le. Long live Chile!
Announcer: Ahora Entel se lleva a los fanáticos del 1-2-3 [uno-dos-tres] a Francia '98 [noventa y ocho].
Now Entel is taking the fans of 1-2-3 to France '98.

3.4 Distributive patterns

[Image of a man cheering].
> *Entel. Un mundo sin límites.*
> Entel. A world without limits.

(Nike, CH)
Man: *El mundo no mira ese. Chile tiene las montañas más hermosas. Chile tiene los mejores vinos. Chile tiene las playas más lindas. Chile tiene los mares como Marruecos. Chile tiene esto. Chile tiene de otro. Pero pregúntate esto. Y piénsalo bien. Porque todas estas cosas valen mucho....Absolutamente a todo lo que tenemos. A cambio de escuchar Chile tiene el mejor fútbol del mundo.* <*Just Do It.*> [Image of Nike swoosh]
The world doesn't see that. Chile has the most beautiful mountains. Chile has the best wines. Chile has the prettiest beaches. Chile has seas like Marroco. Chile has this. Chile has that. But ask yourself this. And think about it well. Because all these things are worth a lot.... Absolutely everything that we have. Contrary to what you hear, Chile has the best football [soccer] in the world.

3.4.4 Summary

Overall, there are more similarities in distribution of pragmatic strategies by country than there are differences. These similarities suggest that the major categories in question are common across dialects and are reflective of Spanish advertising discourse in general. Nevertheless, at a more detailed level, some individual pragmatic strategies pattern differently according to region. The order of preference for speech act strategies differs with respect to expressives and commissives. Furthermore, Univisión (U.S.) ads reveal more of each speech act category as well as a greater variety of individual speech acts than their counterparts, perhaps due to the greater complexity in terms of participants in ads from the U.S. Chilean ads tend to include fewer characters than the U.S. and Spanish ads and contain a smaller repertoire of pragmatic strategies. Although a greater repertoire of strategies does not necessarily mean that an ad is more persuasive, it is likely to hold the audience's attention and interest for a longer period of time. Thus, the greater complexity of Spanish and U.S. ads at least contributes to the attention component of persuasion. Univisión ads also reflect more use of present tense and of speaker considerations. The latter suggests that advertisers are more prone to stereotype U.S. viewers. The relative lack of speaker considerations in Spain may reveal attempts to appeal to a wide audience. Preference for solidarity and positive face is most common in the U.S., followed by Spain and then Chile. The most negative politeness strategies are found in ads on Teletrece (CH), suggesting that in comparison to Spanish and U.S. advertisers, Chilean copywriters do not believe that their audiences wish for speakers in ads to address them in a friendly, informal way. Furthermore, the amount of distancing devices in Chilean ads may reflect a society that is stratified and highly conscious of degrees of status.

With regard to implicature, conversational implicature is slightly more frequent in ads from Spain and Chile, and conventional implicature occurs most often in American ads. Violations of quantity are most common on Teletrece; ads from Chile appear to be more formulaic in their construction and Chilean copywriters perhaps perceive their audience as being more tolerant of predictable ads. The advertising market in Chile is perhaps also less competitive than in the U.S. and Spain. Spain exhibits more ads containing syntactic novelty, explicit novelty, new associations, and situational novelty than the other countries. This fact suggests that Spanish advertisers believe that their viewers require unusual tactics to stimulate their interest in products and services. Shock appeals are probably necessary in Spain because of stiff advertising competition among products from different parts of the world.

3.5 Summary of analysis and results

Returning to the research questions posed at the beginning of the study, the data suggest the following answers with regard to pragmatics in Spanish television advertising.

1. Which pragmatic devices occur most frequently in Spanish television advertising? The major pragmatic factors in the data are speech acts, novelty, indexicals, politeness, implicature, violation of maxims, speaker considerations, and lexicon. These strategies are, therefore, most reflective of Spanish television advertising. Of the major devices, representatives and directives are the most common types of speech acts. The most frequent types of novelty are syntactic and explicit novelty. Deictic items and personal reference are the most frequent indexicals, and positive face and solidarity are the most common politeness strategies. Both types of implicature and each violation of Grice's Maxims occur in the majority of ads. Minor variables include flattery, humor, endorsements, information structure, and phonological elements. Thus, to write a pragmatic formula for Spanish advertising discourse, all of the major strategies would be included and are important when describing and analyzing persuasive discourse.

3.5 Summary of analysis and results

2. How are these pragmatic devices linguistically encoded in the data? The results suggest that the most common class of speech acts in the data, representatives, are typically encoded as assertions of real or supposed fact. The frequency of assertions reveals the attempt by advertisers to appear to be informative and to present opinions as though they are facts. Directives are generally realized as orders, but are really strong suggestions since examples in the data are infelicitous as orders and advertisers do not have the inherent authority to command viewers to do anything. Commissives and expressives are less uniform in their realization. Commissives, particularly those that are specific, are uncommon because they require action from the advertiser. Finally, some speech acts are deliberately formed to be vague or ambiguous in order to allow for more than one interpretation.

Spatial and temporal deixis most often refer to notions of "here and now" in an attempt to draw the audience into the advertiser's point of view. Consequently, past reference is infrequent, generally carrying negative connotations. Advertisers wish to encourage viewers to rush out and buy their products. Second person singular is by far the most common form of personal reference, suggesting the importance of viewers as individuals. Furthermore, positive face conveying concepts of solidarity and proximity is the most frequent form of politeness since advertisers wish to identify with the desires and needs of the public. Negative-face strategies involving distance and power are also common, particularly in the speech of male announcers. Thus, announcers' speech is able to achieve authority over the audience. Written messages and announcers' speech suggest that if a message is formal, the preference is to avoid explicit formality by avoiding any personal reference whatsoever. The reason is that advertisers do not wish to draw attention to their use of announcers.

Conventional implicature is achieved through presupposition and embedded assertions and through implicatures derived from the semantics of lexical items. Such implicatures generally are used by advertisers to presume that they know the individual consumer and that the audience agrees with the viewpoint presented. Conversational implicature, on the other hand, is more difficult to categorize and more often consists of hints or inferences as a result of violations of Grice's Maxims. Repetition, metaphor, implied relations, and vagueness are the most common types, respectively, of violations of quantity, quality, relation, and manner. Implicatures arising from violations of these four maxims suggest, among other things:

- importance and a stronger claim or association than can be literally stated without being literally "untruthful", and
- avoidance when ads have little real information to present.

Furthermore, implicatures are also used to avoid responsiblity for an ad's literal message, to make minor associations constitute inherent similarity between a product and selected notion, and to convey a product's positive characteristics via vague language.

3. Are any pragmatic differences evident between dialects of Spanish? There are generally more similarities in distribution of pragmatic strategies by country than there are differences, suggesting that the major categories in question are common across dialects and Spanish regions. Nevertheless, at a more detailed level, some differences become apparent. The order of preference for speech act strategies varies with respect to expressives and commissives, perhaps suggesting that U.S. advertisers emphasize their viewers' individuality. Univisión ads reveal a greater variety of speech acts and indexicals than their counterparts, perhaps due to the greater complexity in terms of participants in ads from the U.S. Chilean ads tend to include fewer characters than the U.S. and Spain. Univisión (U.S.) ads also reflect more varieties of tense and more speaker considerations. The greater variety of pragmatic strategies may contribute to the persuasiveness of ads. Ads from Spain and the U.S. tend to be less alike and more complex, which may help hold the audience's interest. Preference for solidarity and positive face is most common in the U.S., followed by Spain and then Chile. The most negative politeness strategies were found in ads on Teletrece (CH), suggesting that advertisers there see Chilean society as being more stratified and less egalitarian than advertisers in Spain and the U.S.

Conversational implicature is slightly more frequent in ads from Spain and Chile, and conventional implicature occurs most often in American ads. Violations of quantity are most common on Teletrece (CH), and violations of relation are least frequent on Univisión (U.S.). As previously stated, Chilean ads seem to follow a similar format and this may partially account for the high frequency of quantity violations. It is also likely that Chilean advertisers believe that their audiences are more tolerant of repetition and ellipsis. Furthermore, Chilean ads contain fewer female announcers than their counterparts, suggesting that women are less likely to represent power or authority in Chile than in the U.S. or Spain. Syntactic novelty, explicit novelty, new associations, and situational novelty are more frequent in ads from Spain than in the other countries. The high frequency of novelty in Spanish ads contributes to the shock appeal that advertisers there seem to believe is necessary to attract viewers' interest. Finally, U.S. ads contain more of the minor pragmatic strategies than Spain or Chile, particularly strategies that emphasize and flatter the viewer as an individual. Advertisers in Spain may view strategies such as flattery, endorsements, and tautologies as being superficial and unappealing to a public that they perhaps imagine to be cynical.

3.5 Summary of analysis and results

Thus, the results of research questions (1-3) reveal major pragmatic strategies across regions, as well as patterns in the linguistic realization of these strategies. Furthermore, dialectal patterns of individual pragmatic strategies and their distribution become evident when ads are compared with one another according to country. I address the fourth research question concerning the role of pragmatics in persuasion in chapter 4, as the main point of this study.

4
Pragmatics and Persuasion

4.1 Introduction

As discussed in chapter 1, the general framework or theoretical model for this study comprises three areas of linguistics:

- the macro-context of persuasive discourse in advertisements,
- the pragmatic strategies within this context, and
- the linguistic realization of these pragmatic strategies in the form of syntax, phonology, and lexicon.

Pragmalinguistics in this study (information structure, phonological highlighting, and lexical selection) consists of linguistic categories that are linked with pragmatic strategies in order to achieve the goal of persuasion. The theoretical model for the study is depicted in (63). The macrocontext consists of Spanish television advertising in three different countries. Pragmatic strategies such as politeness, speech acts, and implicatures are selected for the macrocontext of advertising, in which the overall intent is to persuade the viewing audience to buy. Furthermore, the type of effect desired determines the type of strategy selected. Advertisements are created for particular effects, such as solidarity, indirectness, and emotional appeal. Finally, the pragmatic strategies important to this study are ultimately achieved via linguistic forms. That is, they are spoken (or written) and have syntactic, phonological, and lexical representations.

(63) Theoretical model for the study

Macro context
Television advertising in Spain, Chile, the United States
↓

Pragmatic strategies
Politeness/indexicals	Speech acts	Implicatures
(degree of distance	(direct/indirect)	(conventional/
solidarity/power)		conversational)
↓

Linguistic realization
| Syntax | Phonology | Lexicon |

Research questions (1–3) address the relationship depicted in (63) and describe the nature of Spanish television advertising. I now turn to the fourth research question, *How are pragmalinguistic features of television advertising used to effect persuasion?* The parameters of persuasive discourse (advertising discourse) include being nonreciprocal, unilateral, scripted, fragmented, and containing a formal/informal mix and a natural/unnatural mix of style. Its intent is to be remembered and to have an appropriately forceful message (Lakoff 1990). Persuasion in advertising is aimed at convincing the audience to purchase a particular product or service. Even in the case of ads that attempt to create a particular image of a company, rather than selling an individual product, the ultimate purpose is to create goodwill toward the company so that viewers will be loyal and either continue to buy or change their product preference. The principal components of persuasion found in this study are MEMORABILITY, FORCE, and PARTICIPATION. Clearly, other elements of persuasion exist; however, these are key goals of persuasion and are those found most often in the data.

In this chapter I discuss the role of pragmatics in persuasion. Conclusions from results of the research questions in the study and support of previous literature, as well as applications, limitations, and further research are also addressed.

4.2 How pragmatic strategies effect persuasion in the data

4.2.1 Goals of persuasion

The goals of persuasion selected for this study are supported by previous literature, including Rank (1988) and Leech (1966). Following

4.2 How pragmatic strategies effect persuasion in the data

Cicero's classical oration and Aristotle's ethos, Rank (1988:10) suggested a basic persuasive formula for advertisements, political speech, and other types of persuasive discourse. His five components were (a) attention-getting, (b) confidence-building, (c) desire-stimulating, (d) urgency-stressing, and (e) response-seeking. Leech (1966:27) similarly argued that to be successful, a typical ad must accomplish four things in sequence, as shown in (64).

(64) Leech's components for persuasive ads
1. It must draw attention to itself. (Attention value)
2. It must sustain the interest it has attracted. (Readability/listenability)
3. It must be remembered, or at any rate recognized as familiar. (Memorability)
4. It must prompt the right kind of action. (Selling power)

Both Rank and Leech's components roughly correspond to the persuasive goals noted and analyzed in the present study, i.e., Memorability (M), Force (F), and Participation (P). Memorability includes attention-getting, but goes beyond this simple goal to that of making viewers remember the message. That is, attention-getting is a means of making sure that the ad is noticed and ultimately remembered or recognized. Memorability generally corresponds to Rank's attention-getting and a combination of Leech's attention value and memorability.

Force refers to emotional and logical appeals to viewers and the degree of impact or strength of a particular message. It includes the intensity and power that a message has in appealing to an audience. The degree of force is generally relative to the nature of the product/service advertised. Force corresponds to a combination of Rank's confidence-building, desire-stimulating, and urgency-stressing and corresponds to Leech's readability/listenability.

Participation refers to the desire for a response or viewer involvement in the message and, ultimately, to the purchasing of the advertised product or service. Participation is comparable to Rank's response-seeking and Leech's selling power. Given the key components of persuasion addressed in the study, I turn to the specific results. The goals of persuasion are presented in the context of advertising and are not necessarily reflective of other discourse contexts.

4.2.2 Results: speech acts

Research question (4) asks, *How are pragmalinguistic features of television advertising used to effect persuasion?* The contribution to persuasion for each speech act is based on a compilation of the analysis of individual examples in every ad in the database. Thus, after reviewing all ads containing a given speech act, patterns emerged regarding how the speech act (and other pragmatic strategies in the data) contributed to persuasion. I find that most speech acts contribute to the force component of persuasion, and that only certain types of speech acts attempt viewer participation. I summarize the contribution of each class of speech acts in (65). Declarations are not listed because they contain repeated information shown in other classes of speech acts. Items in parentheses indicate persuasive goals that are optional and that occur only in certain types within the class. I determined that a combination of Leech (1966) and Rank's (1988) components of persuasion occur in all of the ads. Consequently, the persuasive components of Memorability, Force, and Participation were selected as representative goals of persuasion in Spanish television advertising.

(65) Speech acts and their contribution to persuasion

    Representatives
      Assertions - F
      Announcements - M
      Reports - (M), F

    Directives
      Orders - F, P
      Requests - F, P
      Warnings - F, P
      Suggestions - F, (P)
      Recommendations - F, (P)
      Invitations - P
      Instructions - (M), P
      Attention-getters - M

    Commissives
      Offers - M, F, (P)
      Apologies - (M), P
      Promises - F
      Guarantees - F
      Disclaimers - F

4.2 How pragmatic strategies effect persuasion in the data

Expressives
Compliments/flattery/praise - (M), F, P
Introductions - M, (P)
Greetings - M, (P)
Leave-taking - M, (P)
Thanks - F, (P)
Congratulations - F, (P)
Insults - F

Key: M = Memorability, F = Force, P = Participation

The primary contribution of representatives to persuasion is that of Force. Assertions in the data are frequent because their intent is to influence viewers by declaring information to be true, thereby building confidence in the product. Claims made via assertions are stronger than those made, for example, in suggestions or questions because assertions insist on the validity of the propositions they contain. Thus, the notion of Force as a component of persuasion is partly reflected by the illocutionary force of speech acts. Assertions such as those in (66) contribute only to Force and do not directly contribute to Memorability or Participation, whereas the announcements in (67) clearly contribute to the goal of attention and memory because they attract notice or are meant to be remembered. If the examples in (66) contribute to Memorability or Participation it is due to lexical items or syntactic novelty, rather than the nature of assertions themselves. Instead, the assertions in (66) enhance the Force component of persuasion by providing definitive statements to impress the audience regarding a product's reliablity and superiority.

(66) Assertions: Force

Para la mayoría de los malestares estomacales, el remedio es el mismo.
For the majority of stomach problems, the remedy is the same. (Pepto Bismol, U.S.)

Priority Mail. La decisión más fácil para su negocio.
Priority Mail. The easiest decision for your business. (Priority mail, U.S.)

Y cubre perfectamente las canas.
And it perfectly covers gray hairs. (L'Oreal, SP)

Head & Shoulders. El fin de la caspa y el principio de un cabello hermoso.
Head & Shoulders. The end of dandruff and the beginning of beautiful hair. (Head & Shoulders, CH)

(67) Announcements: Memorability

¡Y por primera vez en Austin viene Alberto Benitta!
And for the first time in Austin, Alberto Benitta is coming! (Club Carnaval, U.S.)

¡Ganamos! ¡Ganamos!
We won! We won! (Lotto Texas, U.S.)

El programa de extensión de la Escuela de Arte de la Pontificia Universidad Católica de Chile abre una nueva temporada de cursos. Pintura, historia, grabado, cerámica, fotografía y escultura, dibujo y computación gráfica.
The extension program of the art school of the Pontifical Catholic University of Chile is opening a new season of courses. Painting, history, engraving, ceramics, photography and sculpture, drawing, and computer graphics. (Universidad Católica, CH)

Some assertions reflect other persuasive goals than Force. Nevertheless, the goals of Memorability or Participation are not due to the nature of the speech act, but rather, due to other pragmatic strategies embedded within the assertion. For example, the sentence in (68a) expresses Force because of its assertive nature, but also Memorability because of the lexical item *chispa* 'sparkle' and its novel association with cereal. Similarly, (68b) contains an assertion that contributes to the persuasive goal of Memorability, not because it is an assertion but because it is a short slogan and the purpose of slogans is to be remembered. It also contains an absolute contrast between the unimportant image of other soft drinks and the thirst the viewer supposedly feels for Sprite. Sentence (68c) may contribute to Memorability because it is a slogan. The utterance also contributes to Participation because of the possessive pronoun *tú* 'you (INFRML)'. It attempts to draw the viewer into the message by presuming that the audience likes and owns the product in question and because of the wordplay on sweetness. Finally, (68d) contributes to Participation via ellipsis, a violation of the Maxim of Quantity. Viewers are forced into the position of interpreting the implicature that the product is more effective than it was before, yet this forced participation is not due to the nature of the speech act of asserting. Thus, all of the rest of the examples in this section contribute to Force because of their assertive illocutionary force. Contribution to other persuasive goals (Memorability and Participation) is not inherent to the nature of assertions and is dependent on pragmatic factors that are embedded within the assertions and are outside the

4.2 How pragmatic strategies effect persuasion in the data

arena of speech acts. By nature, assertions in ads mainly attempt to build confidence in a product (part of the Force component of persuasion).

(68) Assertions: other persuasive goals

    a. *Apple Jacks de Kellogg's. El cereal con* **chispa.**
       Kellogg's Apple Jacks. The cereal with **sparkle.** (Apple Jacks, U.S.)

    b. *La imagen es nada. La sed es todo.*
       Image is nothing. Thirst is everything. (Sprite, CH)

    c. *Nueva Arcor Golosinas.* **Tu** *dulce compañía.*
       New Arcor Delicasies. **Your** sweet company. (Arcor candy, CH)

    d. *Ahora hay un nuevo desodorante aún* **más eficaz.**
       Now there is a new, even **more effective** deodorant. (Sanex, SP)

In a similar way, announcements may contain lexical elements that connote audience participation in a particular context, even though the speech act's primary persuasive goal is Memorability. For instance, the announcements in (69) contain the lexical items *ya* 'now' and *oportunidades* 'opportunities', which both connote Participation. That is, viewers are expected to do something about the message—to purchase products or to seize the opportunity of enrolling in a raffle. Use of *ya* 'now' in the Opel ad helps viewers work out the implicature that the viewer has been waiting for the new model to arrive. Therefore, Participation is a persuasive goal of only certain types of announcements, due to contextualized connotations included as information within the announcement. Participation is not due to the inherent nature of announcements in advertising because announcements inherently contribute to Memorability.

(69) Announcements: other persuasive goals

    Ya están aquí.
    They are now here. (Opel Astar, SP)

    Eres ya está a la venta.
    Eres is now on sale. (*Eres* magazine, U.S.)

    Anna and the Freebies. Ya en tu tienda de discos.
    Anna and the Freebies. Now in your record store. (Pilosa CD, U.S.)

Y hay tres oportunidades para ganar...de cualquier premio!
And there are three opportunities to win...from any prize!
(Harina Selecta, CH)

Recall from chapter 3 that reports present information about present or past events or studies. Their primary persuasive goal in the data is to inform viewers, but to do so in the form of a factual presentation. Thus, reports contribute to the persuasive goals of Force because they suggest that the message is factual and reliable, and to Memorability because they present important information that is intended to be remembered. Consider, for example, the reports in (70) and the factual, newsworthy effect that they attempt. Reports in Spanish ads serve to build the viewer's confidence in a product.

(70) Reports: Force, Memorability

Financiado por la comunidad europea.
Financed by the European community. (Mosto, SP)

Los doctores recomiendan Advil para el dolor de espalda.
Doctors recommend Advil for back pain. (Advil, U.S.)

Claro, ocho de cada diez de aquí a Córdoba recomiendan usar tampones.
Of course, eight out of ten from here to Cordoba recommend using tampons. (Tampax, SP)

Me dijo, "Virgo, sacúdete y anda que tu trabajo está allí mismo. ¡Y el día siguiente, ya encontré trabajo!"
He told me, "Virgo, get up and get going because your work is right there. And the following day, I had already found work!" (Walter, U.S.)

The principal goal of persuasion for the class of directives in ads is both Force and Participation. Directives may reflect varying degrees of illocutionary force and their purpose is to get the hearer to do a desired act. As previously noted, orders are the most frequent directives in the ads. As the type of directives with the strongest impact on the hearer, orders contribute to Force. They also contribute to Participation because they attempt to evoke obedience from the audience. Orders demonstrating Force and Participation appear in (71a–b). Furthermore, orders containing the phrases *no te olvides/no se olvide* 'don't forget' and *recuerda/recuerde* 'remember' are also tied to the goal of Memorability, as in (71b). Hence, the examples

4.2 How pragmatic strategies effect persuasion in the data 141

in (71b) contribute to Memorability because of particular lexical items, rather than the inherent forceful and interactional nature of all orders.

(71) Orders: Force, Participation

    a. *Llame ahora sin compromiso a los números que aparecen en pantalla.*
Call now without obligation the numbers that appear on the screen. (Inglés Sin Barreras, U.S.)

       Ven por el tesoro Copec.
Come for the Copec treasure. (Copec, CH)

       Compre como siempre. Disfrute como nunca.
Buy, as always. Enjoy like never before. (Travel Club, SP)

       Sé práctica. Usa Linic Plus.
Be practical. Use Linic Plus. (Linic Plus shampoo, CH)

    b. *No te olvides. Es Kanibal.*
Don't forget. It's Kanibal. (Kanibal, SP)

       Recuerda, disponible en tres colores. Azul, hueso y estampado de cuadros.
Remember, available in three colors. Blue, bone, and plaid. (El Back Relax, SP)

Though not as forceful as orders, requests not directed to the viewer are also linked with the persuasive components of Force and Participation because they are a direct means of getting the audience to act. Likewise, the one warning to the audience contributes to Force and intended Participation because it dramatically alerts viewers (who are young boys) toward the supposed frightening aspects of the product and attempts to provoke them to buy the action figures.

(72) Requests and warnings: Force, Participation

    Request: *Yo quiero más ketchup Watt's.*
I want more Watt's ketchup. (Watt's, CH)

    Warning: *¡Advertencia! Crece hasta seis veces su tamaño. Jurassic Park de Bresler.*
Warning! It grows to six times its size. Jurassic Park from Bresler. (Bresler, CH)

Other types of directives, such as recommendations and suggestions also communicate Force and Participation, but Participation is optional. Viewers are given more of a choice as to whether or not to buy than they are with orders and requests.

(73) Suggestions and recommendations: Force, (Participation)

> Recommendations
> *Necesitan los nuevos Zucosos de Nestle.*
> You (PL) need the new Zucosos [sugary flakes cereal] by Nestle. (Nestle, CH)
>
> *Y yo se lo recomiendo.*
> And I recommend it to you. (Aceite Rosa Mosqueta, U.S.)
>
> Suggestions
> *¿Por qué no confiar en la marca que cada uno de dos hogares en el país prefiere?*
> Why not trust the brand that every one in two households in the country prefers? (Sears, U.S.)
>
> *Ya lo puedes conseguir en compacto o cassette.*
> Now you can get it on compact or cassette. (Industria del Amor, U.S.)
>
> *Es hora de darle fuerza con los nuevos champús Johnson's pH 5.5 [cinco punto cinco].*
> It's time to strengthen it with the new Johnson's pH 5.5 shampoos. (Johnson's shampoo, SP)

Of the remaining directives, invitations increase Participation because, by nature, they suggest a response.

(74) Invitations: Participation

> *Amigos y amigas, les invito a mi concierto a través de la revista TV y Novelas.*
> Friends (MASC, FEM), I invite you (PL) to my concert by way of the magazine, TV, and Soap Operas. (TV y Novelas, CH)

Instructions also require active or passive participation with the message from the audience. It is also possible that instructions have a secondary goal of attempting to help the audience remember. In contrast, the sole purpose of

4.2 How pragmatic strategies effect persuasion in the data 143

attention-getters is to attract the viewer's notice in hopes that something about the ad (an offer, sale, or free gift) will be remembered.

(75) Other directives

> Instructions: (Memorability), Participation
> *La aplicas templada. La retiras sin esperar y el resultado dura semanas.*
> You apply it (while) warm. You remove it without waiting and the result lasts for weeks. (Cera Tibia Veet, SP)
>
> Attention-getters: Memorability
> *¡Atención! ¡Oferta especial!*
> Attention! Special offer! (Viva Inglés, U.S.)

Thus, there are two primary contributions to persuasion by directives: Force and Participation. I now turn to the class of speech acts known as commissives.

Offers are the most common type of commissives in Spanish ads and generally contribute to persuasion in their strength of appeal or Force. They also attract attention and are used in the data as a means of making the audience remember what they can get as a free gift. Participation, however, is optional, depending on whether or not the offer is appealing to the viewing audience (see 76a). Nevertheless, some types of offers evoke mandatory participation from viewers by proposing conditional offers of the form, "If you do X then we will give you Y." The latter are shown in (76b).

(76) Offers: Memory, Force, (Participation)

> a. Optional Participation
> *Ahora Danone te ofrece el sabor natural de las naranjas frescas.*
> Now Danone offers you the natural flavor of fresh oranges. (Minute Maid, SP)
>
> *A quiénes toman la vida con interés, les ofrecemos una buena inversión.*
> To those who take life with interest, we offer a good investment. (Bonos ICO, SP)
>
> b. Mandatory Participation
> *Cambia a AT&T y recibe dos entradas a un juego de MLX.*
> Change to AT&T and receive two tickets to a game of MLX. (AT&T, U.S.)

> *Y si te cambias a Sprint ya, recibirás cien minutos gratis.*
> And if you change to Sprint now, you will receive one hundred minutes free. (Sprint, U.S.)
>
> *Ahora con un curso de ciudadanía gratis.*
> Now with a free citizenship course. (Inglés sin barreras, U.S.)

The one apology in the data that is addressed to viewers contributes to persuasion by attempting to evoke a response from viewers (Participation) and possibly by attracting attention because it is an unexpected statement (Memorability).

(77) Apology: (Memorability), Participation

> Toilet: [to audience after making a burping noise] *¡Perdón!*
> Pardon! (Clorox, CH)

Promises, guarantees, and disclaimers are other types of commissives; however, they only contribute to the persuasive goal of Force in Spanish ads. That is, promises and guarantees are the means of making products or services appealing to the audience; they help make an item sound like a great deal and thus build viewers' confidence in the product or service. In contrast, disclaimers provide a way for advertisers to protect themselves from complaints and suggest honesty and forthrightness, thereby contributing to Force.

(78) Other types of commissives

   a. Promises: Force
   > *Y McDonald's donará dinero a Ronald McDonald House Charities.*
   > And McDonald's will donate money to Ronald McDonald House Charities. (McDonald's, U.S.)
   >
   > *También te los entregamos y te los acomodamos en tu domicilio.*
   > Also, we will bring them to you and situate them for you in your home. (Rent-A-Center, U.S.)
   >
   > *Nuevos precios bajos todos los días.*
   > New low prices every day. (H-E-B, U.S.)

4.2 How pragmatic strategies effect persuasion in the data

b. Guarantees: Force

Y con la garantía de una de las casas relojeras suizas de mayor autoridad al nivel mundial.
And with the guarantee of one of the most authoritative Swiss watch companies in the world. (Christian Duvenet, SP)

Si no queda satisfecho, le devolvemos su dinero.
If you aren't satisfied, we'll return your money to you (FRML). (Set Arcobaleno, SP)

Y si encuentra algo en Weiners que no esté en rebaja, es gratis.
And if you find something in Weiners that isn't discounted, it's free. (Weiners, U.S.)

c. Disclaimers: Force

Las muñecas no se mueven solas. Se venden por separado.
The dolls do not move alone. Sold separately. (Barbie Fashion Avenue, CH)

Announcer 2: *Este anuncio es de un medicamento. Lea detenidamente las instrucciones de uso. En caso de duda consulte a su farmacéutico.*
This ad is for a medicine. Carefully read the instructions for use. In case of doubt, consult with your pharmacist. (Regaine, SP)

Other factors besides the illocutionary intent of speech acts can help effect persuasion, but these factors are again due to lexical connotations and pragmatic devices embedded within the speech act itself. The following promises illustrate this point. They contribute to the persuasive goal of Participation, not because they are promises, but because they contain a second person pronoun that refers to the audience and thereby attempts to draw the viewer into the message.

(79) Promises: Participation due to other factors

Yo y mis psíquicos atenderán a tus problemas.
I and my psychics will attend to your problems. (Walter, U.S.)

Cada experiencia en el nuevo Camry te llevará a la grandeza de sus cambios.
Every experience in the new Camry will carry you to the grandeur of its changes. (Toyota, U.S.)

Es una sorpresa tan grande que te dejará con la boca abierta.
It's a surprise so big that it will leave you with your mouth open. (McDonald's, SP)

The last type of speech acts, expressives, form the least unified class in Spanish commercials. Compliments, flattery, and praise (hereafter designated as flattery) contribute to at least two goals of persuasion. Flattery contributes to Force because of the strength of its claims. By appealing to viewers' vanity, the impact of flattery is emotional rather than logical, as shown in (80a). Furthermore, it is unlikely that viewers will deny or disagree with such complimentary descriptions of themselves. Flattery is linked with Force if it is about the audience, about a character as an example to the audience, or about the product/entity itself. Flattery contributes to Participation only if it is flattery of the audience and not self-praise or flattery of other characters as examples. Compliments about other characters, and by implication, of the audience, appear in (80b). Flattery of the audience involves viewers in the message, whether or not they are aware of their involvement, because it is personal and describes them as if they were known individually by advertisers. It augments Force by making viewers feel good about themselves and relates to Participation by enticing the audience to respond to the message. Finally, it may be argued that flattery optionally contributes to Memorability by attracting attention and by being remembered because of its positive and personal description of the viewing audience. Flattery in slogans is particularly memorable because of the brief nature of slogans.

(80) Flattery: (Memorability), Force, Participation

a. *Tú sí que sabes.*
You are the one who knows. (Burger King, U.S.)

Usted merece más.
You deserve more. (Reyes y Asociados, U.S.)

Te queremos en Alcampo.
We love you at Alcampo. (Alcampo, SP)

b. *Mamá no daría otra cosa.*
Mom wouldn't give anything else. (Nestum, CH)

¡Genial! ¡Mami, nunca fallas!
Fabulous! Mommy, you never fail! (Dodot Excel, SP)

Introductions outside of an advertising context would probably evoke some sort of a response from the hearer. Indeed, there are a few such genuine

4.2 How pragmatic strategies effect persuasion in the data

introductions in the data, and they contribute to persuasion by drawing attention (Memorability) and by implying a response such as, "Nice to meet you" on the part of the audience (Participation). Nevertheless, what is interesting about introductions in advertising discourse is that they tend to sound like announcements and, therefore, often do not contribute to the persuasive goal of Participation. Instead, such introductions only contribute to Memorability by focusing the viewer's attention on the product or entity being presented. The two types of introductions appear respectively in (81a) and (81b). The ad for Belmont in (81a) introduces a well-known tennis player in Chile, and the ad for *Eres* magazine presents characters with diminutive nicknames that contribute to warmth and humor. In contrast, the ads in (81a) seem more like announcements since they are introductions of products.

(81) Introductions: Memorability, (Participation)

   a. *Young woman:* [Pointing to man.] *El es Carlitos.*
      He is Carlitos.

      Young man: Y ella es Shakirita.
      And she is Shakirita. (Eres, U.S.)

      Yo soy Patricio Cornejo.
      I'm Patricio Cornejo. (Aceite Belmont, CH)

   b. *Bounty presenta las nuevas toallas reusables 'Rinse and Reuse'.*
      Bounty presents the new reusable towels, Rinse and Reuse. (Bounty, U.S.)

      Nintendo 64 [sesenta y cuatro] presenta lo último en videojuegos.
      Nintendo 64 presents the latest in videogames. (Nintendo, SP)

For other types of expressives involving habitual utterances such as greetings and leave-taking, their persuasive contribution is generally that of Memorability; the speaker attempts to get the viewer's attention. Participation is likely, but not required by the speech acts themselves. Indeed, in contexts such as public meetings, sermons, and advertisements; greetings and leave-taking are largely rhetorical and no response is expected.

(82) Greetings, leave-taking: Memorability, (Participation)

   Greetings
   ¡Hola, Austin!
   Hello, Austin! (Texas Discount Furniture Outlet, U.S.)

Leave-Taking
Y nos vemos próximo viernes.
See you next Friday. (Carozzi, CH)

Finally, the expressives of thanks, congratulations, and insults also contribute to persuasion in different ways. All three augment the strength of the message (Force) because they are social courtesies that are considered polite and that evoke positive feelings in their listeners. Giving thanks further contributes to the goal of Participation. A response to an utterance of thanks is likely in ordinary conversation, but is unlikely to be actually spoken by a television viewer, even though the viewer may mentally process a response. I, therefore, consider expressions of gratitude in Spanish advertisements to optionally contribute to Participation because they attempt to draw the viewer into the message. In contrast, congratulations do not increase Participation because they do not imply or attempt to evoke a response. Likewise, insults in the data, although forceful, do not necessitate a response from the viewer and, therefore, only contribute to the persuasive goal of Force (generally via humor) and Memorability (by capturing the audience's attention).

(83) Other expressives

Thanks: Force, (Participation)
Gracias por escuchar y ayudar a hacer mi McDonald's su McDonald's.
Thanks for listening and helping to make my McDonald's your McDonald's. (McDonald's, U.S.)

Congratulations: Force
Alicia, felicidades [to a viewer after winning raffle].
Alicia, congratulations! (Carozzi, CH)

Insults: Force
¿No tienen nada mejor que hacer que ver comerciales?
Don't you have anything better to do than to watch commercials? (Nectar Andina, CH)

4.2.3 Results: novelty

Results of research question (4) for novelty suggest that novelty is used primarily to make the ad be noticed and, ultimately, remembered (Memorability). Results for novelty are summarized in (84).

4.2 How pragmatic strategies effect persuasion in the data

(84) Contribution to persuasion by novelty

Explicit - M
Lexical - M
Pragmatic - M
Situational - M
Morphological - M, (F)
Syntactic - M, (F)
Associational - M, F, (P)
Semantic - F, P

Explicit, lexical, pragmatic, and situational novelty all simply serve to attract the viewer's attention (Memorability) and do not contribute to other persuasive goals. Instead, they are pragmatic devices for making the audience notice the ad and product/service being advertised.

(85) Explicit, lexical, pragmatic, and situational novelty: Memorability

Explicit
Ahora hay un nuevo desodorante aún más eficaz.
Now there is a **new,** even more effective deodorant. (Sanex, SP)

Nuevas Choco Zucaritas de Kellogg's. Son chocorricas.
New Choco Zucaritas [chocolate frosted flakes] from Kellogg's. They're chocorich. (Kellogg's, CH)

Cambio drástico.
Drastic **change.** (Toyota Corolla, CH)

Lexical
Filtrohelada
Filtercooled (Coors, U.S.)

Sprimido
Sprimmed (Sprim, CH)

Zoorpresa
Zoorprise (Nestle, CH)

McVaso
McGlass (McDonald's, CH)

MoviLine
Mobile line (MoviLine, SP)

Pragmatic
Announcer: *Quesadillas de Kraft Singles. La leche las hace....*
Quesadillas from Kraft Singles. The milk makes them....

Daughter: *¡Sabrosas!*
Delicious! (Kraft, U.S.)

Mother: *Para poder triunfar....*
To be able to triumph....

Captain Crunch:...lo tienes que intentar.
...you have to try it. (Captain Crunch, U.S.)

Situational
M&M's that talk (M&M's, U.S.)
Surprise party (Miller, U.S.)
Recipe contest (La Lechera, CH)
Cows that dance (Lechera Asturiana, SP)
Images of people kissing each other's underarms (Sanex, SP)

Besides contributing to Memorability by attracting viewers' attention, morphological and syntactic novelty also increase the force of a given message in many, but not all ads. Thus, they optionally contribute to the persuasive goal of Force. Morphological novelty contributes to force in two ways: (a) by describing an impersonal entity not normally possessed by a possessive pronoun; and (b) by using adjectival chaining to attribute multiple features to a given product. The possession of soup and Budweiser in (86a) strengthens the personal appeal of the message and is used to suggest that viewers want to own the products. Similarly, the multiple adjectives in (86b) serve to emphasize positive qualities in an attempt to stimulate the audience's desire for the products. Syntactic novelty contributes to Force by including only essential ingredients of the message and by omitting extraneous items such as articles, understood subjects, copula verbs, and other implied information. Syntactic novelty forces viewers to focus only on the important and desirable portions of an advertising message.

(86) Morphological, situational, and syntactic novelty: Memorability, (Force)

Morphological
a. *Porque ahora tomar **tu sopa** va a ser divertido, asombroso, delicioso y genial.*
Because now eating **your soup** is going to be fun, surprising, delicious, and fabulous. (Maggi Comics, CH)

*Para que disfrutes más del sabor fresco de **tu Budweiser**, la protegemos contra la luz con botellas oscuras.*
So that you further enjoy the fresh flavor of **your Budweiser**, we protect it from light with dark bottles. (Budweiser, U.S.)

b. *Pones una pequeña cantidad en esta suave esponja y gracias al agua de la ducha, se convierte en **una maravillosa espuma humectante**.*
You put a small quantity in this soft sponge and thanks to water from the shower, it converts into **a marvelous moisturizing foam**. (Oil of Olay, CH)

*Una nueva fórmula que le da a tu cabello **fuerza vital en colores más brillantes, vibrantes y mucho más duraderos**.*
A new formula that gives your hair **vital strength in more brilliant, vibrant, and much more lasting colors**. (Koleston, CH)

La primera hidratante detoxificante natural.
The first natural detoxifying moisturizer. (Biotherm, SP)

Syntactic[15]
Té Supremo. Con toda la calidad del mundo.
Supreme Tea. With all the quality in the world. (Té Supremo, CH)

Para tener un viaje feliz, sólo autobuses San Luis.
For a happy trip, only San Luis autobuses. (Autobuses San Luis, U.S.)

Preparación. Concentración. Técnica. Destreza.
Preparation. Concentration. Technique. Dexterity. (AT&T, U.S.)

---

[15]Lakoff (1982) defines syntactic innovation (syntactic novelty in the present study) as sentence fragments involving the absence of subjects or verbal auxiliaries and odd uses of the definite article. All examples of syntactic novelty in this study contain missing subjects or verbs.

Novel associations also contribute to both Memorability and Force. Often these associations are means of both attracting viewers' attention and also making them remember the item being advertised by first remembering the association. Novel associations augment the force of the message by making a product seem better than it really is or by implying additional traits not normally associated with the product. In this way, novel associations also optionally contribute to Participation via free gifts and offers. Novel associations consisting of free gifts and offers are a means of drawing viewers into the message and encouraging them to take action.

(87) Novel Association: Memorability, Force, (Participation)

Sexy women and beer. (Miller, U.S.)
Relay race and dishwashing liquid. (Fairy Ultra, CH)
Royal Club Evian health spa and shampoo. (Pantene, SP)
Topless woman and vitamins. (Revalid, SP)

The last category of novelty, semantic novelty, contributes to both Force and Participation. Since semantic novelty consists of elliptical comparisons, as shown in (88), such comparisons strengthen the force of the message by implying, rather than overtly stating comparisons. In doing so, more than one comparison is often possible. For example, the statement that a product is "better" may be interpreted in several ways: the product is better than other products in its class; the product is better than it used to be and has improved in some way; or the product is both better than others in its class and better than it was before. A statement that implies stronger claims than can be literally stated is more forceful than its literal counterpart. Furthermore, because elliptical comparatives force the audience to interpret the claim and to select a meaning, they thereby contribute to Participation.

(88) Semantic: Force, Participation

Summa es más.
Summa is more. (Summa, CH)

Rasch líquido lava mejor y conviene más.
Rasch liquid washes better and is more convenient. (Rasch, CH)

Siempre conviene más.
It's always more convenient. (Manquehue Larga Distancia, CH)

4.2.4 Results: indexicals and politeness

Indexicals in the data generally contribute to the Force component of persuasion in advertising, as in (89).

(89) Contribution to persuasion by indexicals

    Deixis - F
    Personal reference - (M), F, (P)
    Tense - F

Deixis primarily contributes to the persuasive goal of Force by directing the viewer toward the goal of buying. As Sánchez Corral (1991) suggested, verbs of motion serve to bring the product and the audience closer together and spatial deictics such as *aquí* 'here' and *este* 'this' combine the "here" of the product and speaker with the "here" of the viewer. Temporal deixis in Spanish ads generally refers negatively to the past and offers before/after contrasts that emphasize the preference for "now" as opposed to "before". Deictic items, therefore, strengthen the impact of the message on the viewer. The overwhelming preference for present tense in Spanish ads also contributes to the force of a message by making the product seem less remote and by attempting to combine the "now" of the ad with the time of purchase.

Personal reference, on the other hand, not only contributes to Force but also to Memorability and Participation. Second person reference is utilized to address viewers and involve them in the message. When first person is used in a testimonial, it often contributes to Memorability because it draws attention to speakers and attributes anecdotal credibility to merits of the product. Both first and second person are employed far more often than third person, because they more directly refer to the audience and perhaps attract more attention than third person. First person reference often is used in testimonials to help the audience remember the speaker and, by implication, the product or ad itself. Furthermore, first person reference sometimes can be interpreted as combining the "I" of the speaker with that of the audience, as if the viewer were actually producing the message. I illustrate first person reference in (90).

(90) <*Nuevo Toyota Camry. Estás hecho para mí.*>
      <New Toyota Camry. You're made for me.> (Toyota, U.S.)

      <*Mi McDonald's.*>
      <My McDonald's.> (McDonald's, U.S.)

Vocalist [Rapping]:
Yo quiero más. Yo quiero más. Yo quiero más. Más ketchup Watt's. Quiero mucho, mucho, mucho más ketchup....
I want more. I want more. I want more. More ketchup Watt's. I want much, much, much more ketchup.... (Ketchup Watt's, CH)

Third person reference in Spanish advertising frequently contributes to Force by using a character as an example for the viewer to either avoid or imitate, depending on the context. Examples of third person reference include ads for medicines where a character is told how to avoid indigestion, as in (91a). The excerpts in (91b) illustrate use of third person as examples for viewers to imitate.

(91) Third person reference: Force

a. (Pepto Bismol, U.S.)
Puppet [Grandfatherly, as if reading a story]:
Hoy quiero hablarles de Javier. El come por gusto y placer.
Today I want to talk to you about Javier. He eats for desire and pleasure.

Javier:	*Suegrita, estaba muy rica. Sírveme otro poquito.* Mom-in-law, it tastes delicious. Serve me a little bit more. [Image of him grimacing and holding his stomach.]
Mother-in-law:	*Y también sé como aliviar cualquier malestar.* And I also know how to alleviate any ailment.
Puppet:	*El único remedio que necesita es Pepto Bismol que cubre suavemente su estómago.* The only remedy that you need is Pepto Bismol, which softly coats your stomach.
Javier:	*Siento aliviado. ¿Todavía hay helado?* I feel better. Is there any ice cream left?
Puppet:	*Disfruten la ocasión. Para la mayoría de los malestares estomacales, el remedio es el mismo. ¡Pepto Bismol!* Enjoy the occasion. For the majority of stomach problems, the remedy is the same. Pepto Bismol!

b. (Café Monterrey, CH)
Monterrey Gold. Para los que valoran el café.
Monterrey Gold. For those who value coffee.

(Matarazzo, CH)
Announcer: [Images of a boy and girl.]
Al final, ellos siempre se salen con su gusto. Y disfrutan en grande la más rica elección. Porque saben lo que quieren. Matarazzo. Todos los días un instante de gloria.
In the end, they always get what they like. And greatly enjoy the most tasty selection. Because they know what they want. Matarazzo. Every day, a moment of glory.

Politeness strategies generally contribute to Force and sometimes to Participation, as in (92).

(92) Contribution to persuasion by politeness

Positive Face - F, P
Negative Face - F, P
Distance: F
Solidarity: F
Power: F

Positive politeness contributes to the force of the message because it suggests that the viewer and speaker's desires are one and the same and, through a friendly appeal, encourages the audience to participate in the message. Ads employing positive politeness that also contain flattery or announcers that make specific personal reference to the audience also contribute to Participation by drawing the viewer closer to the speaker and message. Use of directives also contributes to participation as outlined in §4.2.2. In contrast, ads containing negative politeness contribute to the impact of the message on the audience through formality and noninfringement on the viewer's face. That is, negative face supports notions of the speaker's authority and desire not to offend the viewer.

Other strategies in the data that contribute to the persuasive goal of Force are those that connote distance, solidarity, or power. These strategies aid in persuading the viewer to accept the claims of the ad and attempt to draw the audience into the advertiser's point of view. Distancing strategies and items connoting power suggest that the speaker is authoritative or holds a particular status in relation to the viewer. The ad for Margaret Astor Integrité in (93) does not contain any personal reference whatsoever, and the speaker is, therefore, able to remain as distant as possible from viewers. Viewers can therefore look up to the speaker and respect the message presented. Strategies of solidarity instead suggest proximity, egalitarianism, friendliness, and like-mindedness with viewers.

(93) Politeness: Force, (Participation)

> Positive face, Solildarity
> (JC Penney, U.S.)
> Woman: *Sólo hay una tienda para todas tus ocasiones especiales. Es JC Penney.* [Image of bride and groom.] *Allí quedas bien con tus regalos y también quedas bien con tu bolsillo.* [Images of people opening presents.] *JC Penney nos ha ayudado a hacer nuestras celebraciones más especiales con grandes ofertas y buenos regalos.* There is only one store for all your special occasions. It's JC Penney. There you make a good impression with your gifts and also with your pocketbook. JC Penney has helped us make our clebrations more special with great offers and good presents.
>
> Announcer: [Image of a father opening a present.] *Ahorre en las marcas favoritas de papá hasta el 14 [catorce] de junio.* Save on Dad's favorite brands until the 14th of June.
>
> Vocalist: *JC Penney. Te queda bien.*
> JC Penney. It fits you.
>
> Negative face, Power, Distance
> (Margaret Astor Integrité, SP)
> Announcer: *Ahora por la compra de una crema Margaret Astor Integrité, un contorno de ojos gratis. Margaret Astor Integrité. Con oxígeno puro.*
> Now with the purchase of a Margaret Astor Integrité cream, an eye shadow free. Margaret Astor Integrité. With pure oxygen.

4.2.5 Results: implicatures and violations of maxims

Implicatures and violations of the Cooperative Principle are some of the crucial ingredients for persuasion in Spanish television advertising. Violations of Grice's Maxims and the implicatures arising from them occur in advertising and contribute to persuasion because they allow for stronger

4.2 How pragmatic strategies effect persuasion in the data 157

claims to be made than those that are literally true. As Geis (1982) argued, advertisers normally make the strongest claims they can. He believed that advertisers should be held responsible not only for what they assert to be true but also for what they imply to be true, since even children are able to understand conversational implicatures in advertising. We find that advertising claims in the data frequently imply a stronger assertion or emotional argument than that which is factual or logically true. Thus, Grice's Maxims help explain much of the persuasive nature of Spanish advertising.

I will briefly examine the two types of implicatures, before turning to violations of Grice's Maxims and conversational implicatures. Conventional implicatures primarily contribute to the persuasive goal of Force, whereas conversational implicatures contribute to both Force and Participation because, by definition, it is necessary for viewers to work out the meaning of conversational implicatures. Implicatures may also contribute to Memorability when they are in the form of slogans or when an unusual lexical item is used. In such cases, their memorability is probably due to syntactic novelty and lexical novelty, rather than the fact that they are implicatures.

The following examples of implicatures demonstrate the contributions to persuasion. Notice that conventional implicatures are apparent from the lexical meanings of words and from semantic presuppositions. Although conventional implicatures subtly augment the strength of an argument, they are not intended to be analyzed or "worked out" in the Gricean sense. Instead, viewers tend to understand such implicatures automatically, whether they realize it or not.

(94) Conventional implicature: Force

Sabemos la sed que sientes.
We know the thirst you feel. (Coors, U.S.)

Otro World Best de Samsung.
Another World Best from Samsung. (Samsung, CH)

*Saimaza. **Sigue** eligiendo lo mejor.*
Saimaza. **Keep** selecting the best. (Saimaza, SP)

Dos vídeos Disney para tu colección.
Two Disney videos **for your collection.** (Disney videos, SP)

Y ahora puede disfrutar de una gran variedad de deliciosos omelettes desde sólo 2.99 (dos dólares noventa y nueve centavos).
And now you can enjoy a great variety of delicious omelettes from **only** 2.99. (Denny's, U.S.)

Conversational implicatures, on the other hand, do not arise solely from the meaning of particular lexical items or the conventional understanding of phrases. In contrast, conversational implicatures arise from violations of the Cooperative Principle and Grice's Maxims, and their meaning must be worked out using the context, background knowledge, and other factors. Hence, the audience must participate in the message in order to understand it. For example, the sentences in (95a–d) are somewhat open to interpretation. The slogan in (95e) makes sense only if the viewer knows that the beer comes in a green bottle, and the excerpt in (95f) is interpretable based on the background knowledge that women stereotypically like shoes.

(95) Converstional implicature: Force, Participation

    a. *Descubre tu propia belleza y vas a asegurar mucho más.*
       Discover your own beauty and you're going to ensure much more. (All-Day, CH) (Much more beauty/happiness.)

    b. [Image of button with Coca Cola written on it. Button is pushed and begins a series of chain reactions in a machine. Eventually the machine pours a coke.]
       <*Siempre Coca Cola.*>
       <Always Coca Cola.> (Coca Cola, CH)
       (Always drink/choose Coca Cola.)

    c. *Miller Time. Todo puede pasar.*
       Miller Time. Anything can happen. (Miller, U.S.)
       (Drinking Miller beer means that strange/great things happen.)

    d. *Tú sí que sabes.*
       You are the one who knows. (Burger King, U.S.)
       (You are the one who knows that Burger King is best.)

    e. *Piensa en verde.*
       Think of green. (Heineken, SP)
       (Think of Heineken.)

    f. Mom 2: *¿Tú crees que a las mujeres nos gustan los zapatos?*
               Do you think that we women like shoes?

       Mom 1: *No. ¿Cómo crees? Es puro mito*
               No. How can you think that? It's just a myth..
               (Payless, U.S.)
       (Women really like shoes.)

4.2 How pragmatic strategies effect persuasion in the data

One of the fascinating things about advertising language as a discourse form is that neither ordinary conversation nor cooperation truly occurs in advertising, although there is a pretense of appeal to both (Lakoff 1982). For example, frequent imperatives and offers and rhetorical questions do not work well in ordinary conversation, and ordinary conversation cannot occur since advertising discourse is in only one direction. Nevertheless, advertisements are created as if they assume that the viewer is interacting and responding. Cooperation is only a secondary goal of advertising because ads primarily attempt to persuade, manipulate, or change the audience. In a sense, noncooperation occurs in advertising more often than true cooperation, and, therefore, advertising violates/flouts Grice's Maxims as a rule and obeys them only incidentally. What makes advertising discourse especially persuasive, however, is that it pretends to cooperate and communicate in accordance with the Cooperative Principle.

A summary of the contribution to persuasion by violations of Grice's conversational maxims and the implicatures that tend to arise from these violations are listed in (96).

(96) Contribution to persuasion by violations of maxims

Quantity:
    Ellipsis - F, P
    Repetition - M, F
    Lack of information - F, (P)

Quality:
    Metaphor - (M), F, P
    Hyperbole/understatement - F, P
    Irony - F, P
    False assertions - F, (P)

Relation:
    Relation - (M), F, P
    Nonrelevance - (M), F, P

Manner:
    Rhetorical questions - F, P
    Vagueness/ambiguity/obscurity - F, P
    Verbosity - M, F

The only violations of Grice's Maxims that do not seem to contribute to Participation are strategies of repetition and verbosity/too much information, which are both violations of Quantity. Repetition and verbosity generally occur as mnemonic devices to make the audience pay attention and remember (Memorability). Repetition, nevertheless, contributes to Force because it serves to highlight elements of the message that the advertiser considers important. Verbosity contributes to Force because it makes the message seem to contain more information than it really does. That is, if an ad enumerates features of the advertised product in several ways, the overall effect is to sound like the product has many merits and that there is a lot to say about the product.

(97) Repetition, Verbosity: Memorability, Force

    a. Repetition
       < *El misterioso poder de Cornetto Frigo.* >
       < The mysterious power of Cornetto Frigo. >
       [Image of young people at the beach eating ice cream.]
       < *¡Atención! Cornetto Frigo. Activa los músculos faciales.*
       ¡Atención! Cornetto Frigo. ¡Atención! Acelera el corazón.
       !Atención! Cornetto Frigo provoca ataques de espontaneidad. >
       < Attention! Cornetto Frigo. Activates facial muscles. Attention! Cornetto Frigo. Attention! Accelerates the heart. Attention! Cornetto Frigo provokes attacks of spontaneity. >
       Announcer: *El poder de las emociones. Cornetto Frigo.* < *El poder de las emociones.* >
                     The power of emotions. Cornetto Frigo. < The power of emotions. > (Cornetto Frigo, SP)

    b. Verbosity
       El nuevo envase individual grande de papitas Evercrisp tipo americano.
       The new big individual package of American-type Evercrisp potato chips. (Evercrisp, CH)

Metaphors, implied relations, and nonrelevance contribute to all of the persuasive goals in this study, though they only optionally contribute to Memorability. Some metaphors and implied relations are incidental and not necessarily used to attract attention or be remembered. They do, however, contribute to Force by strengthening the description and associations surrounding a given concept or product, and they contribute to Participation because they generally require the audience to interpret or work out the implied associations. The examples in (98a) contain metaphors that contribute to all three persuasive goals, whereas those in (98b) contain metaphors that do not contribute to Memorability.

4.2 How pragmatic strategies effect persuasion in the data

(98) Metaphors: (Memorability), Force, Participation

    a. *¡Nestlé Gold hizo crujiente la miel!*
Nestlé Gold made honey crunchy! (Nestlé, CH)

    Bebe Mosto. La energía natural.
Drink Mosto. The natural energy. (Mosto, SP)

    La vida es como un deporte. Saboréala con Gatorade.
Life is like a sport. Savor it with Gatorade. (Gatorade, U.S.)

    b. *Dígale adiós a las venas varicosas con Venacilin.*
Say goodbye to varicose veins with Venacilin. (Venacilin, U.S.)

    Los nuevos diseños Pullups motivan a los niños a aprender.
The new Pullups designs motivate children to learn. (Pullups, U.S.)

    La solución: Pantene ProV que ayuda a mantenerlo fuerte y celebrarlo.
The solution: Pantene ProV, which helps to keep it [hair] strong and enhance it. (Pantene, CH)

Implied relations and nonrelevance contribute to Force by associating one or more factors with the advertised product, thus increasing the strength of the claim. It contributes to Participation by forcing viewers to make these associations. Implied relations and nonrelevance are effective strategies for creating multiple associations beyond those inherent to the product. Only some examples contribute to Memorability, particularly ads that include vivid visual images, as in the ad for Kotex in (99b), or when they occur in slogans, as in the army ad in (99a).

(99) Implied relations and nonrelevance: (Memorability), Force, Participation

    a. Implied relations
        Woman 2: *Queda tan suave...*
                        It stays so soft...

        Woman 1: *que me hace muy feliz.*
                        that it makes me very happy.

Woman 2: *Y al ser muy feliz, me siento muy bonita.*
And being very happy, I feel very pretty. (Dove, U.S.)
(Dove, beauty, and happiness)

Army. Sé todo lo que puedes ser.
Army. Be all that you can be. (Army, U.S.)
(Army and success)

Nada te llevará a un viaje tan refrescante como Solero de Frigo.
Nothing will take you on as refreshing a trip as Solero de Frigo. [Images of various exotic places]. (Frigo, SP)
(Frigo and travel to exotic places)

b. Nonrelevance
¿Te vas de viaje? ¡Qué bueno! Pero antes pasa por Sears Auto Center donde ahora todas las llantas Bridgestone Roadhandlers están en oferta.
You're going on a trip? How great! But first go by Sears Auto Center where now all Bridgestone Roadhandlers tires are on sale. (Sears, U.S.)
(Travel and Sears)

Woman 1: ...*¿Qué es GelSec?*
...What is GelSec?
[Sanitary pad falls into bathtub, absorbs all the water, and Woman 2 is left naked] (Kotex, CH)
(GelSec, absorption, and humor)

Oye, vive más y aprende. Y compra Luv's.
Listen, live more, and learn. And buy Luv's. (Luv's, U.S.)
(Luv's and essential advice for living)

Finally, ellipsis, lack of information, hyperbole/understatement, irony, false assertions, vagueness/ambiguity/obscurity, and rhetorical questions all contribute to Force and Participation. Ellipsis and a lack of information contribute to Force by implying information not present in the ad, as in (100–101), and evoke Participation by causing the audience to fill in the missing parts of the message. A lack of information only optionally contributes to Participation, since not all examples require that the viewer infer or work out the ad's meaning.

4.2 How pragmatic strategies effect persuasion in the data

(100) Ellipsis: Force, Participation

Descubre tu propia belleza y vas a asegurar mucho más.
Discover your own beauty and you're going to ensure much more. (All-Day, CH)

Fortalece su cabello un cincuenta y cinco por ciento.
Strengthen your hair [by] 55 percent. (Alberto VO5, CH)

(101) Lack of information: Force, (Participation)

[Image of a woman's face.]
Woman: ¡Paco!
Paco!
Announcer: ¡Paco!
Paco!
[Image of a cologne bottle. Six other faces, each say, ¡Paco! The announcer repeats after each speaker.] (Paco Rabanne, SP)

[Image of a man with a grey beard looking at the sky. Image of a dog searching for something. The sky starts raining Skittles.]
Voice: *[whispering] Skittles. Saborea el arco iris.*
Skittles. Savor the rainbow. (Skittles, U.S.)

Violations of Quality also contribute to Force and Participation. For example, hyperbole/understatement are means of asserting that a product is better than can be stated literally. Viewers are expected to understand such statements to be only slight hyperbole or understatement and to be mostly true. The audience is therefore left to decide which part(s) of the message are true and which are overstated. Irony in the data generally contributes to Force by adding humor to the message and by implying something different from the literal statement. Irony also contributes to Participation because the audience is expected to use prior knowledge to interpret its meaning. False assertions contribute to Force by asserting information as if it were true and only optionally contribute to Participation, since not all examples require that the viewer infer or work out the ad's message.

(102) Violations of Quality

Hyperbole/understatement: Force, Participation
El lubricante más avanzado del mundo.
The most advanced lubricant in the world. (Mobil 1, SP)

A cambio de escuchar, Chile tiene el mejor fútbol del mundo.
Contrary to what you hear, Chile has the best football in the world. (Nike, CH)

Un poco de pasta basta.
A little pasta is enough. (Gior, SP)

Irony: Force, Participation
Mother: O te comas todo o te quedas sin postre.
Either you eat everything or you don't get any dessert.
[Image of child eating his food, then eating the flowers, tablecloth, chunks of the wall] (Postres Caricia, CH)

False assertions: Force, (Participation)
El refresco que siempre te ha refrescado.
The refreshment that always has refreshed you. (Coca Cola, U.S.)
Quieres un Ford nuevo.
You want a new Ford. (Ford Contour, U.S.)

Es tiempo de pintar tu casa.
It's time to paint your house. (Sears, U.S.)

Vagueness, ambiguity, and obscurity all contribute to Force because they blur claims and imply that the audience is meant to understand how wonderful the product is. Thus, the ad for Tylenol in (103) implies that *all* doctors recommend Tylenol more than other brands, when in reality, the statement can also mean that just some doctors prefer Tylenol. These violations of Manner also contribute to Participation because messages are worded in such a way that a claim is unclear and viewers have to interpret in order to understand.

(103) Violations of Manner

Vagueness/ambiguity/obscurity: Force, Participation
Para el dolor causado por la cirugía, los doctores recomiendan Tylenol más que otras marcas.
For the pain caused by surgery, doctors recommend Tylenol more than other brands. (Tylenol, U.S.)

Y si también combinas Fattaché con un poco de ejercicio de grado, vas a obtener estupendos resultados.
And if you also combine Fattaché with a little of the right amount of exercise, you're going to obtain stupendous results. (Fattaché, U.S.)

4.2 How pragmatic strategies effect persuasion in the data

Cien por ciento café. Cien por ciento sabor.
One hundred per cent coffee. One hundred per cent flavor.
(Monterrey, CH)

Mantenemos tu AutoMóvil.
We keep your automobile (Sears Auto Center, U.S.)

Many rhetorical questions are interpretable simply because of their conventional meanings and, therefore, result in conventional, rather than conversational implicatures. Nevertheless, rhetorical questions resulting in conversational implicatures contribute to Force by implying an assertion. They contribute to Participation by making the audience interpret what the implied assertion and assumed answer are, as in (104b), where the question together with the context and tone of voice imply doubt.

(104) Rhetorical questions: Force, Participation

    a. (Nivea, SP)
    ¿Que cuántas cremas usa?
    You use how many creams?

    Assertion: *Usa demasiadas cremas.*
    You use too many creams.

    b. (Cash 5 Lottery, U.S.)
    [Setting - in a restaurant with a ship motif.]
    Waitress: *Bienvenidos abordo. ¿Qué les sirvo?*
              Welcome aboard. What can I serve you?

    Woman 1: *A mí huachinango al mojo de ajo con poco ajo y mucho mojo.*
              I'll have red snapper in garlic sauce with little garlic and a lot of sauce.

    Waitress: *Sí.*
              Yes.

    Man 1: *Yo quiero una mojarrita empanizada.*
            I want a breaded mojarra [fish].

    Woman 3: *Con camarones.*
              With shrimp.

    Man 2: *No asada.*
            Not roasted.

Waitress (not paying attention): *Sí, está bien.*
Yes, okay.

Woman 2: [Patrons keep adding to their orders.] ...*porque quiero caldo, ¿eh?*
...because I want soup, eh?

[Waitress responds, "uh-huh" to each person as they make their requests.]

Man 3: *Pero, ¿si no ha apuntado nada?*
But, since you haven't written anything down?

Waitress: *Sí, sí. Me acuerdo.*
Yes, yes. I remember.

Announcer: *¿**Tú crees**? Es más probable que ganes con Cash 5 [cinco]. Sólo necesitas igualar cinco, cuatro o tres números de treinta y nueve para ganar.*
You think so? It's more probable that you'll win with Cash 5. You only need to match five, four, or three numbers out of thirty-nine to win.

4.2.6 Results: speaker considerations

Particular characteristics of speakers contribute to persuasion in the data. It is unusual and, therefore, memorable when the announcer or presenter is female or when there is a mix of male and female announcers in Spanish ads. Female speakers also contribute to the persuasive goal of Force when the intention is to identify with the audience, as in advertisements that include mothers or women, as in (105a). Use of male announcers/presenters, on the other hand, is extremely common and primarily contributes to Force by conveying authority, power, or status. Male announcers even appear in ads only addressed to women and serve to communicate importance and material of an informational nature about the product/service, as in (105b).

4.2 How pragmatic strategies effect persuasion in the data

(105) Gender: (Memorability), Force

    a. (Color Stay, SP)

Announcer (Female):	*Nuevo Color Stay de Revlon.* *<Hidratación para tus labios.> Porque nosotras merecemos unos labios así.* *<Revlon.>* New Color Stay from Revlon. <Hydration for your lips.> Because we [PL, FEM] deserve lips like this.
<Revlon.>	

    b. (EPT, U.S.)

Daughter:	*Ay, Mami. Estoy tan nerviosa. ¿Tú crees que estaré embarazada?* Oh, Mom. I'm so nervous. Do you think that I'm pregnant?
Mother:	*Bueno, hija, con EPT lo vamos a saber con certeza porque fíjate que EPT usa el mismo método que usan los doctores.* Well, daughter, with EPT we're going to know for sure because, notice that EPT uses the same method that doctors use.
Announcer (Male):	*EPT. Es tan fácil de usar y confiable como siempre. Sólo EPT tiene una punta absorbente así de ancha y una ventanilla sellada a prueba de derrames.* EPT. It is so easy to use and reliable as always. Only EPT has an absorbent point this wide and a sealed little window prevents spills.
Mother:	*¿Estás lista?* Are you ready?
Daughter:	*Sí, ¿y tú?* Yes, and you?
Mother:	*Lista para ser abuela.* Ready to be a grandmother.

Announcer (Male): *EPT. Para la respuesta correcta.* < *EPT. Para la respuesta correcta.* >
EPT. For the correct answer. <EPT. For the correct answer.>

Ads in which the age or profession of speakers is important or obvious contribute to Force by identifying with the audience, conveying authenticity, or, in the case of testimonials, by implying that the speaker is an authority on the product. The age of speakers is commonly a factor for identification in ads directed at audiences who are children or are elderly, as in (106). The speaker's profession is particularly a means of identification with viewers or of communicating authority in ads addressed to mothers, as in (107a). Thus, characteristics of speakers contribute to the Force component of persuasion by attempting to build the viewer's confidence in the credibility of a speaker.

(106) Age: Force

a. Children (Kanibal, SP)
[Image of kids on a beach.] [Camy]
Kids [rapping]: *Oye, mira. Mira. Si te gustan los helados, Camy tiene uno que se come a dos manos. Que se coge por abajo. Que se coge por arriba. No te olvides el de Camy.* <*Camy*> *No te olvides. Es Kanibal.*
Hey, look. Look. If you like ice cream. Camy has one that is eaten with two hands. That you hold from below. That you hold from above. Don't forget the one from Camy. <Camy.> Don't forget. It's Kanibal.

b. Elderly (Aleve, U.S.)
Grey-haired woman [Seamstress]: [Sighs.]
Cuando me duelen las manos no me puedo dar el lujo de parar. Durante el día puedo tomar cuatro Advil u ocho Tylenol. O puedo tomar sólo dos Aleve. Como dice la etiqueta. Tú decides.
When my hands hurt, I can't give myself the luxury of stopping. During the day I can take four Advil or eight Tylenol. Or I can take just two Aleve. Like the label says. You decide.

(107) Profession: Force

    a. Mother (Palmolive, U.S.)
       [Mother and Daughter cooking in kitchen]
       Mother: [Looking dismayed.] *¡Los frijoles!*
                   Beans!

       Daughter: *Mami, ¿cómo limpiamos todo esto?*
                    Mommy, how do we clean all this?

       Mother: *Con Palmolive para ollas y sartenes.*
                   With Palmolive for pots and pans.

       Daughter: *Ah, por eso se llama Palmolive for pots and pans.*
                    Oh, that's why it's called Palmolive for pots and pans.

       Mother: *Especializado para ollas y sartenes, hace que la comida grasosa pegada se despegue fácilmente.*
                 Especially for pots and pans, it makes it so that greasy, stuck-on food is easily removed.

    b. Employee (Parma, CH)

       Woman: [Going up escalator, looking at people.] *Para ser una buena pasta, no es viajar y juntar un ingrediente con otro. Es que los ingredientes son como las personas. Para que se junten, algo especial debe haber entre ellos. Así la pasta se transforma en algo único. Lo veo todos los días. Soy Andrea. Trabajo en Parma.*
       To be a good pasta, it isn't travelling and mixing one ingredient with another. It's that ingredients are like people. In order for them to mix, there ought to be something special in them. In that way, pasta is transformed into something unique. I see it every day. I'm Andrea. I work at Parma.

Attractive physical features are commonly used in advertisements to make viewers notice and perhaps remember the speaker (Memorability) and to invoke notions of power or identification with the audience (Force), thereby lending authority and authenticity to the message. In ads for beauty products, a speaker that is attractive supports the message that the product really works, has worked for the speaker, and that it can make the viewer beautiful as well. Inclusion of attractive female speakers may also help to convey a sensual appeal or association with the product.

Speakers who are ordinary looking are also often used to communicate authenticity and identification with the audience. It is interesting to note that the U.S. ads generally include speakers who have dark hair and who are stereotypically Hispanic looking.

(108) Physical characteristics of speakers

> Beauty: Memorability, Force
> [Image of a woman's silhouette]
> Woman [Slender, attractive]: *Me gusta cuidar de mi silueta. Y he descubierto cómo hacerlo de la forma más sana y natural.*
> I like to take care of my figure. And I've discovered how to do it in the most healthy and natural way. [She holds up a loaf of bread.]
>
> *Y sobre todo, deliciosa.*
> And more than anything, deliciously. (Silueta bread, SP)
>
> Ordinary looking—Force
> Woman [Ordinary looking, slightly overweight, middle-aged.]: [Cutting shrubs] *Corta, corta, corta. Yo corto todo, sobretodo mis gastos y así mis ahorros crecen. Con Collect en español. ¡Claro!*
> Cut, cut, cut. I cut everything, especially my expenses and that way my savings grow. With Collect in Spanish. Of course! [She runs to answer the telephone.] (Collect en español, U.S.)

4.2.7 Results: minor categories

Other minor pragmatic categories in the data also contribute to persuasion, as shown in (109).

(109) Contribution to persuasion by minor categories

> Flattery: F, P
> Humor: (M), F, P
> Endorsements: (M), F
> Syntax: M, F
> Phonology: M, F
> Lexicon: M, F

Flattery contributes to the force component of persuasion. Flattery of the audience is an attempt to make viewers feel good about the product/service and to emotionally align themselves with the product. When flattery is of a character as part of a secondary dialogue, it is generally to flatter by example anyone who uses the product/service advertised. In this way, flattery of characters indirectly strengthens the ad's message. When flattery is of the product itself, its purpose is to boast about the merits, thereby communicating a willingness to publicly express pride in the product. Only flattery of the audience also contributes to Participation by playing on the viewers' vanity and attempting to draw them into the message.

Humor primarily contributes to the force and participation components of persuasion via implicatures and reference to the audience's background or contextual knowledge. Humor that is conveyed through visual antics is less common but contributes to Memorability in its attempt to be noticed.

Endorsements either directly or indirectly contribute to Force by strengthening the personal appeal and, therefore, the impact of an ad on viewers. Those ads containing testimonials about a product that are directly addressed to the audience try to convince viewers of the endorser's experience and that their recommendation is, therefore, authoritative and valid. Endorsements that occur in dialogues between characters likewise endeavor to convince the audience of a product's superiority, but do so indirectly and as an example for viewers. Endorsements by celebrities also contribute to Memorability.

The pragmalinguistic strategies of information structure (syntax), phonological selection, and lexical selection all contribute to both Memorability and Force. Fragments in slogans assist the audience in remembering key portions of the message (Memorability), and information structure is employed to emphasize or focus the viewer's attention on important words and phrases within a sentence (Force). Phonological elements such as alliteration, rhyme, and jingles are mnemonic devices aimed at making the audience take notice or remember certain phrases. In contrast, use of foreign accents implies legitimacy and, therefore, helps portray the desired image for a product. Use of stress also contributes to the persuasive goal of Force by emphasizing particular words. Finally, lexical selection of foreign words, neologisms, the product name as a mini-ad, and jargon all attempt to attract the viewers' attention and to make them remember. Use of jargon also contributes to Force because it is a means of describing a product/service in lofty or pseudoscientific terms, thus sounding newsworthy, factual, and intelligent.

4.2.8 Summary

I have demonstrated the contributions to persuasion of each pragmatic strategy in the study. In general, speech acts contribute to the component of Force, whereas novelty primarily contributes to Memorability. Both indexicals and politeness also contribute to Force more than any other persuasive goal. Conventional and conversational implicatures contribute to Force, but Participation is important for the effectiveness of conversational implicatures. Violations of Grice's Maxims differ in their contributions to persuasion; however, they generally add to the goals of Force and Participation. Speaker considerations also tend to augment the force of an ad's message. Finally, minor strategies such as flattery, humor, endorsements, information structure, phonological elements, and lexical selection do not form a uniform class and, therefore, individually contribute to persuasion in varying ways.

5
Conclusions and Implications

5.1 Conclusions

5.1.1 Reorganization of categories

Following is a summary of the key findings of my analysis in answer to the four general questions presented in §1.2.2. (1) Which pragmatic devices occur most frequently in Spanish television advertising? Based on the results of the first research question and the interrelation of some strategies, I propose the following as major pragmatic strategies that are representative of Spanish television advertising.

(110) Major pragmatic strategies

    Speech acts
    Indexicals
    Politeness
    Violations of Grice's Maxims
    Implicature
    Speaker considerations

(2) How are these pragmatic devices linguistically encoded in the data? Based on results of the second research question, I present common strategies within each major class in table 5.1. Minor categories in the study are recategorized and are indicated by italics. For example, the initial database was created with categories such as flattery, endorsement, and

humor that were relatively infrequent in Spanish advertising. After analysis, I found these items and some other features in the database to be subsumed by the major categories in the data. Thus, flattery is a type of expressive speech act and is reclassified as such. Similarly, endorsements are reclassified as speaker considerations, since their purpose is to imply the authority and authenticity of a speaker as a means of selling products/services. Like gender, age, profession, physical characteristics, and endorsements draw attention to the speaker, who is typically a celebrity, an ordinary person, or an authority about a product (such as a mother or lottery winner). Another possibility for endorsements might be to include them as a type of representative speech act or to include them as both speech acts and speaker considerations. Nonvisual or slapstick humor is recategorized as a result of implicature. To be successful, this type of humor generally must be worked out as a result of context, background knowledge, and the Cooperative Principle. Hence, the humor found in Spanish ads typically involves some sort of implicature and relies on knowledge shared with the viewer for it to be successful.

Novelty is also recategorized under Grice's Maxims since classes of novelty are a violation of at least one maxim, as discussed in chapter 3. Thus, ellipsis and semantic novelty are two names for the same strategy and are violations of quantity. Ellipsis/semantic novelty may also be considered as a type of vagueness, and thus, a violation of manner. Similarly, novel associations and implied relations are both names for the same violation of relation. They also may violate manner because they are pragmatic strategies for capturing the viewer's attention. Information structure, phonological selection (such as rhyme or alliteration), explicit, syntactic, and situational novelty are likewise violations of manner because they serve to attract attention and help the audience remember a product or an ad. Finally, the category of lexicon in the database generally overlaps with the category of lexical novelty. I therefore consider the two names to identify the same type of strategy and to violate the maxim of manner. Lexical selection/lexical novelty includes devices such as foreign words and neologisms whose primary purpose is to attract attention.

5.1 Conclusions

Table 5.1 Reclassification of major and minor pragmatic strategies (Key: italics = reclassified strategies; bold print = most typical strategies.)

Speech acts	Representatives:	**assertions** (statements of assumed facts), reports (past or implied studies), announcements (statements about existence)
	Directives:	**orders** (commands), suggestions (imperatives, interrogatives, declaratives with *poder*), recommendations (explicit, implicit), invitations (explicit, ambiguous), requests, attentiongetters, instructions, warnings, ultimatums
	Commissives:	**offers** (explicit, contingent), promises (statements assuring future action), guarantees (explicit, contingent), disclaimers (negative statements), apologies (polite imperatives)
	Expressives:	*flattery* (assertions of emotional alignment), introductions (explicit, people and products), thanks, congratulations, greetings, leave-taking, insults
Indexicals	Deixis:	**here and now,** before/after contrast, verbs of motion
	Personal ref.:	preference for **second person**
	Tense:	**present tense,** past/present contrast
Politeness	Positive face:	**identification with audience,** friendliness
	Negative face:	formal, offers options
	Distance:	second person formal
	Power:	**second person formal**
	Solidarity:	**second person familiar**
Violation of Maxims	Quantity:	**ellipsis** *(semantic novelty),* **repetition,** lack of information, too much information

	Quality:	**metaphor,** hyperbole, irony, false assertions
	Relation:	**implied relation** *(novel associations),* nonrelevance
	Manner:	**vagueness** (any type, including *semantic novelty*), verbosity, rhetorical questions, *explicit novelty, lexical novelty (lexical selection), syntactic novelty, situational novelty, novel associations, information structure, phonological selection*
Implicature	Conventional:	**presupposition,** lexical items
	Conversational:	**via Grice's Maxims,** background knowledge, *humor (not visual or slapstick)*
Speaker Considerations		**Gender** (masculine)
		Age (elderly or child)
		Profession (mother or other profession)
		Physical characteristics (beautiful or ordinary looking)
		Endorsements

The results indicate that Spanish advertising discourse primarily uses assertions of assumed facts and directives such as orders, suggestions, and recommendations in various linguistic forms to attempt to persuade the viewer to buy. In contrast, the most commonly used commissives, such as offers and promises, and expressives, such as flattery, are secondary means for attempting persuasion. If you only examine speech acts in Spanish advertising, you might argue that much of Spanish advertising language is direct and explicit and, therefore, that the audience is considered to be most influenced by overt persuasion. Nevertheless, as indicated in chapter 3, many speech acts are ambiguous and convey more than one illocutionary force. Moreover, violations of Grice's Maxims are frequently used to achieve an indirect message. Spanish ads regularly employ devices such as ellipsis, metaphor, vagueness, implied relations, and novelty to create conversational implicatures. Conventional implicatures occur because of both presupposition and the meaning of lexical items; Spanish

5.1 Conclusions

ad writers assume that the audience agrees with them. Since implicatures are so frequent, violations of Grice's Maxims and presupposition are the main ways in which Spanish advertisers attempt to indirectly persuade viewers.

Spanish advertisers emphasize solidarity and familiarity slightly more than authority and distance in ads. Identification with the viewing audience serves to create emotional ties to a product and to create a positive overall impression. It is often expressed with informal second person reference. On the other hand, authority and power are generally communicated through announcers' speech and written messages that include formal personal pronouns. Thus, Spanish advertisers blend the use of two politeness strategies. Advertisers also emphasize concepts of "here" and "now" to create impressions of proximity and urgency. Second person personal reference is most frequent because advertisers wish to focus on and identify with the audience above all other individuals. Finally, gender distribution in Spanish commercials reveals that it is males who communicate power and authority. Apparently, Spanish advertisers believe that their viewing public is most influenced by male speakers.

(3) Are any pragmatic differences evident between dialects of Spanish? Results for the third research question suggest that the three dialects generally have more similarities than differences in distribution of pragmatic strategies and that persuasive discourse in Spanish television advertising is highly conventionalized. The similarities listed in (111) reveal pragmatic strategies of Spanish advertising discourse in general.

(111) Similarities in distribution across varieties

> Major versus minor pragmatic categories
> Speech acts—preference for *representatives* and *directives*
> Novelty—preference for *syntactic* and *explicit novelty*
> Indexicals—*deixis, personal reference,* and *present tense*
> Implicature—both types, with a preference for *conversational implicature*
> Violations of Maxims—all occur, with a preference for *violation of Relation*
> Violation of Quantity—preference for *repetition* and *ellipsis*
> Violation of Quality—preference for *metaphor* and *hyperbole*
> Violation of Manner—preference for *vagueness*

Nevertheless, at a more detailed level, some differences are apparent in individual pragmatic strategies according to country. Since advertisers in each country write ads that stereotype their views of the audience and culture, variations in distribution reveal differences between stereotypical representations of the three countries in this study. I summarize these differences are in (112).

(112) Differences in distribution of strategies by country

    United States (Univision)
      Speech acts:
        Different order of preference for speech acts
        Greatest variety and frequency of speech acts

      Indexicals:
        Most personal reference
        Greatest variety of tenses

      Politeness:
        Most positive politeness, solidarity
        Least negative politeness, power

      Implicature:
        Most conventional implicature

      Violations of maxims:
        Most violations of manner, most pragmatic novelty
        Least violations of relation
        Most false assertions, irony, nonrelevance, rhetorical questions

      Speaker considerations:
        Most speaker considerations, female speakers
      Minor categories:
        Most flattery, endorsements, information structure
        Most complex in terms of participants

    Spain (Antena 3)
      Indexicals:
        Least personal reference

      Politeness:
        Least distancing strategies

      Violations of maxims:
        Most syntactic, explicit, situational novelty, new associations
        Most examples of lack of information, too much information

      Speaker considerations:
       Fewest age, physical, professional speaker considerations

5.1 Conclusions

    Minor categories:
      Least flattery, endorsements, information structure
      Most sexual appeals
      Shortest and longest ads

    Chile (Teletrece)
      Speech acts:
        Least variety and frequency of speech acts

      Indexicals:
        Least variety of tenses

      Politeness:
        Least positive politeness, solidarity
        Most negative politeness, power
        Most distancing strategies

      Implicature:
        Least conventional implicature
        Violations of maxims:
        Most violations of quantity, ellipsis

      Speaker considerations:
        Fewest female speakers

      Minor categories:
        Most phonological elements
        Most appeals to nationalism
        Least complex in terms of participants

    The greater variety of speech acts in U.S. ads when compared to those of Chile reflects the greater complexity in terms of participants and situations that is found in U.S. ads. This difference in complexity between the U.S. and Chile is also revealed in the larger repertoire of verb tenses found in U.S. commercials. There are a few possible reasons for the differing complexity:

- Chilean copywriters operate on a smaller budget than their U.S. counterparts,
- the advertising market is not as competitive in Chile as in the U.S. and, therefore, ad writers do not need to go to as great lengths to entertain the audience, and
- Chilean advertisers do not consider the viewing public to be as desirous of complex ads.

The emphasis on personal reference in U.S. ads may reflect the importance of individuality in U.S. society, which probably influences the design of Spanish ads here. In contrast, the relative lack of personal reference for ads in Spain is likely due to the brevity of the average ad on Antena 3 (ten seconds).

Positive politeness strategies are most frequent in the U.S. and Spain whereas they are least common in Chile. This difference suggests that U.S. and Spanish advertisers consider egalitarianism to be highly valued by their viewers. In contrast, the higher degree of negative politeness, power, and distancing strategies in Chile may reveal a society seen by advertisers as being stratified and class conscious. The least distancing strategies are found in Spain, and this is perhaps partially explained by the fact that formal reference (*usted* 'you [FRML]') is less frequent in colloquial use. Furthermore, the small number of female speakers, and particularly female announcers, in Chilean ads probably reveals advertisers' concepts of women and their subordinate role to males. Even in U.S. ads, females portrayed as authority figures or role models are uncommon. U.S. ads, however, do reveal more stereotypes of age, physical characteristics, and profession. U.S. advertisers perhaps believe that they have an understanding of the composition of their viewing public. The small number of speaker considerations in Spain is probably again due to the brevity of ads and lack of time to develop characters, although it may also reflect a strategy of advertisers to appeal to a wide audience.

Chilean ads contain the most violations of repetition, ellipsis, and phonological elements such as alliteration and rhymes, which are well-known devices in advertising language. This frequent usage may reflect the more formulaic ads found in the data. Similarly, pragmatic novelty is only found in U.S. ads and seems to be an advertising device borrowed from English ads. Frequent false assertions are probably not possible in Chilean ads because of station restrictions; however, they are common in U.S. ads. This fact may suggest that viewers in the U.S. are believed to be more tolerant of untruthfulness. Quantity violations regarding a lack of information or too much information occur in ads from Spain because of the combination of extremely brief (ten seconds) and very long (two minutes) ads in the data. The larger variety of maxim violations in the U.S. probably reflects the greater complexity of ads on Univisión than on other stations in the study.

Commercials from the U.S. also contain the most examples of flattery and endorsements. These strategies for persuasion perhaps suggest that Spanish advertisers on Univisión believe that viewers wish to be complimented and valued as individuals and that personal testimonies of a product's worth are influential in persuading U.S. viewers to buy. On the other hand, ads from Spain rarely contain flattery or endorsements; Spanish viewers may consider

5.1 Conclusions

these strategies to be too superficial and obvious. Spanish viewers are perhaps more cynical than their counterparts in the Americas. Advertisers in Spain believe that their audience requires ads that are shocking or sexually stimulating in order to capture their attention. Spanish advertisers seem to think that their viewers have become desensitized to the messages in ads. Finally, advertisers in Chile conceive of their viewers as being influenced and swayed by elements of nationalism. Such elements do not occur at all on the other two stations.

Thus, the pragmatic differences between commercials from Chile, Spain, and the U.S. reveal the different perceptions of ad writers from these three countries. Ads are constructed based on stereotypes of societies and their supposed cultural values and mores. In general, U.S. ads convey supposed values of a positive self-image, individuality, and egalitarianism, yet they are more prone to stereotype Spanish speakers and seem to be influenced by the wider U.S. (English-speaking) population. Ads from Spain suggest that sophistication, egalitarianism, and sensuality are considered appealing by Spanish society. Finally, Chilean ads emphasize nationalism, consciousness of status and class, and tradition and uniformity as societal values. Regardless of whether or not these values are true of the respective societies, advertisers *believe* that they are representative, and they are concepts used to persuade and to sell.

5.1.2 Summary of pragmatics and persuasion

(4) How are pragmalinguistic features of television advertising used to effect persuasion? Pragmalinguistic strategies in the data contribute to at least one of three components of persuasion: Memorability, Force, or Participation. As previously discussed in this chapter, representatives are the most widely used speech acts in Spanish advertising discourse. They are used primarily to strengthen the force or impact of the message, and they do so via assertions and reports. Because announcements refer to future events, they emphasize novelty and attract attention (Memorability).

Directives are also frequent in the data and generally augment both Force and Participation. For example, orders, suggestions, and recommendations are more direct than hints and threaten the viewer's fece more than representatives, commissives, and expressives do in the data. Most directives also require Participation, or a future act, on the part of the viewer (although the viewer may choose to ignore this requirement). Commissives and expressives are less unified classes than representatives and directives, but commissives tend to add to Memorability and Force. Expressives generally contribute to either Memorability or Force, although flattery also contributes to viewer participation.

Indexicals and politeness generally augment the Force component of persuasion. For example, deictic items and tense emphasize proximity and urgency to buy. Politeness strategies help to create emotional bonds with viewers or an illusion of freedom from imposition. Furthermore, both positive and negative politeness are employed as attempts to evoke responses from viewers (Participation).

Conventional implicatures add to Force by presupposing shared knowledge and opinions with viewers and by implying more than what is literally stated. Violations of Grice's Maxims and the resulting conversational implicatures contribute to both Force and Participation. That is, they serve to strengthen the message of an ad through metaphor, vagueness, and other means of creating additional nonliteral interpretations. Since viewers must "work out" implicatures, Participation is required from the audience for comprehension. Certain types of violations, such as repetition and most types of novelty, additionally contribute to the Memorability component of persuasion by drawing attention to a product or ad.

Finally, speaker considerations serve to augment the Force of a commercial by conveying authenticity, importance, and the implicit suggestion that viewers can become or are already beautiful, young, and successful. Furthermore, male announcers are important in Spanish advertising; they convey authority and power and are used frequently throughout the data.

Table 5.2 summarizes the contribution of all of the pragmatic strategies found in this study to effect persuasion, and they all contribute to at least one goal of persuasion.

Table 5.2 Summary of pragmatics and persuasion
(Key: ( ) = optional, — = no contribution)

Strategies	Memorability	Force	Participation
Speech acts:			
Representatives	—	Assertions	—
	(Reports)	Reports	—
	Announcements		—
Directives	—	Orders	Orders
	—	Requests	Requests
	—	Warnings	Warnings
	—	Suggestions	(Suggestions)
	—	Recommendations	(Recommendations)

5.1 Conclusions

Strategies	Memorability	Force	Participation
	—	—	Invitations
	(Instructions)	—	Instructions
	Attention-getters	—	—
Commissives	Offers	Offers	(Offers)
	(Apologies)	—	Apologies
	—	Promises	—
	—	Guarantees	—
	—	Disclaimers	—
Expressives	(Flattery)	Flattery	Flattery
	Introductions	—	(Introductions)
	Greetings	—	(Greetings)
	Leave-taking	—	(Leave-taking)
	—	Thanks	(Thanks)
	—	Congratulations	(Congratulations)
	—	Insults	—
Indexicals:	—	Deixis	—
	(Personal reference)	Personal reference	Personal reference
	—	Tense	—
Politeness:	—	Positive	Positive
	—	Negative	Negative
	—	Distance	—
	—	Solidarity	—
	—	Power	—
Implicature:	—	Conventional	—
	—	Conversational—	Conversational—
	(humor)	humor, other	humor, other
Violation of maxims:			
Quantity	—	Ellipsis/novelty—semantic	Ellipsis/novelty—semantic
	Repetition	Repetition	—
	—	Lack of information	(Lack of information)

Quality Strategies	(Metaphor) Memorability	Metaphor Force	Metaphor Participation
	—	Hyperbole	Hyperbole
	—	Irony	Irony
	—	False assertions	(False assertions)
Relation	(Implied relations)	Implied relations	Implied relations
	(Nonrelevance)	Nonrelevance	Nonrelevance
	—	Novelty—associational	Novelty—(associational)
Manner	—	Vagueness	Vagueness
	—	Rhet. questions	Rhet. questions
	Verbosity	Verbosity	—
	Novelty: explicit, pragmatic, lexical, syntactic, morphological, situational, associational	Novelty: — (lexical) (syntactic) (morphological) — associational, semantic	Novelty: — — — — (associational) semantic
	Phonology	Phonology	—
	Info. structure	Info. structure	—
Speaker considerations:	(Gender)	Gender	—
	—	Age	—
	—	Profession	—
	(Physical)	Physical	—
	(Endorsements)	Endorsements	—

5.2 Support of existing literature

The present study supports much of the existing literature on pragmatics, persuasion, and advertising. For example, it supports Rank (1988) and Leech's (1966) goals of advertising, with minor adjustments, and discusses many of the grammatical and rhetorical categories from Bolinger (1980) in pragmatic rather than grammatical and anecdotal terms. Since to date I am not aware that any large scale study of pragmatics in Spanish television advertising has been done, this study adds a new dimension to previous

5.2 Support of existing literature

linguistic studies of Spanish advertising. Furthermore, it expands on discussions of novelty found in Lakoff (1982) and of implicature found in Geis (1982). It also suggests that Lakoff's (1990) argument that politeness supersedes intelligibility in conversation may also be true in advertising. Moreover, her contention that women's speech is stereotypically illogical, submissive, and of secondary status seems true for advertising, since female announcers are seldom used. Men's language, on the other hand, is reflected as important talk, as she suggested. The present study goes beyond Lakoff's work in that it offers more pragmatic strategies by which those in power (advertisers) attempt to persuade their audiences to agree with them.

This study also supports literature specifically on the Spanish language. It goes beyond the so-called Spanish "barbarism studies" to discuss these anomalies in terms of violations of manner via novelty. My findings support Sánchez Corral's (1991) discussion of the effects of deixis in advertising; however, in this study I examine Spanish deixis in terms of pragmatics rather than classical rhetoric. I support Delbecque and Leuven's (1990) presentation on Spanish nonrational arguments with examples of implicature and violations of quality via metaphor in the data. Fant's (1984) argument that the more known a theme is, the less it is syntactically represented is reinforced in the data through syntactic novelty and slogans, in which missing information is assumed or implied and through information structure, which advertisers use to emphasize previously unknown information. Use of word order for emotional highlighting, as described by Silva-Corvalán (1983), is also found in the data.

This study lends support to Kumatoridiani's (1984) study of the underlying communicative act of advertising discourse. He maintained that opinion was the primary speech act for ads. This is supported in that representatives, and specifically assertions, form the most frequent class of speech acts. Koike's (1994) continuum for directives in Spanish is supported by the directives found in this study and their contribution to the force of the message, based on varying degrees of illocutionary force. Haverkate's (1990) suggestion that the conditional may imply distance is supported in the data by the fact that it is infrequently used in ads, since ads attempt proximity rather than distance from the audience. Finally, Haverkate's (1993:178) statement that commissives are a less uniform class than expressives is true in the data if we apply it to their contributions to persuasion. Thus, the results of the present study generally support previous analyses of pragmatics, persuasion, and advertising, but it is unique in offering a combination of these three areas as applied to Spanish data and goes beyond previous studies of Spanish advertising language by specifying how pragmatic strategies contribute to persuasion. It is an in-depth pragmatic analysis of Spanish persuasive discourse as found in television advertising.

5.3 Applications, limitations, and implications

5.3.1 Applications for teaching

Results from this study's pragmatic approach to persuasion hold valuable applications to Spanish teaching (and perhaps, by extension, to the teaching of other foreign languages). At the elementary level of Spanish, videos of advertisements might be useful in consciousness-raising regarding pragmatic strategies such as basic politeness. Contrastive ads using positive and negative politeness strategies might be used to illustrate differences in communicating similar messages. Although the goal is not for our students to speak Spanish as if they are in an advertisement, teachers can use short, easily comprehended ads as examples of discourse and how to avoid insulting one's audience. Ads might also be contrasted with video clips of ordinary conversation to demonstrate the differences between persuasive and nonpersuasive speech.

In a similar way, contrastive videos of advertising and ordinary conversation could be used in conversational classes to show both the differences and similarities between the two forms of discourse. That is, ads could be discussed in terms of the ways in which they attempt ordinary conversation. They could also be used to illustrate the importance of context in speech. Pragmatic strategies that are effective within the context of advertising may not be desirable or effective in other contexts. The importance of context could also be brought into cultural elements of Spanish classes at all levels, via the contrast mentioned. Furthermore, ads might be used to illustrate elements of Hispanic culture, since advertising largely reflects desires, mannerisms, accent, humor, and perceptions that copywriters have of their audiences. Spanish ads also illustrate stereotypes and generalizations about Hispanic society. Thus, examples from Spain, Chile, and the U.S. are useful for portraying generalizations about culture in the Spanish-speaking world and for discussing the problems with stereotyping.

Advertising can also be used in writing and reading components of courses at all levels as examples of persuasive/hortatory discourse, especially when contrasted with other discursive forms. Writing classes might use ads to illustrate the types of speech acts, politeness, and implicature commonly used in persuasive speech and writing. Moreover, discussion of advertising discourse might be helpful in teaching students how to "read between the lines" and how to interpret implicatures and some types of humor.

An understanding of conventional and conversational implicatures would also be important in Spanish classes for special purposes such as law. For example, violations of quantity are frequently used in law. Lawyers should learn how to be as informative as necessary for the purpose of a conversational exchange. Advertising discourse provides examples where speakers regularly violate quantity. Medical Spanish classes could also be taught how to directly and indirectly persuade via varying speech acts, politeness, and implicatures. Viewing ads portraying speakers that convey power or status might also be helpful for future medical personnel, especially if they are young and wish to be respected.

This study also has applications for Spanish linguistics classes in that videos of ads could be used to teach persuasion in a specified context. Sample ads could be shown in class to illustrate various subtleties of the Spanish language with pragmatic examples in a context that students are familiar with in English. Hence, students might be able to grasp abstract pragmatic concepts such as politeness and implicature from viewing numerous examples and describing what they believe the intent of the strategy to be. Similarly, different types of speech acts within a given class, such as directives, might be discussed with respect to their varying degrees of forcefulness and whether or not they require participation from the hearer/audience in a specified context. In this way, students might be given not just an awareness but also practice with varying degrees of persuasion.

Finally, and perhaps most obviously, pragmatics and its relation to persuasion have applications to teaching Spanish for business students, both in university and workplace settings. In many ways, the goal of Business Spanish is to learn how to encourage consumerism and how to persuade in a foreign language. More importantly, future businessmen and women need to learn how to avoid offense and the subtleties of using language in a particular context. They must learn, for example, the importance of family in Hispanic culture and of showing an interest in the audience before getting down to business. This and other contextual knowledge might be illustrated via video examples of ads. One of the primary goals of advertisers is to avoid offense; they, therefore, employ politeness strategies based on perceptions of their audience. Understanding and the contribution of major pragmatic strategies to the three components of persuasion (Memorability, Force, and Participation) would be especially important for students of marketing, entrepreneurialship, advertising, and public relations. Students might be asked to discuss whether strategies that they see in Spanish examples would sell to an English audience. Class discussion might also focus on contrasts between ads from different cultures. Ultimately, the goal in teaching the pragmatics of persuasion in Business Spanish classes would be to help students practice the art of persuasion and be able to persuade using the language of the Hispanic business world.

5.3.2 Limitations of the study

One limitation of the present study is that it does not include every aspect of pragmatics. To cover every possible pragmatic strategy would pass far beyond the scope of this study. Nevertheless, I believe that the major pragmatic strategies are accounted for. Another limitation is that ads were transcribed due to the lack of original copywritten texts for analysis. Translations and many of the transcriptions were checked by native speakers in an attempt to avoid errors. Furthermore, the television stations used in this study, although as similar as possible, are not identical in nature. Ideally, all three would have been private and nonreligious stations, but this was not possible for stations with large audiences in Chile. Although I consulted with native speakers, I did not have the luxury of a complete analysis by another investigator to further corroborate the results. Finally, this study only looked at the illocutionary intent of speech acts and did not measure the perlocutionary effect of the message on native speakers.

5.3.3 Implications of study and further research

Further research would obtain native speaker reactions and look at perlocutionary effect of pragmatic strategies. Native speaker reactions might also reveal interesting dialectal differences in interpretations and ad preference. A study of native speaker reactions might contribute more to our understanding of the pragmatics of persuasion in Spanish. Research in the future could also reveal interesting issues regarding the diachronic study of linguistic and pragmatic changes in the Spanish language as seen in an advertising context. An in-depth study involving teaching the pragmatics of persuasion might also yield interesting results. For example, a study into the nature of misunderstanding and misinterpretation of pragmatics in advertising might be undertaken using reactions to ads by nonnative Spanish students. Finally, examination of the role of pragmatic strategies in other contexts of persuasive discourse such as televangelism and political speeches might add to our understanding of Spanish pragmatics and its contribution to persuasion.

5.4 Conclusion

Although advertising generally tries to make its products and services appear novel, the language and pragmatic strategies of Spanish ads are highly conventionalized. These strategies are related to three primary goals of persuasion: Memory, Force, and Participation. Furthermore, all of the pragmatic categories used for analysis occur in the majority of ads and are reflective of advertising discourse. The pragmatic strategies found in the data also reveal distributive patterns according to the country of origin.

My hope is that this study will contribute to the cross-linguistic understanding of the pragmatics of persuasion by providing (1) an application of supposed universal pragmatic concepts to the Spanish language and (2) another large database from which to compare other languages in future research. This study may also add to a cross-dialectal understanding of Spanish pragmatics, an area in which there is little information in the literature. The study provides a detailed account of a specific genre or register of Spanish discourse, that of television advertising, to offer further insight into ways of persuading in Spanish.

As noted, the study also has potential applications to the teaching of pragmatics in Spanish language classrooms, with particular applications to the teaching of Spanish for Business. The ability to appropriately weave linguistic form around meaning in a given context is an essential part of functioning successfully in a language and culture. Advertisements provide a clear context for examples of language in use and, as such, real-life examples for language teaching.

Given the vital role of the media in society and on language, Spanish television advertising reflects the pragmatic and sociolinguistic communication of persuasion by and to Spanish speakers. As Lakoff (1990:2) stated, "Knowledge of special language is power, normally reserved for the professionals; but there is no law that prevents the power from being spread around the larger community through greater understanding....The trick for all of us is to grasp the generalizations, the larger picture" between the form of a communication and the power it provides its user. This study into the pragmatics of persuasion helps us understand how writers of Spanish ads wield power over their viewers and how they attempt to both create and reflect the public's conceptions, values, and mores.

Finally, the same components of persuasion demonstrated in advertising are also present in this study. I hope the role of pragmatic strategies in persuasion as described in this study may attract additional study and be useful for Spanish linguists and teachers. If so, then this study will have met its goals and will also have applied three components of persuasion (Memorability, Force, and Participation) to influence the reader's understanding of pragmatics in Spanish persuasive discourse.

Appendix A
A Critical Review of Literature

A brief history of advertising

Consumer advertising as we know it today developed in the latter half of the nineteenth century, with the ordinary housewife as its primary target. Nonetheless, some conventional elements of advertising language were discovered as far back as ancient Roman times in lost and found notices. Leech (1966:168) asserted that by the 1920s the character of modern advertising language had emerged and that one of its primary features was a simple, personal, colloquial style unlike the formal one of older advertisements. Great Britain was the first country to introduce a public television service in 1936 (Henry 1986), but the American advertising industry seems to have the greatest influence on international television advertising.

The 1960s seem to have marked a turning point in advertising trends in the United States. Previously, ads had been fairly conservative and the typical catchphrase for advertising agencies was, "Don't make waves" (Buxton 1972:43). The decade of 1960 to 1970, however, witnessed a creative shift in advertising strategy because of increasing competition. In the 1970s, marketing research and governmental regulations became responsible for the bulk of changes in advertising strategy (ibid:80). Other changes in American advertising strategy from the 1960s to the 1980s included

- emphasis on individual rather than mass audiences and on warm feelings as opposed to a hard sell approach,
- a more complex lexicon,
- advances in technology,

- an increasing number of foreign accents,
- wider variation in voice selection for announcers, and
- shorter commercials (Franklin, 1984).

In the United States, the primary carrier for television advertising in Spanish is Univisión, followed by Telemundo (Tobenkin 1997). One of its main platforms has been via *Sábado Gigante,* Spanish television's most popular show (Treister 1988). Roslow and Nicholls (1996) found that both Spanish-dominant and bilingual viewers were more persuaded when exposed to commercials in Spanish embedded in Spanish television programs, than similar commercials in English embedded in English television programs. Their measure of persuasion was based on the viewers' intention to purchase. U.S. advertising directed at Spanish and bilingual speakers is often based on the ideas of Latino marketing specialists, who try to define Latino culture and its preferred goods and use. They may assign buying practices to a stereotypical Latino culture and promote this constructed culture as general knowledge (Astroff 1997). For example, Maso-Fleischman (1997) asserted that unlike general market ads that tend to be postmodern, ads for Hispanic audiences were more traditional.

In Spain there were only two television channels until 1983: TVE 1 and TVE 2, both run by the state (Palacio 1993). Six regional channels, each supported by its own regional government began in the 1980s. In 1989, Canal+, Antena 3, and Tele 5 were issued licenses as private channels. Growth of advertising expenditures slowed in 1990, provoking stiff competition. Thus, Antena 3 and Tele 5 were forced into the position of offering advertisers free ad space. Between 1991 and 1992, air time allotted to advertising rose from 2,368 hours to 3,354 hours, resulting in cheaper ad time. Competition between both private and public channels remains fierce. Nevertheless, Spain was the only major European market that was able to continue its double-digit growth in ad spending in 1991 and forecasters predicted continued growth (Advertising 1991). The top ten advertisers in 1987 were Citroën, El Corte Inglés, Renault, Ford, Henkel, the Ministry of the Economy, Peugeot, SEAT, Nestlé, and Unilever (European Advertising 1990).

In Chile private television arrived following the 1990 takeover from Pinochet by a more democratic government (Ehrmann 1991). In the early 1990s, foreign investors scrambled to get into Chile; however, due to sizable losses in 1996, an overcrowded broadcast market, and low ratings for foreign shows, investors were hurrying to get out of the Chilean market (Paxman 1996).

This brief overview of television advertising in its historical context demonstrates the variety of external influences on the industry.

The language of advertising

Copywriting

Clever copywriters are best able to write a persuasive commercial and are adept language users, though not necessarily aware of the pragmatic strategies and linguistic devices they employ. Five masters of the art of writing advertising are: William Bernbach, Leo Burnett, George Gribbin, David Ogilvy, and Rosser Reeves. Bernbach stated, "I think the most important element in success in ad writing is the product itself." (Higgins 1990:23). Gribbin similarly discussed the importance of knowing a great deal about a product and its consumers and encouraged the use of the vernacular, using language that surrounds us in colorful ways. He also maintained that the first thing to mark a good writer "is that he avoids the cliché" (p. 61). Burnett suggested that the ad writer should always be tuned in to ways of "putting usual things in unusual relationships that get attention and aptly express an idea" (p. 47). Reeves and Ogilvy emphasized the problem of writing an ad to shock or entertain in order to be remembered and how useless such a strategy was if the product itself was forgotten. From such statements it is evident that the focus of copywriters tends to be more psychological than linguistic in nature.

Consider also a list of advice from the well-known advertising genius, David Ogilvy (1985), which demonstrates that copywriting is primarily focused on consumer product loyalty. He noted research suggesting types of commercials that were above and below average in their ability to change the audience's brand preference. Those that were above average included testimonials with loyal users and unusual characters, truly funny commercials, slice of life playlets, demonstrations, problem-solution ads, talking heads (a pitchman extolling the virtues of a product), relevant characters, Reason Why commercials (give a rational reason for buying the product), created news, and emotion. Those types that were below average included testimonials by celebrities, cartoons for adults (although they were successful for children), musical vignettes with fleeting images and no words, and explicit comparisons of a product with its competitor (viewers tended to regard the disparaged competitor as the hero of the ad).

Ogilvy also suggested the following auditory and visual tips for creating a good commercial, paraphrased as follows (110–112).

Auditory
1. Identify the brand name within the first ten seconds.
2. When you have nothing to say, sing it.

3. Use sound effects, such as sausages sizzling in a frying pan.
4. Reinforce the promise by superimposing it auditorily (or in type).
5. Use mnemonic devices.
6. Make commercials crystal clear. (Between nineteen and forty percent of viewers may misunderstand a given ad.)

Visual
1. Show the package.
2. Show food in motion to make it look appetizing.
3. Use close-ups of the product.
4. Grab the attention in the first frame with a visual surprise.
5. Have actors talk on camera rather than as voice-overs.
6. Avoid visual banality.
7. Use a plethora of short scenes.
8. Show the product in use.
9. Technicians can produce anything you want.
10. Cut actors out of the ad if you need to save money.

Note that his suggestions do not include advice on how to achieve linguistically the goal of persuasion, yet he himself argued that ads without words are below average in their ability to sell a product.

Pragmatics in advertising discourse

The art of persuasion or rhetoric is at least as old as early Greek literature although the rhetorical practices of persuasion are not always the same in all cultures. Persuasive discourse is the nonreciprocal "attempt or intention of one party to change the behavior, feelings, intentions, or viewpoint of another by communicative means" (R. Lakoff 1982:28). Propaganda, political rhetoric, and religious sermons are a few examples of persuasive discourse. Moreover, advertising is clearly one type of persuasive discourse, since its purpose is to change the buying behavior of its audience. By constructing taxonomies, Lakoff contrasted various types of persuasive discourse. Hence, advertising discourse, which is nonreciprocal, nonegalitarian, scripted, publicly accessible, and constrained by time, was contrasted with ordinary conversation, which is reciprocal, egalitarian, spontaneous, and not generally constrained by time. Schmidt and Kess (1986) likewise found many similarities between two types of persuasive discourse, television advertising, and televangelism, particularly in the area of novelty and use of implicature.

Pragmatic study is useful in analyzing advertising, a particular context of persuasive discourse. The definition of pragmatics used in this study is "the study of the relationship between language, its communication, and its contextualized use" (Koike 1996). There have been a number of linguistic studies on advertising language, though few have explicitly emphasized pragmatics. Some of the major linguistic works are as follows.

Leech (1966) detailed the linguistic devices most often found in standard advertising English of Great Britain. He argued that a successful ad typically must accomplish four things in sequence. An ad must:

- draw attention to itself,
- sustain the interest,
- be remembered or recognized as familiar, and
- prompt the right kind of action.

He further argued that the most important linguistic means of conveying television advertising messages is by means of the spoken commentary. Some of the devices emphasized included: direct address, or speech directed to the viewer as opposed to other secondary participants such as characters in an ad; the public-colloquial style of ads; grammatical categories such as imperatives, adjectives, sentence coordination, and rhetorical questions; and semantic items such as vagueness of reference, novelty, and figurative language. His primary purpose was to characterize the most common features of advertising language.

Though not a quantitative study per se, Bolinger (1980) described the use of language as a "loaded weapon" and cited numerous examples from advertising. Like Leech, he detailed common linguistic strategies found in advertising, with emphasis on the use of literalism, euphemism, economic metaphors of time, power, and value, and nice sounding illogic. While much of his book is anecdotal in nature, it provides a useful overview of strategies of persuasive and manipulative language.

In a collaborative report with advertising practitioners, O'Barr (1979) researched the cause-effect relationship between advertising message structure and its memorability. He divided the message structure into three semantic units: the condition or problem necessitating use, the product or service advertised, and the qualities or benefits to be derived. Of particular interest was the effect of various ways of linking these units. His study may be applicable when analyzing types of selling arguments across languages.

Another study, emphasizing semantics/pragmatics, was that of Garfinkel (1978) who analyzed over 200 American television commercials in terms of their truthfulness and structure. He analyzed notions of assertion, presupposition, and implication and discovered that most ads relayed information by means of implication. Furthermore, the truth of such propositions depended on the viewer's assumptions. He also analyzed the structure of ads with respect to openings and closings. Many of his findings were of a preliminary nature and, as he admitted, required future study.

Kumatoridiani (1984) analyzed the organizational structure of advertising discourse based on the underlying communicative acts. He examined taxonomies of discourse and from these first concluded that the initial communicative act of OPINION is the universal communicative act of advertising discourse (AD). The supporting act of INFORMING was also considered to be a universal act of AD, although its propositional content varies according to the type of ad (product, quality, or situation). Thus, the act of opinion occurs regardless of the type of ad and expresses the copywriter's belief/judgment. The act of informing is performed in order to strategically achieve the goal of expressing an opinion and is accomplished by means of different types of information units. Finally, these units lead to shallower communicative acts that vary greatly and are not universal in AD. The following schema was, therefore, proposed to account for the communicative process in advertising (p. 116).

> OPINION   You ought to buy our product.
>
> Strategy   Give accounts by explicating the basis of OPINION.
> ↓
> INFORM   Presentation of information units: product, quality, and situation
>
> Shallower communicative acts

In another pragmatic analysis, Lakoff (1982) used advertising examples to argue that clear examples of persuasive discourse involve violations of Grice's Cooperative Principle and the Maxim of Manner. She considered advertising to thrive on novelty and suggested that neologisms in advertising flout the Maxim of Manner by attracting attention and making the audience remember. She maintained that advertising superficially adheres to the Cooperative Principle in order to conceal appeals to the audience's emotions. They, therefore, contain an appeal to our knowledge of how the Cooperative Principle works. Some of Lakoff's neologisms are illustrated in example (1) in chapter 1. Lakoff's essay is helpful in that it analyzes just one common pragmatic feature of ads. A few other studies of novelty in advertising include the study of wordplay in product names (Nilsen 1979) and of prosodic cues and semantic selection in information processing of commercials (Coleman 1983).

In another pragmatic analysis, Geis (1982) examined ways in which advertisers use conversational implicatures to persuade and manipulate their audience. Some of the persuasive strategies he analyzed included:

conventional, theoretical, and conversational implicatures; use of modal verbs, comparatives, special words and phrases, styles and registers; and disclaimers. He also demonstrated that even children are able to understand conversational implicatures in advertising, arguing for a pragmatist theory of truth in advertising in which advertisers would be held responsible for what they conversationally implicate. That is, Geis asserted that advertisers normally make the strongest claims they can. Therefore, he believed that advertisers should be held responsible not only for what they *assert* to be true but also for what they *imply* to be true.

Thus, in the studies examined above the authors focused on the most common linguistic devices in English advertising, linguistic strategies of manipulation, units of advertising message structure, openings and closings in commercials, the underlying communicative acts of advertising, the use of novelty to violate Grice's Maxim of Manner in ads, and the use of conversational implicature to manipulate viewers.

Studies of Spanish advertising

Linguistic studies of Spanish advertising language have generally focused on: the corrupting phonological and lexical influences on the Spanish language by television ads, the rhetoric of persuasion with examples from advertising, or on a particular discursive element. Some of these Spanish studies are as follows.

Fernández (1988) examined phonetic and phonological anomalies and "barbarisms" now found in Spanish as a result of the media and its introduction of foreign elements. Fontanillo and Riesco (1990) likewise enumerated the lexical "perversion" of the Spanish language by television. In a departure from such studies, Ávila (1994) examined the quantity and types of lexical borrowing found on the radio and television. His conclusion, based on a statistical comparison between media language and *la lengua culta* 'the language or intellectuals', was that there were more similarities than differences and that television does not impoverish the language. Nevertheless, he argued for unity within diversity, stating the need for television to generally utilize a Spanish dialect that is understood internationally and use regionalisms within the context of natural conversation such as in soap operas.

Other studies of Spanish advertising have concentrated on the rhetoric of persuasion with examples from advertising (Briz Gómez et al. 1987; Delbecque and Leuven 1990; Moreno Fernández 1990). Briz Gómez, Pruñonosa Tomás, and Serra Alegre (1987) examined the use of classical rhetoric in five television ads for television sets, demonstrating the similarity between ad structure (clincher, body, and slogan) and rhetorical structure (beginning, development, denouement).

Delbecque and Leuven (1990) also examined the power of suggestion in a year's worth of newspaper ads from *El País Semanal*. They particularly emphasized the use of prelogic, or nonrational arguments, to create psychological and emotional ideas about a product, and they determined which values were promoted the most. They found images and language depicting friendship and male-female relationships to be central concepts. Connotation or implication by means of association with these and other concepts was seen as a key method of achieving persuasion. Furthermore, exploitation of metaphor was considered a basic mechanism.

Moreno Fernández (1990) described manipulation in the media of elements such as orthography and phonetics (alliteration and intonation), grammar (syntactic ambiguity), creation of gender-neutral morphemes such as *nueves ministris* 'new ministers'), the lexicon (euphemism, use of qualifying adverbs), and metalanguage based on politics or economics (use of statistics, technical jargon). The intent of the article was to expose some linguistic methods of manipulation in the media.

Finally, Sánchez Corral (1991) examined deictic markers as a persuasive strategy in advertising discourse. He examined the egocentric elements, *yo/nosotros-aquí-ahora* 'I/we-here-now' and their transmission of proximity. First person is contrasted with the use of second person, both to refer to and link the audience with the product, as in *Los Seat y tú estáis de moda* 'Seats and you are in style.' Third person reference, however, is generally absent, creating the idea that first and second person participants are positive members of the discourse, whereas third person members connote negative ideas of exclusion and indefiniteness. Moreover, use of possessive deictics create an identification between the imaginary you and the image of the product, as though the product had actually been acquired. Verbs of movement and changes of spatial deixis are often used to suggest the possibility of change from unhappiness (or not wanting to buy) to happiness (wanting the product/buying it). Similarly, temporal deixis often presupposes a transformation, a before and after for the acquisition of a product, as well as the identification of the product with urgency and the euphoric moment (now). Indeed, the function of deixis in advertising is to unidirectionally direct the viewer's attention and simultaneously organize his attention in order to avoid any deviation from the desired interpretation. Thus, Sánchez Corral viewed deictic markers as pragmatic strategies for persuasion.

In summary, the authors of these Spanish studies of advertising focused on

- neologisms or so-called perversion of the language by the media,
- the use of classical rhetorical devices in ads,

- exploitation of metaphor as a method of achieving persuasion,
- linguistic methods of manipulation, and
- deictic markers as pragmatic strategies of persuasion in ads.

Pragmatic categories addressed in this study

In the present study, I draw from four major categories in the field of pragmatics that I believe are especially relevant to persuasion in advertising. The areas of particular interest concern speech acts, indexicality, politeness, and Grice's theory. Relevant literature on these theories is presented in the following sections.

Speech acts

Speech acts, as defined by Goffman (1974), are frames with a conventional meaning or intent, such as requests, orders, and apologies. The concept of speech acts was developed by the philosophers, Searle and Austin, from the basic insight that language is not just to describe the world, but to perform a range of actions that are identifiable from the performance of the utterance itself (Schiffrin 1994). The study of speech acts, therefore, focuses upon knowledge of underlying conditions for production and interpretation of acts via words. Speech acts are relevant to persuasion in advertising because the intent of an ad is reflected in the types of speech acts selected. Moreover, the linguistic realization of particular speech acts and the context of utterance help shape the degree to which a commercial is successful in persuading viewers to buy.

Austin (1962) noted three basic types of acts: locutionary, the physical utterance; illocutionary, the communication of intent; and perlocutionary, how the intent is acted on. Speech acts are primarily understood in terms of felicity conditions and illocutionary force, the conventional way that a speaker communicates an intent. Drawing from Austin's ideas, Searle (1969) proposed a number of felicity conditions for speech acts. Each speech act contains a proposition and an illocutionary force expressing the speaker's psychological state (the sincerity condition), the speaker's linguistic goal (the essential condition), and the relation of the speaker's words to the state of the world (direction of fit). As one example, Searle proposed the following conditions for directives: a propositional content condition wherein the speaker predicates a future act of the hearer, a preparatory condition of ability (the addressee has the ability to perform the action), a sincerity condition (the speaker wants the hearer to do the act), and the essential condition (the speaker attempts to get the hearer to do the act).

Mey (1993:132) summarized the meaning of Searle's term, 'fit,' stating that it describes the correspondence between reality and language. Thus, in a words-to-world fit, language is fitted to the environment, as in describing scenery, or reporting an event. In a world-to-words fit, however, the speaker changes the world by what is said, as in directives and commissives. The bidirectional fit of declarations creates a state of reality that is based on a previous state. Finally, when there is no fit at all, as in expressives, there may not be any strict correspondence between what the speaker says and what the situation is like.

Austin's (1962) classification of speech acts consisted of five categories: verdictives, expositives, exercitives, behabitives, and commissives. In later work, Searle (1976, 1977, 1979) similarly proposed five major classes for speech acts based on the illocutionary point of the act and its fit with the world. They are adapted from Reiss (1985:31) as follows.

>Representatives
>*decir, insistir, quejarse de, jurar (que), deducir*
>state, insist, complain, swear, deduce
>
>Directives
>*sugerir, mandar, invitar, advertir, aconsejar*
>suggest, order, invite, warn, advise
>
>Commissives
>*prometer, ofrecer, negar, amenazar, garantizar*
>promise, offer, refuse, threaten, guarantee
>
>Expressives
>*agradecer, disculparse, felicitar, dar la bienvenida a, condolerse*
>thank, apologize, congratulate, welcome, condole
>
>Declarations
>*nombrar, nominar, maldecir, bautizar, excomunicar*
>name, nominate, curse, baptize, excommunicate

The illocutionary point of representatives (more recently known as ASSERTIVES) is to represent a state of affairs with a words-to-world fit. Their function is to convey information. The speaker's belief is expressed and any proposition can occur. The point of directives, however, is to use a world-to-words fit to direct the hearer towards doing some future action. Commissives commit the speaker to doing some future action and the direction of fit is world-to-words. They create stable expectations about speakers' behavior. Expressives, on the other hand, merely express some psychological state and there is no direction of fit. Haverkate (1984) defines expressives as acts that establish a particular interpersonal relation between the speaker and the hearer. Reiss (1985:35) further suggested that expressives "convey the feelings and attitudes of speakers toward hearers." Finally, the point of declarations (also called PERFORMATIVES) is to bring about some action. The direction of fit is both words-to-world and world-to-words and no psychological state is expressed. Thus, a declaration may contain any type of proposition and the verb generally names the action taking place. Declarations consequently "create facts of language and classification" (Reiss 1985:34).

See also Reiss 1985:29 for a summary of the kinds of illocutionary acts.

Table A.1 Kinds of illocutionary acts (Reiss 1985:29)

	Essential condition	Sincerity condition	Direction of fit	Propositions
Assertives	Commits speaker to something being described	Speaker believes (X)	Speaker tries to get words to match the world	(X)
Declarations	Successful performance guarantees correspondence of words to world	No psychological state expressed	Saying makes the world and words match	(X)
Commissives	Commits speaker to some future course of action	Speaker intends (to do action)	Speaker tries to get the world to match words	Speaker does action in the future
	Essential condition	Sincerity condition	Direction of fit	Propositions

Directives	Counts as an attempt by speaker to get hearer to do something	Speaker wants (hearer to do action)	Speaker tries to get the world to match words	Hearer does action in the future
Expressives	Commits speaker to the expression of psychological state	A psychological variable (attitude toward hearer)	World and words assumed to match	Speaker/ hearer + property

Directives seem to be the most frequently studied type of speech act. Haverkate (1984), using Spanish and English data, further divided this class into two categories: IMPOSITIVES and NONIMPOSITIVES. The former refers to speech acts that influence the hearer to perform an action for the benefit of the speaker, such as orders and requests. Nonimpositives are seen to be different in that the result of the action is supposed to primarily benefit the hearer, as in advice, recommendations, and invitations.

Directives may be direct or indirect in force. Generally, the most direct forms of speech acts are legitimized when the power-differential between participants is great. Nevertheless, explicit directives are common in advertising, perhaps because straight talk is assumed to be honest or because the consumer feels that he is not threatened by the imperatives because he can opt not to obey them (Fowler, Hodge, Kress, and Trew 1979). Indirectness requires the addressees to infer meaning and rely on shared knowledge between the speaker and themselves. Lakoff (1990) pointed out that when conversation is on a risk-free topic, indirectness is puzzling and unlikely.

Conventional indirectness, according to Blum-Kulka (1989), consists of pragmatic duality. The speaker makes a conventional implicature and the hearer makes an inference, passing over the literal interpretation to infer the implicit intent of the speaker. The illocutionary force of a directive may also be softened through mitigation and deictic strategies that distance or defocalize the speakers from their deictic center (Koike 1992; Haverkate 1984). Blum-Kulka (1989) noted that conventional indirectness was most frequently used across languages for requests and that Spanish speakers were more hearer-oriented than the other languages in her study, using few mitigation strategies in requests.

Nonconventional indirectness, on the other hand, is pragmatically ambiguous and forces the hearer to rely on knowledge other than conventions. If an utterance is entirely nonconventional, the utterance is not understood as a speech act. Thus, Grice's Maxims are crucial to interpreting nonconventional implicature.

Although there is some disagreement about how to determine the exact illocutionary force of speech acts, Wierzbicka (1991) argued that illocutionary force is indeed determinable through analysis of BUNDLES of semantic and syntactic components of speech act verbs. She suggested a trial and error approach to analysis by comparing the illocutionary force of related acts and describing them in terms of semantic primitives. She argued that this method was the best way to avoid language specific classification of speech acts. While her analysis is intriguing, it is labor-intensive and allows for more speech act classes than are useful for the present study. I, therefore, prefer Searle's classification in that it is more widely accepted and more practical for the purposes of this study.

One problem with both Austin and Searle's theories of speech acts is that they tend to operate on the one sentence—one case principle and they refer to isolated utterances without discussing the context (Mey 1993:170). Furthermore, Searle (1975:76–77) regarded differences in indirect speech forms from one language to another to be due to conventionalized idiomatic expressions. Wierzbicka (1991) criticized his view, arguing that the general mechanisms for indirect speech acts are not universal and that they are motivated by differences in cultural norms. She instead considered the general mechanisms for speech acts to be culture-specific and argued for descriptions of speech acts in terms of "natural semantic metalanguage" (1991:130). Fitch and Sanders (1994) also argued against a universalist approach to the study of directives. Using data from three cultures, they instead concluded that directives are often preferred and their use is influenced by situational social factors and culture-specific beliefs about relationships and power. Unfortunately, speech act theory has tended to use English as its basic model.

Two pragmatists who have examined speech acts in Spanish are Haverkate (1984, 1993) and Koike (1992, 1994). (Although data from Koike 1992 are from Brazilian Portuguese, her analysis and conclusions also apply to Spanish.) Haverkate (1984) examined various types of speech acts in Spanish, including linguistic forms that serve to mitigate, defocalize, and reflect politeness. In a more recent article, Haverkate (1993) examined Spanish expressives and commissives. He noted that it is courteous in Spanish to reestablish the cost-benefit balance through expressions such as *de nada* or *no hay de qué* 'it's nothing'. Haverkate found expressives to be a somewhat uniform class in which the predominant courtesy was negative and strategies relied on a cost-benefit analysis. Commissives, however, predominantly relied on positive courtesy and were less uniform, containing an extensive list of strategies.

Koike (1994) examined two types of directives: Spanish and English requests and suggestions. She found that negation does not always communicate politeness or mitigation in all speech acts and that it may actually have the opposite effect. Her study illustrates some other cross-linguistic differences in expressing speech acts. In English suggestions, negation is optional and connotes a stronger force. In Spanish, however, a negative element is part of the conventional formula for interrogative suggestions, yet there is no demanding effect or stronger illocutionary force. Furthermore, negation is optional in both English and Spanish requests, but a negative element in English is often used for a more insistent second request after the initial request has already been rejected once. The Spanish counterpart sounds more like a plea and the speaker generally expects an affirmative answer. (See Koike 1994:518, 524 for illustrations of suggestions and requests in English and Spanish.)

Speech acts are relevant to persuasion in advertising because they convey the conventional meaning or intent of a commercial. Classification of speech acts in ads according to Searle's five major categories helps reveal the intent of copywriters and the degree of illocutionary force employed to achieve their goal of persuading viewers to purchase the advertised product or service. The underlying context of advertising determines the felicity conditions of a particular ad. Although an ad may order the viewer to buy, the advertiser does not have the inherent authority to do so. Hence, the illocutionary force of directives is diminished. Advertisers use the concept of FIT (whether they are aware of it or not) to attempt to make language describe their view of reality, or at least the view they want their audience to have. Furthermore, the type of speech act selected determines how direct/indirect the message of an ad will be. A speech act that is ambiguous as to its illocutionary intent or that is indirect is less likely to be offensive to a viewer.

In light of the criticisms of Searle's speech act theory, studies of speech acts in Spanish are important when examining how speech acts are effected in individual languages. Both Haverkate's (1984, 1993) and Koike's (1992, 1994) studies reveal differences in the way that speech acts are communicated in Spanish when compared with other languages such as English and Dutch. Their studies also relate to the pragmatic categories of indexicals and politeness.

Indexical expressions

Another important area of pragmatics is the study of indexicality. Indexical expressions are words or phrases whose reference cannot be determined without taking into account the context of the utterance (Green 1989). Hence, indexical expressions point to elements of the context of utterance such as time, place, speaker, and topic of utterance. Such expressions are commonly referred to by the term DEIXIS, or words that signal. Green (1989) stated that deictic reference involves a relation between an object in the world and a linguistic form with no semantically determined reference. Similarly, Levinson (1983:54) stated that deixis "concerns the ways in which languages encode or grammaticalize features of the *context of utterances,* or *speech event.*" Generally, deictic elements are organized in an egocentric manner. Deixis is, therefore, an orientational device to give some system for one's perspective. Thus, deictic strategies are often used in advertising to try to organize the audience's understanding of an ad and to convey the advertiser's perspective.

Fillmore (1971) suggested three types of deixis: person, space, and time. Person, or social deixis, refers to the roles of participants in discourse. Social deixis includes pronominal alternates, honorifics, humiliatives, and vocatives. Lakoff (1990) described, for example, how first person plural pronouns may be used as a powerful emotional force to convey inclusion and united common interests or exclusion and power/authority. Koike (1989b) noted how use of second person reference in Spanish may convey status to the hearer and may distance the proposition from the speaker's deictic center. She found hearer-based propositions to be more polite than speaker-based ones.

The deictic center is generally the speaker's point of reference, although expression of this center may shift in order to emphasize particular meanings. For instance, Haverkate (1984:56–58) described certain focalizing expressions that "bring into prominence the role of the referent in the state of affairs described." These were contrasted with defocalizing expressions that "keep silent the role of the referent in the state of affairs described." Thus, egocentric reference is a method of focalizing and bringing the speaker's role into prominence, whereas certain expressions such as *su servidor* 'your servant' may serve to defocalize or show modesty on the part of the speaker. The framing of an utterance to reflect the hearer's perspective is one way that the deictic system is used to convey politeness. Shifting the deictic center may, therefore, account for varying pragmatic effects of politeness.

Spatial deixis includes demonstrative adjectives in Romance languages and spatial adverbs such as *aquí* ('here' of the speaker) and *allá* 'over there'.

As an example, Jensen (1982) noted the constraints on the use of come/go and *venir/ir* 'come/go' in English and Spanish. He determined that the fundamental factor in determining the choice of verb is direction of movement in relation to conversational participants. Motion into Deixis I (the 'here' of the speaker) is indicated by *venir,* but, unlike English, the addressee is never the goal of *venir* in Spanish unless both the speaker and hearer are in the same place.

Deictics of time include temporal adverbial expressions such as *ahora* 'now' and *luego* 'later', as well as verb tense and aspect. Haverkate (1984) and Koike (1989) suggested that use of the conditional in requests may distance the proposition in the verb tense from the speaker's deictic center in that the conditional is linked to the past while being semantically oriented to the coding time. Consequently, requests using the conditional in Spanish are more polite than those coded in the present tense.

A further category of discourse deixis refers to macrodiscursive elements of both oral and written discourse. Fleischman (1990) argued that we conceptualize discourse as time or as space, depending on whether we are orienting our addresses around spoken or written discourses. Although drawn from both space and time deictics, the deictics of written discourse refer only to the discourse itself or the argument structure. She suggested that only written discourse may become detached from the speaker and context and acquire a sense of timelessness. In contrast, spoken language relies exclusively on discourse grounded in time. Thus, certain discourse markers may reflect deixis of person, space, time, the context of utterance, and combinations thereof. For example, Koike (1991) found that the adverbial *ya* in narratives reflects aspect, the speaker's emotional intensity toward what is being said, as well as textual cohesion.

Deixis is an underlying orientational device used in advertising to attempt to frame the way in which a viewer sees the product or service being advertised. While not overtly persuasive in nature, social, spatial, and time deictics serve to include or exclude and move viewers closer or distance them from a product. In doing so, they covertly persuade the audience to enter into the advertiser's point of view.

Politeness

Another major area of pragmatics is the study of politeness, since all societies have rules for politeness that are interpreted in different ways. Politeness may be defined as the weightedness of an imposition in terms of degrees of emotional distance between a speaker and hearer. One reason why the concept is relevant to persuasion in advertising is that an ad that is viewed as being too impolite may cause offense and actually persuade a viewer *not* to buy. Advertisers walk a fine line between causing offense and helping the audience to feel good about a product or service.

Brown and Levinson's (1987) seminal treatment of politeness is based on the notions of rationality and FACE, one's public self-image. They also proposed three supposedly universal psychological/sociological factors that influence what we say: power (the similarity or difference in ranking between the speaker and hearer), distance (the degree to which one can impose one's own face), and rank (the cultural and situational ranking of impositions). Politeness may be expressed as payment to one's positive or negative face. Thus, positive politeness consists of expressions of solidarity and the desire to have one's values approved, whereas negative face permits one's freedom to remain unimpeded and allows distance and a preservation of status. Formal politeness is generally an expression of this type of politeness.

Brown and Levinson also proposed a number of face-saving strategies that reflect the choices speakers have when making a speech act. The speakers may choose to do the act or to avoid it. If they choose the act, they may go on record (baldly or with redress) or may speak off the record via metaphor, irony, and hints. Finally, if they choose redressive action, they may appeal to either positive or negative face, either the hearer's face or their own.

Mey (1993) argued that one problem with the basic notions of rationality and a conversational contract is that the notions are promoted as being universal, an assumption that must be proven across languages. Furthermore, he argued that there are intercultural differences regarding what people assume to be cooperative behavior. Finally, Mey criticized the fact that certain forms of behavior are preferred and rewarded within Brown and Levinson's framework while others are "subject to sanction" (p. 75).

Fraser and Nolen (1981) described politeness in terms of abiding by a conversational contract, the initial set of rights and obligations that determine the limits of an interaction. They argued that there are two types of terms of the contract: general and specific. General terms govern all ordinary conversations and are seldom negotiated away (speak the same language, wait for your turn, and speak sufficiently loudly). Specific terms, such as the kinds of speech acts permitted and what the content may be, are maintained because of the particulars of the conversation. For example, a child ordinarily does not authorize a parent to do something. Fraser and Nolan also suggested that the conditional is responsible for mitigation and thus politeness in Spanish assertives and directives, an argument that both and Haverkate (1990) and Koike (1994) dispute.

Koike (1989b) defined politeness as the communication of respect for the social relationship between a speaker and hearer through use of communicative strategies that are recognized by a society as carrying a particular illocutionary force. Recall from the discussion of deixis that politeness may be related to tense and person and that shifting the deictic center of orientation may account for varying pragmatic effects of politeness. Deference is defined by Koike (1989b) and Brown and Levinson (1987) as the maintenance of distance between a hearer and speaker, a component of negative politeness. Koike, therefore, posited a continuum for politeness in Spanish directives based on directness/indirectness of illocutionary force; see Koike 1989a:280.

Table A.2 Continuum of Politeness in Spanish. (Koike, 1989a:280)

Less polite	*Hable* Speak (FRML)	(commands)
	Necesita hablar You (FRML) need to speak	(assertion)
	Sugiero que hable I suggest that you (FRML) speak	(suggestion)
	¿Puede hablar? Can you (FRML) speak?	(request)
	Todo el mundo está callado. Everyone is quiet	(hint)
More polite	∅	(avoidance)

Various other principles have been proposed relating to politeness. Leech's (1983) Tact Maxim, for example, states that maximizing benefit to the hearer and minimizing the cost to the speaker will usually result in politeness. R. Lakoff (1977) similarly posited three rules of politeness from the speaker's point of view: (1) don't impose; (2) offer options; and (3) encourage feelings of camaraderie. Lakoff suggested that the basic politeness strategies are distance, deference, and camaraderie. Furthermore, she maintained that politeness supersedes any other strategy, even at the cost of intelligibility.

Politeness is relevant to persuasion in advertising because it helps determine the type of relationship between the advertiser and viewer. Concepts such as positive and negative face may contribute to a tone of solidarity or power with respect to the viewer. The face-saving strategies selected for an ad reflect the degree to which advertisers wish to impose on their audience.

Furthermore, off-record strategies involving metaphor, irony, or hints may be less threatening to viewers than those that are baldly on record. Fraser and Nolen's (1981) conversational contract determines the limits of an interaction with respect to an advertiser and viewer. Koike's (1989b) continuum for politeness in Spanish reflects the degree of imposition for each speech act. The degree to which a viewer is persuaded to buy a product is determined by the choice of speech act appropriate for the language and context. Finally, Lakoff's (1977) suggestion that politeness supersedes other strategies, even at the cost of intelligibility, may be a factor in explaining the vagueness of some commercials.

The Cooperative Principle and Grice's Maxims

The key to understanding persuasion in advertising is perhaps best explained by the Cooperative Principle, Grice's Maxims, and Implicature. Grice's Maxims are an extension of the Cooperative Principle (CP) that arose from Grice's belief that natural language does not diverge from formal logic. Instead, speakers converse in a maximally efficient way by making use of background knowledge and flouting or violating a maxim in order to convey meaning through an implication. The CP derives explanatory power from what happens when behavior appears not to conform; it is honored as much in the breach as in its observance. As long as participants each assume that the other is adhering to the CP, meanings that are conveyed without being said follow as inferences from the fact that a maxim appears to be violated.

The fundamental assumption of the CP is that communication is primarily a cooperative activity. Grice's (1975:45) Cooperative Principle states: "Make your conversational contribution such as is required, at the stage at which it occurs, by the accepted purpose or direction of the talk exchange in which you are engaged." It is clear that Grice did not believe that every communicative encounter is cooperative. He merely asserted that there is an underlying cooperative basis by which conversation is organized.

Echoing Kant, Grice named the four categories under this principle: Quantity, Quality, Relation, and Manner. While he suggested the existence of other aesthetic, social, or moral types of maxims, the conversational maxims promote a maximally effective exchange of information.

Conversational Maxims (Grice 1975:45-46)

Maxim of Quantity
1. Make your contribution as informative as is required (for the current purposes of the exchange).

2. Do not make your contribution more informative than is required.

Maxim of Quality
1. Do not say what you believe to be false.
2. Do not say that for which you lack adequate evidence.

Maxim of Relation
Be relevant.

Maxim of Manner
1. Avoid obscurity of expression.
2. Avoid ambiguity.
3. Be brief (avoid unnecessary prolixity).
4. Be orderly.

Nevertheless, a participant in conversation may break a maxim by violating the maxim, which in some cases may cause the speakers to mislead the listener. They may also opt out from the CP by making it plain that they are unwilling to cooperate, or they may be faced by a clash of maxims which forces them to violate a maxim. Finally, they may blatantly flout a maxim in order to create a conversational implicature, an ordinary conversational strategy whereby the hearer must work out the meaning conveyed. This inference may be accomplished by using the conventional meaning of words and their references, the CP, context, background knowledge, and mutual knowledge. Grice (1975:52–56) offered the following examples of conversational implicatures.

Conversational Implicatures

Violation of quantity
a. Women are women.
b. In a recommendation letter for a candidate for a philosophy job: "Dear Sir, Mr. X's command of English is excellent, and his attendance at tutorials has been regular. Yours, etc."
[Implicates that the writer thinks Mr. X is no good at philosophy]

Violation of quality
a. Irony: X is a fine friend.
[Implicates the opposite meaning.]
b. Metaphor: You are the cream in my coffee.
c. Meiosis: Of a man known to have broken up all the furniture, one says, "He was a little intoxicated."

d. Hyperbole. Every nice girl loves a sailor.

Violation of Relation
a. Mrs. X is an old bag.
b. The weather has been quite delightful this summer, hasn't it? [Implicature that A's remark should not be discussed.]

Violation of Manner
a. Ambiguity: I sought to tell my love, love that never told can be.
b. Obscurity: A and B, having a conversation in the presence of a child. By means of euphemism, etc. A implicates that the contents of his communication should not be imparted to the third party.
c. Failure to be brief or succinct: Miss X produced a series of sounds that corresponded closely with the score of "Home Sweet Home." [Implicature that Miss X cannot sing well.]

While Grice's maxims have received strong application and support (Geis 1982; R. Lakoff 1982; Leech 1983; Brown and Levinson 1987), they have also been subject to sharp criticism with regard to their universality. Keenan (1974, 1976) challenged the universality of Grice's Maxims in her study of Malagasy society. She maintained that the Malagasy regularly provide less information than is required in conversation, even when they have access to the necessary information. She found that new information is a valuable commodity to the Malagasy and that they, therefore, are hesitant to reveal such information. As Chen (1991) argued, however, it is more likely that the Maxim of Quantity is violated by the Malagasy not to be uninformative but in order to maintain prestige over the rest of the community. Furthermore, Chen suggested that there may be a social convention that one should not ask for certain types of information to begin with, just as Americans generally do not ask someone they have just met about their salary or age. Thus, Keenan's example does not seem to refute Grice's Maxims. Furthermore, as Lakoff (1990) noted, it may be possible for a particular maxim to play a greater or less important role in a given society, as in the reduced role of clarity (from the Maxim of Manner) in Japanese discourse.

Sperber and Wilson (1986) challenged the explanatory power of Grice's Maxims. They proposed reducing the maxims to a single principle of relevance. Horn (1984) similarly reduced the maxims to two principles, the Q- and R-principles, referring to quantity and relation. Mey (1993) noted that one problem with relevance theory is the fact that it says little about real communicative interaction and the social dimensions of language. Furthermore, Mey argued that the language Sperber and Wilson use is borrowed from economics and computer science, causing the theory to view the computer as a metaphor for human thinking processes and to see such processes as economically rational behavior.

Another theoretical argument against Grice's CP and Maxims concerns the treatment of irony as a violation of the Maxim of Quality (Leech 1983; Sperber and Wilson 1986; Chen 1991). Leech (1983) proposed the addition of an Irony Principle to the established maxims. Chen (1991) likewise suggested additional principles to account for all types of irony, and Sperber and Wilson (1986) argued that irony is interpretable through a single maxim of relevance. In this study irony is treated as a type of conversational implicature that minimally stems from flouting the Maxim of Quality.

Despite the criticisms of Grice's CP and Maxims, a better theory has yet to be offered. Furthermore, most criticisms and proposed changes have been directed at a single aspect of Grice's theory and have failed to invalidate the usefulness of his proposal. The CP and maxims are relevant to persuasion in advertising because they allow the advertiser or speaker in an ad to communicate more than what is actually said. Conversational implicatures are difficult to refute and in comparison to direct statements or even conventional implicatures, hearers are often unaware that a conversational implicature has been made. Grice's Maxims, therefore, lie at the heart of persuasion in advertising.

Other strategies in advertising

Though not explicitly pragmatic in nature, a few items remain for discussion. Advertising is controlled by its social context; therefore, sociolinguistic concepts such as gender, power, and solidarity are key strategies for effecting audience reaction. Hodge and Fowler (1979), for example, stressed the Orwellian principle that society is organized upon a principle of unequal power and is realized through forms of public communication. One such example is the power distribution often demonstrated in linguistic choices in women's speech.

Lakoff (1990) asserted that some form of women's language exists in every culture investigated thus far. She argued that while special forms may differ from language to language, most functional characteristics are widespread and include "alleged illogic, submissiveness, sexual utility to men, secondary status" (p. 202). Men's language, in contrast, is said to be the language of the powerful and of "important" talk. Lakoff further stated that the superficial traits of women's language represent a conventional avoidance of the appearance of holding or desiring power (p. 206). This claim is particularly interesting in advertising since men dominate American advertising. Even in commercials featuring women, men are almost always employed to read voice-over messages (Geis 1982:154–155).

In advertising, stereotypes are generally employed to establish a consumer as a product authority (Geis 1982), which is one way of conveying power. Brown and Gilman (1960) described another widespread linguistic means of conveying power or solidarity by means of pronominal address. They proposed a connection between social structure, group ideology, and the semantics of pronouns, the so-called T-V phenomenon, referring to the Latin pronoun *tu* of intimacy and the *vos* of formality. They described the nonreciprocal power semantic in which the superior says *T* and receives *V* and the reciprocal solidarity semantic in which equal participants use *T* (and *V* as solidarity declines). Furthermore, they claimed that solidarity has largely won out over power. Wierzbicka (1991) contrasted the T-V phenomenon with the English *you*, arguing that it is both a social equalizer and distancer in that it is unable to convey the familiarity of the *T*. She maintained that the absence of an intimate *T*-form reflects and fosters the culturally expected psychological distance or need for privacy; *you* implies informality but not intimacy.

Thus, the sociolinguistic context of advertising is reflected through speaker choices regarding gender, power, and solidarity. Such choices help link the ad with the desired set of viewers and often reveal the supposed values of the commercial's audience.

One last topic remains for discussion, the use of pragmalinguistic devices such as prosody and information structure to achieve distinct meanings. Both devices are commonly used in advertising. Bolinger (1954:152) noted how word order in Spanish may achieve similar effects to that of contrastive stress in English. Spanish utilizes word order to emphasize the information point, as in *Su marido está enfermo.* 'Her husband is sick' and *Está enfermo su marido.* 'Her husband is sick.'

Fant (1984) disagreed with Bolinger's analysis, arguing for the primacy of a verb-subject order in Spanish. Instead, he posited that the final position in Spanish is used for new information and that the context of utterance is crucial to determining the information structure. Although his analysis is complex, what is useful for the present study is his idea that the more known a theme is, the less emphasis tends to be syntactically represented.

Silva-Corvalán (1983) supported Bolinger's belief that the distribution of sentence accents is not determined by syntactic structure but by semantic and emotional highlighting. She suggested that the communicative purpose of object-verb (OV) constructions was to establish discourse cohesion. This purpose is accomplished through a smooth transition from older to newer information to signal that the object is contrary to expectation.

Bolinger, Fant, and Silva-Corvalán's arguments are necessary background information when examining the role of phonology and syntax in advertising. Advertisements are crafted using phonological and syntactic devices as tools for pragmatic ends, such as emphasizing particular elements to the audience and drawing attention to new versus given information.

Appendix B
Database Sample

Basic Information

[Back] [Forward] [New] [Backup]

Status: ○ Needy ○ Almost ○ Done!   235

- Ad Name — Taping Period
- Station — Counter Start
- Program — Counter Stop
- Date — Time of ad

Ad Information

- Ad Class — Ad Setting
- Ad Type — Characters
- Target Audience — Slogan

Text of Ad

Features

| Flattery Type | Example | Contribution |
| ○ Yes ○ No | | |

| Humor | Example | Contribution |
| ○ Yes ○ No | | |

| Endorse. | Example | Contribution |
| ○ Yes ○ No | | |

Database Sample

	Example	Contribution
Syntax ○ Yes ○ No		
Phonology ○ Yes ○ No		
Lexicon ○ Yes ○ No		

	Examples	Form	Contribution
Speech Acts ○ Y ○ N Representatives ○ Y ○ N Declarations ○ Y ○ N Commisives ○ Y ○ N Directives ○ Y ○ N Expressives			

	Examples		Contribution
Novelty ○ Y ○ N Explicit ○ Y ○ N Lexical ○ Y ○ N Morphological ○ Y ○ N Syntactic ○ Y ○ N Semantic ○ Y ○ N Pragmatic ○ Y ○ N Other			

Politeness | Examples | Contribution

- O Y O N Deixis
- O Y O N Personal Refer.
- O Y O N Tense
- O Y O N Positive Face
- O Y O N Negative Face
- O Y O N Power
- O Y O N Distance
- O Y O N Rank
- O Y O N Other

Implicature | Examples | Contribution

- O Y O N Conventional
- O Y O N Conversational

Violations of Maxims | Examples | Contribution

- O Y O N Quantity
- O Y O N Quality
- O Y O N Relation
- O Y O N Manner

Speaker Considerations | Contribution

- O Y O N Gender
- O Y O N Age
- O Y O N Physical Characteristics
- O Y O N Profession
- O Y O N Distance
- O Y O N Solidarity
- O Y O N Other

General Comments

Appendix C

Number of Comparable Ads by Product in Each Country

Distribution of Strategies
(Key: 1 = most frequent, 2 = second most frequent, 3 = least frequent, "—" the same)

Product (subtype)	U.S.	SP	CH
Foods:			
Cereals	12	1	8
Soft drinks	3	5	13
Coffee/tea	2	2	7
Water	—	2	2
Milk	—	2	3
Other beverages (juices)	4	8	5
Dairy	1	1	2
Pasta	—	1	7
Bread	—	3	1
Frozen vegetables	—	3	1
Supermarket	2	3	1
Meals and Snacks			
Fast food restaurants	6	2	3
Candy	5	3	3

Product (subtype)	US	SP	CH
Cookies	2	2	1
Chips	—	2	2
Popsicles/ice creams	—	13	3
Yogurt snacks	1	5	8
Baby food	—	1	4
Health and Beauty			
Hair loss	3	2	—
Special "medications"	4	5	—
Pain relief	6	1	1
Deodorant	1	1	5
Oral hygiene	4	2	6
Feminine hygiene	1	3	4
Toilet paper	1	—	1
Shampoo	3	8	9
Soap	2	—	3
Lotions	2	4	5
Hair color	1	3	2
Makeup	—	2	3
Cleaners			
Paper towels	1	—	2
Dish soap	1	3	2
Laundry detergent	—	6	1
Kitchen/bath	—	2	4
Roaches	1	1	—
Appliance	1	1	1
Cooking			
Refrigerator	1	1	1
Washer/dryer	1	1	2
General	1	1	—
TV and Video			
Videos	1	4	—
TV magazines	1	1	2

Number of Comparable Ads by Product in Each Country

Product (subtype)	US	SP	CH
Toys			
Girls	—	2	2
Boy	—	2	1
Audio			
Telephone	9	2	6
CD/cassette	15	8	1
Equipment	—	1	4
Home			
Paint	2	1	—
Computer			
Company	—	1	1
Pagers	—	1	3
Alcohol	13	3	—
Vehicles			
Cars	14	18	2
Repairs/parts	6	4	3
Miscellaneous			
Dept. stores	3	2	6
Financial			
Bank	1	2	4
Investment	1	—	1
Bonds	1	—	1
Credit	1	1	1
Lottery	6	2	5
Education	2	—	6
Recreation			
Concert	3	—	2
Movie	4	2	—

Product (subtype)	US	SP	CH
Theme park	1	1	—
Fortune Teller	6	1	—
Travel	2	3	—

Appendix D

Distribution of Pragmatic Strategies: Preference by Country

Distribution of Maxims and Violations
(Key: 1 = most frequent, 2 = second most frequent, 3 = least frequent, "—" the same)

Strategy	U.S.	SP	CH
Speech acts	1	2	1
representatives	—	—	—
declarations	1	2	3
commissives	1	2	3
directives	1	3	2
expressives	1	2	3
Novelty	—	—	—
explicit	2	1	2
lexical	1	1	2
morphological	2	3	1
syntactic	3	1	2
semantic	1	3	2
pragmatic	1	3	2
situational	2	1	1
association	3	1	2

Appendix D

Strategy	US	SP	CH
Indexicals	1	3	2
deixis	1	3	2
person	1	3	2
tense	1	2	3
Politeness	1	2	1
positive face	1	2	3
negative face	3	2	1
distance	3	2	1
power	3	2	1
solidarity	1	2	3
Implicature	2	1	1
conventional	1	2	3
conversational	2	1	1
Speaker Considerations	1	2	3
gender	1	2	3
age	1	3	2
physical	1	3	2
profession	1	3	2
Flattery	1	3	2
Humor	2	1	3
Endorsements	1	3	2
Syntax	1	3	2
Phonology	2	3	1
Lexicon	3	2	1
Maxims	2	3	11
1. Quantity	2	2	
repetition	2	3	1
ellipsis	2	3	1

Distribution of Pragmatic Strategies

Strategy		U.S.	SP	CH
	lack of info.	3	1	2
	too much info.	2	1	3
2.	Quality	1	3	2
	metaphor	1	2	1
	hyperbole	2	3	1
	false assertion	1	2	3
	irony	1	2	2
	tautology	1	2	1
	understatement	—	—	—
3.	Relation	3	1	2
	relation	—	—	—
	nonrelevance	1	3	2
4.	Manner	1	2	2
	vague	2	1	3
	obscure	1	2	1
	rhetorical	1	2	2
	ambiguous	1	2	1
	verbose	3	1	2
	redundant	2	3	1
	euphemism	1	1	2

References

Advertising Age. 1991. Vietnam beckons, European unity broadens, Latin America brightens. 62(54):16–17.
Alonso, Alegría, Beatriz Garza, and José A. Pascual, eds. 1994. II Encuentro de lingüistas y Filólogos de España y México, Salamanca, 25–30 de noviembre de 1991. Salamanca, Spain: Ediciones Universidad.
Astroff, Roberta J. 1997. Capitals cultural study: Marketing popular ethnography of U.S. Latino culture. In Mica Nava, Andrew Blake, Iain MacRury and Barry Richards (eds.), 120–136. New York: Routledge.
Austin, John. 1962. How to do things with words. Cambridge, Mass.: Harvard University Press.
Avila, Raúl. 1994. El lenguaje de la radio y la televisión: Primeras noticias. In Alonso Alegría, Beatriz Garza, and José A. Pascual (eds.), II Encuentro de Lingüistas y Filólogos de España y México, 101–117. Salamanca: Ediciones Universidad.
Bar-Hillel, Yehoshua. 1971. Out of the pragmatic waste-basket. Linguistic Inquiry 2:401–407.
Bell, Allan. 1991. The language of news media. Cambridge, Mass: Blackwell.
Bjerg, Kresten. 1979. The hollow men and the public speech act. In Jacob L. Mey (ed.), Rasmus Rask studies in pragmatic linguistics: vol. 1. Pragmalinguistics: Theory and practice, 131–168. New York: Mouton.
Blum-Kulka, Shoshana. 1989. Playing it safe: The role of conventionality in indirectness. In Shoshana Blum-Kulka, Juliane House, and Gabriele Kasper (eds.), Cross-cultural pragmatics: Requests and apologies, 37–70. Norwood, N.J.: Ablex.

Blum-Kulka, Shoshana, Juliane House, and Gabriele Kasper, eds. 1989. Cross-cultural pragmatics: Requests and apologies. Norwood, N.J.: Ablex.

Bolinger, Dwight. 1980. Language—the loaded weapon: The use and abuse of language today. New York: Longman.

Briz Gómez, Antonio, Manuel Pruñonosa Tomás, and Enrique N. Serra Alegre. 1987. Notas sobre el uso de la retórica en la publicidad televisiva. Estudios de lingüística 4:87–105.

Brown, Penelope, and Stephen Levinson. 1987. Politeness: Some universals in language usage. Cambridge: Cambridge University Press.

Brown, Roger, and Albert Gilman. 1960. The pronouns of power and solidarity. In Thomas A. Sebeok (ed.), Style in language, 253–276. Cambridge, Mass.: MIT Press.

Bruthiaux, Paul. 1996. The discourse of classified advertising: Exploring the nature of linguistic simplicity. Oxford: Oxford University Press.

Buxton, Edward. 1972. Promise them anything. New York: Stein and Day.

Chen, Rong. 1991. Verbal irony as conversational implicature. Ph.D. dissertation, Ball State University. Dissertation abstracts international, 51, 2728A.

Cole, Peter, and Jerry L. Morgan, eds. 1975. Speech acts. Syntax and semantics, vol. 3. New York: Academic Press.

Coleman, Linda. 1983. Semantic and prosodic manipulation in advertising. In Richard J. Harris, (ed.), Information processing research in advertising. Hillsdale, N.J.: Erlbaum.

Delbecque, Nicole, and K. U. Leuven. 1990. El lenguaje de la publicidad y su poder de sugestión. Anuncios publicitarios en El País Semanal: Los tópicos más frecuentes y su formulación. Lingüística Española Actual 12(2):197–213.

Ehrmann, Hans. 1991. Chile ends government broadcast monopoly. Variety 342(11):72.

Elías-Olivares, Lucía, Elizabeth A. Leone, Rene Cisneros, and John R. Guiterrez, eds. 1985. Spanish language use and public life in the United States. Berlin and New York: Mouton.

European advertising, marketing, and media data 1990: A directory and sourcebook. First edition. 1990. London: Euromonitor.

Fant, Lars. 1984. Estructura informativa en español: Estudio sintáctico y entonativo. Uppsala, Sweden: [Uppsala University] Acta Universitatis Upsaliensis.

Fasold, R. W., and Robert W. Shuy, eds. 1974. Studies in language variation: Semantics, phonology, pragmatics, social situations, ethnographic approaches. Washington, D.C.: Georgetown University School of Languages and Linguistics.

Fernández, Joseph A. 1988. La fonología en la televisión española: Violencias fonéticas. Revista de dialectología y tradiciones populares 43:249-258.

Fillmore, Charles. 1971. Towards a theory of deixis. Working Papers in Linguistics. Honolulu: University of Hawaii.

Fitch, Kristine L., and Robert E. Sanders. 1994. Culture, communication, and preferences for directness in expression of directives. Communication theory 4(3):219-245.

Fleischman, Suzanne. 1990. Discourse as space/discourse as time: Reflections on the metalanguage of spoken and written discourse. Paper presented at the International Pragmatics Association Conference, Barcelona.

Fontanillo, Enrique, and María Isabel Riesco. 1990. Teleperversión de la lengua. Barcelona: Anthropos.

Fowler, Roger, and Gunther Kress. 1979. Critical linguistics. In Roger Fowler, Bob Hodge, Gunther Kress, and Tony Trew (eds.), Language and control, 185-213. Boston: Routledge and Kegan Paul.

Fowler, Roger, Bob Hodge, Gunther Kress, and Tony Trew, eds. 1979. Language and Control. London and Boston: Routledge and Kegan Paul.

Franklin, Karol. 1984. Changes in advertising strategy. Unpublished manuscript.

Fraser, Bruce, and William Nolen. 1981. The association of deference with linguistic form. International Journal of the Sociology of Language 27:93-109.

Garfinkel, Andrew. 1978. A sociolinguistic analysis of the language of advertising. Unpublished doctoral dissertation. Georgetown University.

Geis, Michael L. 1982. The language of television advertising. New York: Academic Press.

Giora, Rachel. 1993. On the political message: Pretending to communicate. In Herman Parret (ed.), Pretending to communicate, 104-123. New York: Walter de Gruyter.

Goffman, Erving. 1974. Frame analysis: An essay in the organization of experience. New York: Harper and Row.

Grice, H. Paul. 1975. Logic and conversation. In Peter Cole and Jerry L. Morgan (eds.), Syntax and semantics III: Speech acts, 41-58. New York: Academic Press.

Green, Georgia M. 1989. Pragmatics and natural language understanding. Hillsdale, N.J.: Lawrence Erlbaum Associates.

Harris, Richard Jackson, ed. 1983. Information processing research in advertising. Hillsdale, N.J.: Lawrence Erlbaum Associates.

Haverkate, Henk. 1984. Speech acts, speakers, and hearers: Reference and referential strategies in Spanish. Philadelphia: John Benjamins.

Haverkate, Henk. 1990. Politeness and mitigation in Spanish: A morpho-pragmatic analysis. In Harm Pinkster and Inge Genee (eds.), International Pragmatics Conference. Unity in diversity. Papers presented to Simon C. Dik on his fiftieth birthday, 107–131. Barcelona: Foris.

Haverkate, Henk. 1993. Acerca de los actos de habla expresivos y comisivos en español. In Henk Haverkate, Kees Hengeveld, and Gijs Mulder (eds.), Aproximaciones pragmalingüísticas al español. Diálogos Hispánicos 12:149–180. Atlanta: Rodopi.

Haverkate, Henk, Kees Hengeveld, and Gijs Mulder, eds. 1993. Aproximaciones pragmalingüísticas al español. Diálogos Hispánicos 12. Atlanta: Rodopi.

Henry, Brian, ed. 1986. British television advertising: The first 30 years. London: Century Benham.

Higgins, Denis. 1990. The art of writing advertising: Conversations with masters of the craft. Second edition. Lincolnwood, Ill.: NTC Business Books.

Hodge, Bob, and Roger Fowler. 1979. Orwellian linguistics. In Roger Fowler, Bob Hodge, Gunther Kress, and Tony Trew (eds.), Language and control, 6–25. Boston: Routledge and Kegan Paul.

Horn, Laurence R. 1984. Toward a new taxonomy for pragmatic inference: Q-based and R-based implicature. In Deborah Schiffrin (ed.), Georgetown Round Table on Languages and Linguistics 1984, 11–42. Washington, D.C.: Georgetown University.

IBOPE. 1997. [Online main page]. Accessed June 20, 1997. http://www.tmm.cl/time/timein.htm

Jensen, John B. 1982. Coming and going in English and Spanish. In Rose Nash, and D. Belaval (eds.), Readings in Spanish-English contrastive linguistics, III, 37–63). San Juan: Inter-American University Press.

Jucker, Andreas H. 1986. News interviews: A pragmalinguistic analysis. Pragmatics and Beyond 7(4). Philadelphia: John Benjamins.

Keenan, Elinor O. 1974. The universality of conversational implicatures. In R. W. Fasold, and R. W. Shuy (eds.), Studies in language variation, 255–268.

Keenan, Elinor O. 1976. The universality of conversational postulates. Language in Society 5:67–80.

Klein-Andreu, Flora, ed. 1983. Discourse perspectives on syntax. New York: Academic Press.

Koike, Dale April. 1989a. Pragmatic competence and adult L2 acquisition: Speech acts in interlanguage. The Modern Language Journal 73(3):279-288.
Koike, Dale April. 1989b. Requests and the role of deixis in politeness. Journal of Pragmatics 13:187-202.
Koike, Dale April. (1991). Functions of the adverbial ya in Spanish narrative discourse. Paper presented at the Linguistic Association of the Southwest Conference, Austin, Tex.
Koike, Dale April. 1992. Language and social relationship in Brazilian Portuguese: The pragmatics of politeness. Austin, Tex.: University of Texas.
Koike, Dale April. 1994. Negation in Spanish and English suggestions and requests: Mitigating effects? Journal of Pragmatics 21:1-14.
Koike, Dale April. 1996. Class notes. Spanish Discourse Analysis and Pragmatics. The University of Texas at Austin.
Kumatoridiani, Tetsuo. 1984a. Communicative process and underlying communicative acts of advertising discourse: A pragmatic analysis of what copywriters do with language. Language and Culture 6(1):93-121.
Kumatoridiani, Tetsuo. 1984b. The structure of persuasive discourse: A cross-cultural analysis of the language in American and Japanese television commercials. [CD-ROM]. Abstract from: MLA File: Dissertation Abstracts Item 45(1):171A.
Labov, William. 1972. Sociolinguistic patterns. Philadelphia: University of Pennsylvania Press.
Lakoff, Robin. 1977. What can you do with words: Politeness, pragmatics, and performatives. In A. Rogers, B. Wall, and J. P. Murphy (eds.), Proceedings of the Texas Conference on Performatives, Presuppositions, and Implicatures, 79-106. Center for Applied Linguistics.
Lakoff, Robin. 1982. Persuasive discourse and ordinary conversation, with examples from advertising. In Deborah Tannen (ed.), Analyzing discourse: Text and talk, 25-42. Georgetown: Georgetown University Press.
Lakoff, Robin Tolmach. 1990. Talking power: The politics of language. New York: Basic Books.
Leech, Geoffrey N. 1966. English in advertising: A linguistic study of advertising in Great Britain. London: Longmans.
Leech, Geoffrey N. 1983. Principles of pragmatics. London: Longman.
Levinson, Stephen C. 1983. Pragmatics. Cambridge: Cambridge University Press.
Lipski, John M. 1985. Spanish in United States broadcasting. In Lucía Elías-Olivares, Elizabeth A. Leone, Rene Cisneros, and John R.

Guiterrez (eds.), Spanish language use and public life in the United States, 217–33. Berlin: Mouton.
Margalit, Avishai, ed. 1976. Meaning and use: Papers presented at the Second Jerusalem Philosophical Encounter, April 1976. Dordrecht; Boston: D. Reidel.
Maso-Fleischman, Roberta. 1997. Archetypal research for advertising: A Spanish-language example. Journal of Advertising Research 37(5):81–84.
Mey, Jacob L., ed. 1979. Pragmalinguistics: Theory and practice. Rasmus Rask studies in pragmatic linguistics, vol. 1. The Hague and New York: Mouton.
Mey, Jacob L. 1985. Whose language?: A study in linguistic pragmatics. Philadelphia: John Benjamins.
Mey, Jacob L. 1993. Pragmatics: An introduction. Cambridge, Mass.: Blackwell.
Moore, Linda. 1992. Madrid media mogul a mystery. Variety 347(12):31, 34.
Moreno Fernández, Francisco. 1990. Lengua y manipulación en los medios de comunicación social. Boletín de la Real Academia Española 70(250):429–448.
Morris, Charles H. 1938. Foundations of the theory of signs. In Rudolf Carnap et al. (eds.), International Encyclopedia of Unified Science 2(1):6. Chicago: University of Chicago Press.
Nash, Rose, and D. Belaval, eds. 1982. Readings in Spanish-English contrastive linguistics III. San Juan: Inter-American University Press.
Nava, Mica, Andrew Blake, Iaian MacRury, and Barry Richards, eds. 1997. Buy this book: Studies in advertising and consumption. London and New York: Routledge.
Nilsen, Don L. F. 1979. Language play in advertising: Linguistic inventions in product naming. In James E. Alatis and Richard Tucker (eds.), Georgetown University Round Table on Languages and Linguistics 1979: Language in Public Life, 137–143. Washington, D.C.: Georgetown University.
Newcomb, Peter, and Dolores Lataniotis. 1997. Andrew Jerrold Perenchio. Forbes 160(8):222.
O'Barr, William M. 1979. Language and advertising. In James E. Alatis and Richard Tucker (eds.), Georgetown University Round Table on Languages and Linguistics 1979: Language in Public Life, 272–285. Washington, D.C.: Georgetown University.
Ogilvy, David. 1985. Ogilvy on advertising. New York: Vintage Books.

P&D Net. 1997. El "site" de la televisión, cine y publicidad en español. On-line:www.produ.com/ratings/agosto_chile.html. Accessed June 20, 1997. Source: Time IBOPE Chile.

Palacio, Luis. 1993. Spain's "Crazy Television" irks viewers and guide magazines as broadcast stations vie for limited revenues. Mediaweek 3(7):12.

Parret, Herman, ed. 1994. Pretending to communicate. Berlin and New York: W. de Gruyter. Grundlagen der Kommunikation und Kognition. [Foundations of communication and cognition.]

Paxman, Andrew. 1996. Foreign investors get cool reception in Chile. Variety 363(8):28.

Pike, Kenneth L. 1982. Linguistic concepts: An introduction to tagmemics. Lincoln: University of Nebraska Press.

Pinkster, Harm, and Inge Genee, eds. 1990. 1990 International Pragmatics Conference. Unity in diversity. Papers presented to Simon C. Dik on his fiftieth birthday. Barcelona: Foris.

Rank, Hugh. 1988. Persuasion analysis: A companion to composition. Park Forest, Ill.: Counter-Propaganda Press.

Reiss, Nira. 1985. Speech act taxonomy as a tool for ethnographic description: An analysis based on videotapes of continuous behavior in two New York households. Pragmatics & Beyond 6(7). Philadelphia: John Benjamins.

Rogers, Andy, Bob Wall, and John P. Murphy, eds. 1977. Proceedings of the Texas Conference on Perfromatives, Presuppositions, and Implicatures. Arlington, Va.: Center for Applied Linguistics.

Roslow, Peter, and J.A.F. Nicholls. 1996. Targeting the Hispanic market: Comparative persuasion of TV commercials in Spanish and English. Journal of Advertising Research 36(3):67–77.

ROSLOW Research Group. 1994. In SRDS TV and Cable Source, 79(2). (1997). Second Quarter, 67, A30–34, 1161, 1377, 1422–1424.

Sánchez Corral, Luis. 1991. Los marcadores deícticos en la publicidad: Una estrategia del discurso. Lingüística Española Actual 13(1):133–151.

Schiffrin, Deborah. 1994. Approaches to discourse. Cambridge, Mass.: Blackwell.

Schmidt, Rosemarie, and Joseph F. Kess. 1985. Persuasive language in the television medium: Contrasting advertising and televangelism. Journal of Pragmatics 9:287–308.

Searle, John R. 1969. Speech acts: An essay in the philosophy of language. Cambridge: Cambridge University Press.

Searle, John R. 1975. Indirect speech acts. In Peter Cole and Jerry L. Morgan (eds.), Syntax and semantics III: Speech acts, 59–82. New York: Academic Press.

Searle, John R. 1976. Intentionality and the use of language. In A. Margalit (ed.), Meaning and use, 181–198. Dordrecht: Reidel.
Searle, John R. (1977). A classification of illocutionary acts. In Andy Rogers, Bob Wall, and John P. Murphy (eds.), Proceedings of the Texas Conference on Performatives, Presuppositions, and Implicatures, 27–45. Washington D.C.: Center for Applied Linguistics.
Searle, John R. 1979. Expressions and meaning. Cambridge: Cambridge University.
Sebeok, Thomas A., ed. 1960. Style in language. Cambridge: Technology Press of Massachusetts Institute of Technology.
Silva-Corvalán, Carmen. 1983. On the interaction of word order and intonation: Some OV constructions in Spanish. In Flora Klein-Andreu (ed.), Discourse perspectives on syntax, 117–140. New York: Academic Press.
Sperber, Dan, and Deirdre Wilson. 1986. Relevance: Communication and cognition. Cambridge, Mass.: Harvard University.
Standard Rate and Data Service. 1997. SRDS TV and Cable Source, 79(2). Second Quarter. Wilmette, Ill.: Standard Rate and Data Service.
Tobenkin, David. 1997. Univisión vs. Telemundo. Broadcasting & Cable 127(41):34–42.
Treister, Lisa. 1988. Bigger than ever, "Sábado" sends out clear message. Advertising Age 59(40):S1, S25.
University of Chicago. 1938. International Encyclopedia of Unified Science II (1). Otto Neurath, Rudolf Carnap, and Charles Morris, (eds.). Chicago, University of Chicago Press.
van Dijk, Teun A. 1983. Discourse analysis: Its development and application to the structure of news. Journal of Communication 33(2):20–43.
Wierzbicka, Anna. 1991. Trends in linguistics studies and monographs 53. Cross-cultural pragmatics: The semantics of human interaction. New York: Mouton de Gruyter.

Summer Institute of Linguistics and
The University of Texas at Arlington
Publications in Linguistics

Recent Publications

137. Pragmatics in persuasive discourse of Spanish TV advertising, by Karol J. Hardin. 2001.
136. Quiegolani Zapotec syntax: A principles and parameters account, by Cheryl Black. 2001.
135. A grammar of Sochiapan Chinantec: Studies in Chinantec languages 6, by David Paul Foris. 2000.
134. Grammar of Northern Embera languages: Studies in the languages of Colombia 7, by Charles Arthur Mortensen. 1999.
133. The geometry and features of tone, by Keither Snider. 1999.
132. Desano grammar: Studies in the languages of Colombia 6, by Marion Miller. 1999.
131. The structure of evidential categories in Wanka Quechua, by Rick Floyd. 1999.
130. Cubeo grammar: Studies in the languages of Colombia 5, by Nancy L. Morse and Michael B. Maxwell. 1999.
129. Aspects of Zaiwa prosody: An autosegmental account, by Mark W. Wannemacher. 1998.
128. Tense and aspect in Obolo grammar and discourse, by Uche Aaron. 1998.
127. Case grammar applied, by Walter A. Cook, S.J. 1998.
126. The Dong language in Guizhou Province, China, by Long Yaohong and Zheng Guoqiao, translated from Chinese by D. Norman Geary. 1998.
125. Vietnamese classifiers in narrative texts, by Karen Ann Daley. 1998.
124. Comparative Kadai: The Tai branch, ed. by Jerold A. Edmondson and David B. Solnit. 1997.
123. Why there are no clitics: An alternative perspective on pronominal allomorphy, by Daniel L. Everett. 1996.
122. Mamaindé stress: The need for strata, by David Eberhard. 1995.
121. The Doyayo language: Selected studies, by Elisabeth Wiering and Marinus Wiering. 1994.
120. A discourse analysis of First Corinthians, by Ralph Bruce Terry. 1995.
119. Discourse features of ten languages of West-Central Africa, ed. by Stephen H. Levensohn. 1994.

For further information or a full listing of SIL publications contact:

International Academic Bookstore
SIL International
7500 W. Camp Wisdom Road
Dallas, TX 75236-5699

Voice: 972-708-7404
Fax: 972-708-7363
Email: academic_books@sil.org
Internet: http://www.ethnologue.com

www.ingramcontent.com/pod-product-compliance
Lightning Source LLC
Chambersburg PA
CBHW050137240426
43673CB00043B/1706